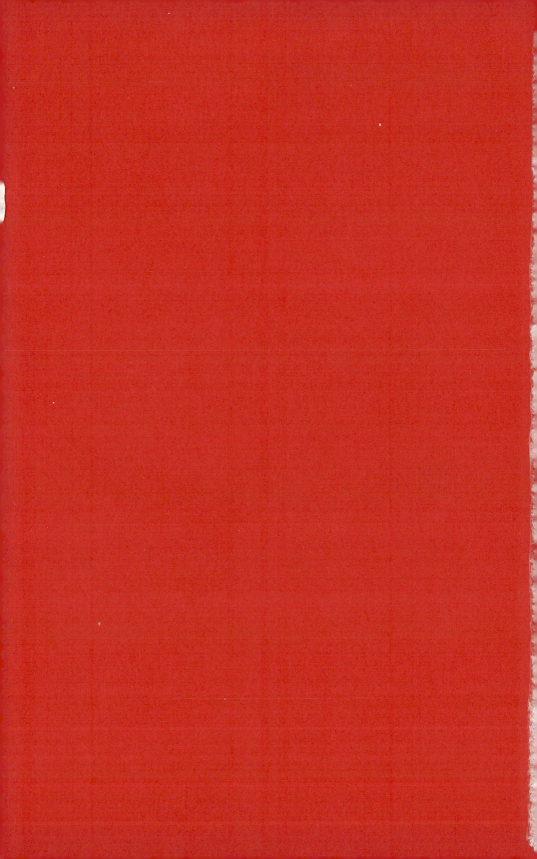

Summon Only the Brave!

In his new book, John W. Brinsfield, Jr. has given everyone—from the casual fan of the Civil War to its most ardent scholar—a very insightful look into the roles of the key participants in the Battle of Gettysburg. He distills the complexity of those three fateful days into an overview of those who were on the field of battle, those who were behind its lines, and those who were left in its aftermath. Of special note is his thoughtful treatment of the mindsets of the front line generals, of the true American pathos of Pickett's charge, and to the role of surgeons and chaplains at the battle—all the while still giving his reader a global view of the three days of carnage at the small Pennsylvania town. This book is a must for any student of the Battle of Gettysburg or the Civil War and will no doubt join the classic tomes by Harry Pfanz, Edward Coddington, Michael Shaara, Kent Masterson Brown, Stephen Sears, Carol Reardon, and others on this most famous battle in all of American history.

—Kenny Rowlette, director of The National Civil War Chaplains Museum and retired professor of English Literature at Liberty University in Lynchburg, Virginia

MERCER UNIVERSITY PRESS

Endowed by

TOM WATSON BROWN
and
THE WATSON-BROWN FOUNDATION, INC.

Summon Only the Brave!

Commanders, Soldiers, and Chaplains at Gettysburg

JOHN W. BRINSFIELD, JR.

MERCER UNIVERSITY PRESS | *Macon, Georgia*
2016

MUP/ H918

© 2016 by Mercer University Press
Published by Mercer University Press
1501 Mercer University Drive
Macon, Georgia 31207

9 8 7 6 5 4 3 2 1

Books published by Mercer University Press are printed on acid-free paper
that meets the requirements of the American National Standard for
Information Sciences—Permanence of Paper for Printed Library Materials.

Library of Congress Cataloging-in-Publication Data

Names: Brinsfield, John Wesley, author.
Title: Summon only the brave! : commanders, soldiers, and chaplains at
   Gettysburg / John W. Brinsfield, Jr.
Description: Macon, Georgia : Mercer University Press, 2016. | Includes
   bibliographical references and index.
Identifiers: LCCN 2016014331 | ISBN 9780881465709 (hardback : alk. paper)
Subjects: LCSH: Gettysburg, Battle of, Gettysburg, Pa., 1863. | Gettysburg,
   Battle of, Gettysburg, Pa., 1863--Personal narratives | United
   States--History--Civil War, 1861-1865--Chaplains. | United States.
   Army--Chaplains--History--19th century. | Confederate States of America.
   Army--Chaplains--History. | Military chaplains--United States--Biography.
   | Military chaplains--Confederate States of America--Biography. | United
   States--History--Civil War, 1861-1865--Religious aspects.
Classification: LCC E475.53 .B848 2016 | DDC 973.7/349--dc23

            LC record available at http://lccn.loc.gov/2016014331

Contents

AUTHOR'S NOTE

All illustrations/images are in the public domain except as noted. In direct quotations the original spelling has been maintained.

For all of the chaplains and chaplain assistants who have served faithfully in America's wars, in peacekeeping or nation-building operations overseas, or in national humanitarian service for the people of this great nation, gratitude is never enough.

For God and Country

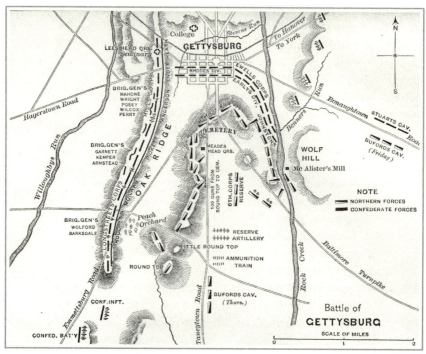

Gettysburg Campaign from Jefferson Davis' *The Rise and Fall of the Confederate Government* vol. 2, (1881) showing roads and rail lines in 1863 Gettysburg battlefield.

Preface

For many years faculty members and students from the United States Army War College in Carlisle, Pennsylvania, have taken staff rides to the nearby Gettysburg National Military Park. Staff rides, originally intended for the ongoing education of staff officers after the Civil War, usually concentrated on a major battle or campaign. Students were challenged to analyze the battle in its strategic, operational, and tactical aspects and address issues such as how timely military intelligence, signal capabilities, the chain of command, logistics, weather, terrain, and, above all, command leadership may have influenced the outcome of the battle.

In general, staff rides were popular with the 320 students and numerous faculty members at the Army War College in any given year. Each seminar or class of students had their own historian to help guide their discussions. If the weather was good, a staff ride was a pleasant way to learn and to socialize away from the daily classroom.

For four years, from 1995 to 1999, I served in the Department of Command, Leadership, and Management at the Army War College as an instructor, seminar historian, director for two elective courses, and the only chaplain assigned to the teaching faculty. In these various capacities, I was able to take students on staff rides and otherwise visit the Gettysburg National Military Park many times. I met some of the licensed guides and sought their insights, expertise, and, at times, physical presence on our seminar bus trips around the park.

As an active duty army chaplain, though assigned to be an instructor, I was naturally interested in knowing more about what the Civil War chaplains did at Gettysburg before, during, and after the battle. I found a statue, a tombstone, and two bronze monuments around the battlefield that mentioned Union chaplains, but nothing about Confederate chaplains.[1] There were no books for sale in the visitor center that provided an overview of chaplain ministries during the conflict. Although the Military History Insti-

---

[1] The statue is that of Chaplain William Corby, 88th New York, the Irish Brigade; the tombstone belongs to Chaplain and Mrs. John H. W. Stuckenberg, 145th Pennsylvania Infantry, the only chaplain buried in the Gettysburg National Cemetery; a bronze, open-Bible marker on the steps of Christ Lutheran Church commemorates the death of Chaplain Horatio Howell, 90th Pennsylvania Infantry; the Pennsylvania State Monument lists all the chaplains assigned to Pennsylvania regiments during the battle.

tute at Carlisle included scores of Civil War regimental histories written by Union chaplains, none provided the summary about Gettysburg I hoped to find. It appeared that these chaplains were historic ghosts, sensed perhaps, but not often seen[2]. I decided to do as much research as I could, first just to identify the chaplains, Union and Confederate, who served at Gettysburg in July 1863. I did not realize it would take another sixteen years to weave the names, memoirs, service records, and civilian church records into one story of their service.

After retirement from active duty and after spending nine years as the Army Chaplain Corps Historian at Fort Jackson, South Carolina, I had managed to author or coauthor three books on Civil War chaplains.[3] Possibly for that reason, I was invited back to Gettysburg during the 150th Anniversary of the battle. In 2012 the Military Chaplains Association of America asked me to give a lecture in April 2013 on "Chaplains at Gettysburg," an invitation I accepted even though the subject demanded more information than I had immediately on hand at that time. At the same time, Dr. Lew Parks, director of the Doctor of Ministry program at Wesley Theological Seminary in Washington, DC, set up a 30-hour seminar for graduate students at the Eisenhower Conference Center in Gettysburg for October 2013. The seminar subject was "Ministry in a High-Stress Environment: Chaplains at Gettysburg." In spite of the understated title, I agreed to teach that course as well.

By fall 2013 it was still the case that there was no single-source book or article that I could find which provided an overview of the ministries of the chaplains, North and South, who served at Gettysburg. I thought the subject was important because I did not believe most officers who took staff rides really understood the mindset of the common soldiers who were preparing to fight on July 2 or July 3, 1863. Most of the regiments in the Army of Northern Virginia and in the Army of the Potomac included veterans of Antietam, Fredericksburg, and Chancellorsville. According to their own journals and letters, written just before the shelling began, many of the sol-

---

[2] The soldiers might have said they were holy ghosts when it came to ministering to the wounded under fire.

[3] John W. Brinsfield, William C. Davis, Benedict Maryniak, and James I. Robertson, Jr., *Faith in the Fight: Civil War Chaplains* (Mechanicsburg, PA: Stackpole Books, 2003); John Wesley Brinsfield, Jr., *The Spirit Divided: Memoirs of Civil War Chaplains—The Confederacy* (Macon, GA: Mercer University Press, 2005) and the companion volume with Benedict R. Maryniak, *The Spirit Divided: Memoirs of Civil War Chaplains—The Union* (Macon, GA: Mercer University Press, 2007).

diers and many of the officers were concerned with the probability of a high death rate, with having bodies identified after battle, with sending messages home to families, and with what may have been a greater dread, the possibility of disfiguring wounds. Some were consumed with revenge for earlier incidents in Virginia, and some were just plain scared. Chaplains recorded in their journals and diaries the comments and concerns the soldiers voiced as they prepared for battle. Commanders made short speeches; chaplains offered prayers. These were all concerns for chaplain ministries, but they were also readiness issues for commanders to weigh as well. Some did, some did not until it was too late.

The following is therefore a case study that seeks to portray not just the events leading to and through the Battle of Gettysburg, but also something of the mood and spirit of the soldiers and commanders on each side. The ministries of some 228 chaplains, Blue and Gray, who marched, camped, sometimes fought, and often prayed with their soldiers, have been placed in context according to the time and location of each chaplain during three days of battle. Many of the quotations from the memoirs, journals, and diaries of the commanders, soldiers, and chaplains have not been published, and certainly not published together, before now.

It would require another chapter to acknowledge the help and encouragement of all the military officers, seminary officials, and historians who gave me suggestions for this book. I am grateful to you all. Yet I must mention with special appreciation those who interrupted very busy schedules to give my manuscript or my project their attention: Col. Leonard Fullenkamp, USA (Retired), professor of History and Strategy, US Army War College; Professor George C. Rable, Sommersell Chair in Southern History, University of Alabama; Dr. Lew Parks, director of the Doctor of Ministries program, Wesley Theological Seminary, Washington, DC; Dr. Kenny Rowlette, director of the National Civil War Chaplains Museum, Liberty University, Lynchburg, Virginia; Dr. James I. Robertson, Jr., Alumni Distinguished Professor Emeritus of History, Virginia Tech and former executive director, US Civil War Centennial Commission, Washington, DC; Chaplain (Colonel-Retired) Kenneth Sampson, former faculty member, National War College, Washington, DC; Chaplain (Colonel-Retired) C. David Reese, former faculty member, US Army War College; the Rev. John A. Wega, director of the US Christian Commission Museum, Gettysburg, Pennsylvania; Dr. Marc Jolley, director, Mercer University Press, Macon, Georgia; and my wife, Patricia Tallon Brinsfield, my proofreader, driver, navigator, adviser, and assistant as I refought the Battle of Gettysburg year after year. She never grew weary, though the result of the battle was always the same.

In all, I have been amazed that it took the brave soldiers on both sides just three days to fight a battle that has taken me over a year just to describe. Yet many of their chaplains at Gettysburg, who left letters, memoirs, and diaries behind, were not just heroes on the battlefield, but also heroes of faith. This study is about them and the valiant commanders and soldiers who were their companions over the roads and fields of history.

—John Wesley Brinsfield, PhD, DMin
Chaplain (Colonel) US Army (Retired)

Introduction

The soldier's heart, the soldier's spirit, the soldier's soul are everything.
Unless the soldier's soul sustains him, he cannot be relied upon and will
fail himself and his commander and his country in the end.
—General of the Army George C. Marshall, 1944.[1]

Visitors to Gettysburg National Military Park are frequently struck by the
serenity of the countryside, the size of the battlefield, the scope of the battle
involving 160,000 men over three days, and the seeming willingness of soldiers to sacrifice themselves for a hill, a ridge, or a stream. The spirits of the
brave and bold, chiseled in stone and cast in bronze, seem to remain. In
1889 Gen. Joshua Chamberlain, former commander of the 20th Maine Infantry during the battle, came back to Gettysburg. In his speech on that occasion, he spoke of the effect the battlefield still had upon him: "In great
deeds something abides. On great fields something stays. Forms change and
pass; bodies disappear; but spirits linger, to consecrate ground for the vision-
place of souls. And reverent men and women from afar, and generations that
know us not and that we know not of, heart-drawn to see where and by
whom great things were suffered and done for them, shall come to this
deathless field, to ponder and dream."[2]

In more recent times, as expert guides take their parties around the battlefield and explain what happened at Gettysburg a century and a half ago,
questions inevitably arise: Why did General Lee invade Pennsylvania? Why
did so many attacks against the Union lines fail? Why did General Lee order
Pickett's Charge, almost a mile across fields laced with five-foot fences, into
devastating fire? And then the question that many ponder but don't always
ask, What drove soldiers to charge so valiantly against cannon belching shell
and canister when most of them must have known that many would be
killed, wounded, or captured?

The answers to some of these questions are often proposed, but complete answers remain in debate because neither General Lee nor General

---

[1] As cited in Robert L. Gushwa, *The Best and Worst of Times: The United States
Army Chaplaincy 1920–1945* (Washington, DC: Office of the Chief of Chaplains,
1977) 186.

[2] As cited in Henry Woodhead, ed., *Voices of the Civil War: Gettysburg* (Alexandria, VA: Time-Life Books, 1995) 171.

Meade wrote memoirs of the battle. Official records, letters, diaries, and other memoirs provide intriguing clues. However, since the Civil War the question of why men summon up their courage for battle, even when they know their survival is at stake, has transcended history.

Since the Civil War military leaders, historians, psychologists, journalists, and members of the general public have pondered the same question. What makes men and women willing to risk their lives for their country?

Sir John Keegan, the late senior lecturer in military history at the Royal Military Academy, Sandhurst, England, distilled four factors that made it easier for soldiers to endure the stresses of prolonged combat:

1. Moral purpose: belief that the war was just, necessary, and important.

2. Unit cohesion: belief that the regiment was well trained and composed of loyal comrades.

3. Selfless leadership: from first-line officers and noncommissioned officers.

4. Spiritual or religious fortification before battle: by prayer, worship, and for some, absolution.[3]

To Keegan's list one might add that soldiers need time to get their personal affairs in order, including sending any last letters home before deployment, preparing equipment, and a reasonable hope for success.[4]

Nevertheless, as the US Army Research Institute for the Behavioral and Social Sciences, in its 1994 study on the effective performance of Army units in combat, concluded:

> When the chips are down, there is no rational calculation in the world capable of causing an individual to lay down his life. On both the individual and collective levels, war is therefore primarily an affair of the heart. It is dominated by such irrational factors as resolution and courage, honor and duty and loyalty and sacrifice of self. When everything is said and done, none of these have anything to do with technology, whether primitive or sophisticated.[5]

---

[3] John Keegan, *The Face of Battle* (New York: Penguin Books, 1976) 279–80, 333.

[4] John W. Brinsfield and Peter A. Baktis, "The Human and Ethical Dimensions of Leadership in Preparation for Combat," in Lloyd J. Matthews, ed., *The Future of the Military Profession*, (New York: McGraw Hill, Custom Publishing, 2005) 485.

[5] *Determinants of Effective Unit Performance* (Alexandria, VA: US Army Research Institute for Behavioral and Social Sciences, 1994) 233.

Will a well-trained, well-led, and combat-hardened regiment with good morale stand up to prolonged conflict even when casualties mount? Certainly such a unit should have a better chance than a regiment of recruits. However, there still should be a realistic hope for success and enough supplies, especially ammunition, food, water, and bandages to sustain the soldiers in the cauldron of battle.

Agents of Hope

During the Gettysburg Campaign there were several agents of hope who could help summon the brave for difficult and dangerous assignments. Among these were commanders, both officers and noncommissioned officers, who sought to inspire their men by word and by example from the front of the battle line, and who were known to care personally for their troops. Second were the regimental chaplains, who led the men in prayer before battle, encouraged them to do their duty, held their last letters home, and helped succor the wounded and bury the dead with dignity. Third were the veteran soldiers themselves, who tried to take care of one another, sharing their ammunition and water and carrying wounded friends off of the field. Fourth were regimental bands, authorized by army regulations to play martial music any time the commander directed and then to serve as stretcher-bearers when soldiers fell in agony. Fifth were the regimental surgeons and assistant surgeons, who, while not morale officers, held out the hope that wounds could be treated and not prove always fatal.

Of course, there were other factors that helped keep the soldiers' morale and spirits up. Mail from home, newspapers, camp games, and sport contests were just a few. Yet when the drummers sounded the long roll and men fell into ranks, when muskets were primed, handshakes exchanged, and the small brass band played a brave song, it was often the commanders, the noncommissioned officers, the chaplain, and the surgeon whose presence gave them hope.

It is the purpose of this study to examine the ways that leaders made a difference in the outcome of the Battle of Gettysburg, including the spiritual leadership of chaplains. There have been many studies of generalship, operations, and tactics at Gettysburg, perhaps more than any other battle of the Civil War. There are also printed memoirs and letters of individual chaplains who were at Gettysburg, but there have not been to date any published studies that included an overview of the ministries of the 238 regimental chaplains and two missionaries, North and South, within the context of the battle. Not only should the service of these chaplains be of interest to the public, but also their memoirs of the battle, more than 150 pages discovered

3

to date. That the chaplains' encouragement and ministry was appreciated by their men is clear from the monuments the veterans erected after the war, including the statue of Father William Corby of the Irish Brigade on the battlefield and the memorial to Chaplain Horatio Howell of the 90th Pennsylvania in the town itself. Their stories should be told, for they helped keep the soldiers' spirits up in a time of national crisis, and like multitudes of others, were faithful to God and their soldiers to the end.

Soldiers of God

Why were chaplains, who were assumed to be noncombatants, included in the organizational tables of the Union and Confederate armies? Although chaplains had served as commissioned officers during the American Revolution, the War of 1812, and the Mexican-American War, their legal warrant for service during the Civil War came in May 1861.

The Provisional Congress of the Confederate States in Montgomery, Alabama, acted first. In passing legislation establishing a war department in February 1861, the Confederate Congress had not addressed the subject of the spiritual and moral welfare of soldiers. Clearly, thousands of young men leaving home to face the hardships of war would need some religious, moral, and morale support if they were to avoid the temptations that camp life supplied, including, in the extreme, the temptation to desert their units before, during, or after a battle. Moreover, by spring 1861 church leaders, parents of young soldiers, and local politicians were already petitioning for the establishment of chaplains in the military forces.

Accordingly, on May 2, 1861, Congressman Francis Bartow of Georgia reported a bill to provide chaplains for the Provisional Army of the Confederate States. After the required three readings, the bill passed and a commissioning process was set up for the president of the Confederate States to appoint chaplains for the duration of the war.[6]

The new law empowered the president to appoint chaplains to as many regiments, brigades, and posts as he deemed expedient, and provided a monthly pay of $85, which was midway between the pay of a second and a first lieutenant.[7] The legislation contained no stipulations regarding age,

---

[6] Herman A. Norton, *Struggling for Recognition: The United States Army Chaplaincy, 1791–1865* (Washington, DC: Office of the Chief of Chaplains, Department of the Army, 1977) 132.

[7] Two weeks after the initial legislation passed, an amendment lowered chaplains' pay to $50 a month since they supposedly worked only one day a week. In April 1862, after many protests, their pay was raised to $80 a month.

physical condition, education, or ecclesiastical status. However, ministers, priests, lay preachers, or even pious soldiers who wished to be commissioned as chaplains, whether they were ordained or not, had to have the approval and written recommendation of a regimental commander.[8] This could be secured by letters from third parties, by direct application to the commander, by transfer of an existing state militia commission, or by simply demonstrating the ability to preach, lead Bible studies, and conduct burial services in the absence of a regimental chaplain. Once a candidate was recommended through the senior commander to Richmond, a commission would be returned from the secretary of war on behalf of President Davis. Eventually, 1,308 men volunteered and served as Confederate chaplains.

While there were no duties for chaplains specified in the body of the Confederate Army Regulations, in the appended Articles of War, Article 2, it is clear that chaplains would be responsible for conducting divine worship, presumably at the time and place specified or allowed by their regimental commanders.[9] It was also stated in Article 4 that "every chaplain, commissioned in the army or armies of the Confederate States, who shall absent himself from the duties assigned him (excepting in cases of sickness or leave of absence) shall, on conviction thereof before a court-martial, be fined not exceeding one month's pay, besides the loss of his pay during his absence: or be discharged, as the said court-martial shall judge proper."[10] Clearly, commanders expected their chaplains to set the example of dedication to duty or submit their resignations if they could not do so.

Although pay was poor, there was some glamour for chaplains in being commissioned officers with the prospect of wearing a military uniform. Many Confederate chaplains dressed in a plain gray uniform coat with gray trousers and such hats, belts, buckles, and buttons as they could find. Some just wore a black suit with a white shirt and a wide-brimmed hat, as they had when they were civilians. There were few overcoats at first because many did not think the war would last long enough to require one.

Chaplains in Black and Blue

The enrollment and commissioning of chaplains for the Union forces was similar but with a few differences. On April 15, 1861, when President

---

[8] As stated in James A. Seddon, Secretary of War, *Regulations of the Army of the Confederate States, 1863* (Richmond, VA: J. W. Randolph, 1863) Article XXIV, paragraph 195, 22.

[9] Ibid., Articles of War, Art. 2,407.

[10] Ibid., Art. 4,407.

Lincoln called for 75,000 state militiamen to serve for three months following the surrender of Fort Sumter, chaplains were already part of the normal militia staff structure. Scarcely two weeks later, on May 3, with Confederate forces in nearby Virginia a threat to the capital, the president called for an additional 42,000 volunteers and an increase in regular army strength of 22,714.[11]

For moral and political reasons, Lincoln wanted chaplains available to both volunteer and regular units. When, on May 4, 1861, the war department issued general orders 15 and 16—the former for the organization of volunteer regiments, the latter making similar provision for new regiments in the regular army—both orders authorized regimental commanders to appoint chaplains on the vote of field officers and company commanders. The man thus chosen by volunteer regiments had to be an ordained minister of a Christian denomination and approved by the state governor. All who met those conditions were officially commissioned chaplains by the war department. While on duty they were to receive the pay and allowances of a captain of cavalry, approximately $100 a month plus allowances, or $1,700 annually.[12]

As in the case of Confederate chaplains, candidates for chaplain positions in the Army of the United States sometimes received direct appointments through personal or political contacts with regimental commanders. Many who applied to state volunteer regiments, however, had to be elected by the officers and sometimes by the men in ranks. When Father Joseph B. O'Hagan, SJ, applied for the chaplain position in the 73rd New York Volunteer Infantry, the men got to vote on his candidacy.

Initially, the men didn't make a very good impression on Father O'Hagan, as he wrote, "Such a collection was never before united in one body since the flood. Most of them were the scum of New York society, reeking with vice and spreading a moral malaria around them."[13] O'Hagan's sense of humor prevailed, however, as his description of his election suggests: "Over 400 voted for a Catholic priest; 154 for any kind of

---

[11] Herman A. Norton, *Struggling for Recognition: The United States Army Chaplaincy, 1791–1865* (Washington, DC: Office of the Chief of Chaplains, Department of the Army, 1977) 83.

[12] Ibid., 83–84. On July 17, 1862, Congress passed an act that substituted "religious denomination" for "Christian denomination," which allowed clergy of the Jewish faith, and ultimately of other faiths, to be commissioned as chaplains.

[13] Pat McNamara, "Fr. Joseph B. O'Hagan, SJ (1826–1878)" *Patheos Newsletter* (15 December 2009) accessed November 2014 at http://www.patheos.com/blogs/mcnamarasblog/2009/12/fr-joseph-b-o'hagan-s-j-1826-1878.html.

Protestant minister; 11 for a Mormon elder; and 335 said they could find their way to hell without the assistance of clergy."[14]

Eventually, Union regimental commanders found 2,154 chaplains to serve in their units during the Civil War.[15] Their uniform was prescribed by the 1861 army regulations: "The uniform for Chaplains of the Army will be plain black frock coat with standing collar, and one row of black buttons; plain black pantaloons; black felt hat or army forage cap, without ornament."[16] Eventually, some chaplains added a cap or hat insignia of the letters US in old English characters, in silver letters on a black velvet background surrounded by a gold-embroidered wreath.[17] Others wore a blue uniform, carried a ceremonial sword, and wore the two silver bars on their shoulders indicating that they were captains. A few were photographed with pistols or cavalry sabers. Commanders didn't seem to mind.

The specified duties of Union chaplains were almost as vague as were those of their Confederate counterparts. Aside from the implied duty of conducting divine services as reflected in the Articles of War, Union chaplains, one per regiment, were required "to report to the colonel commanding the regiment to which he is attached, at the end of each quarter, the moral and religious condition of the regiment, and such suggestions as may conduce to the social happiness and moral improvement of the troops."[18] Any other duties, such as ministering to the wounded, burying the dead, distributing religious literature and Bibles, conducting prayer services and revivals, or assisting surgeons, were left to the individual chaplain's initiative and to the commander's approval.

Neither Union nor Confederate chaplains were assumed to have had any military experience, but there was no Chaplain School for them to attend or even any authorized manuals regarding chaplain duties for them to read.[19] They learned how to do their jobs from their prior experience in

---

[14] Ibid.

[15] Benedict Maryniak, "Union Military Chaplains," as cited in Brinsfield et al., *Faith in the Fight*, 43.

[16] Simon Cameron, Secretary of War, *Revised United States Army Regulations of 1861* (Washington, DC: Government Printing Office, 1863) 524.

[17] Ibid., 466.

[18] Ibid., 507. Perhaps the only army regulation to consider the social happiness of soldiers!

[19] Two Union chaplains, William Y. Brown and Pinkney Hammond, wrote manuals addressing the office, duties, and responsibilities of army chaplains and published them privately in 1863, but they were not official publications and thus were advisory rather than regulatory. Moreover, it is uncertain how widely their pub-

civilian religious organizations, from their commanders, from other soldiers, and from each other when they got to camp.

Chaplain Thomas Caskey of the 18th Mississippi Infantry wrote in *Recollections* about his first days as a chaplain:

> I enlisted in the army as a preacher of the gospel and was assigned the duty of a chaplain. It was the hardest place to fill in the whole army. I was expected to cut my sermons to fit the pattern of our occupation as soldiers. It was expected that my preaching, prayers and exhortations would tend to make the soldiers hard fighters. It was difficult to find even texts from which to construct such sermons. I soon discovered that I would have to close my Bible and manufacture my ministerial supplies out of the whole cloth.[20]

Chaplain William R. Eastman, who served at Gettysburg with the 72nd New York Volunteer Infantry, had a more positive view of his ministry in the army:

> In one word, the significance of the chaplaincy was this: that the government offered to each regiment one man to be a friend to every man. While other officers might be good friends, this man was to make a business of kindliness. Not a commander, not a fighter, not hemmed in by any rules or any rank; left to himself to reach men by their hearts if he touched them at all, and by their hearts to make them better soldiers; a man to be sought in the hour of need; to stand for truth, purity, and all righteousness; for honorable living and hopeful dying; and having done all to stand by, in the spirit of service, according to the pattern of the Master. Many regiments did not understand and did not care; many commanders found it impossible to secure the man they would have gladly welcomed to such a post; many men who undertoook such service fell short, perhaps far short of their opportunities; but many also gained for themselves much love and a good name and a share in the final triumph.[21]

---

lications were disseminated and read by chaplains during the war. Herman A. Norton, *Struggling for Recognition: The United States Army Chaplaincy, 1791–1865* (Washington, DC: Office of the Chief of Chaplains, Department of the Army, 1977) 175, 177.

[20] As cited in John K. Butterworth, ed., *Mississippi in the Confederacy: As They Saw It* (Baton Rouge, LA: LSU Press, 1961) 233.

[21] Brinsfield et al., *Faith in the Fight*, 126.

In June 1863, 110 Confederate and 128 Union chaplains left Virginia for the long march north into Pennsylvania with their respective armies. They were not sure where they were going or what they would find along the way. A month later, at Gettysburg, one was killed, at least two wounded, two captured, and sixteen imprisoned when they volunteered to stay behind with the men too badly wounded to be moved. They performed many functions, from loading artillery pieces to administering chloroform to soldiers in field hospitals, from offering prayers and absolution under fire to advising commanders, from writing letters for soldiers to burying the dead. Their stories of trying to be a friend to all in the context of the largest battle of the Civil War are testaments to faith and courage above and beyond the call of duty.

JOHN W. BRINSFIELD, JR.

Order of Battle for the Union and Confederate Armies

Union Order of Battle
Army of the Potomac
Maj. Gen. George G. Meade, Commanding
93,000 Men

First Corps: Major General John R. Reynolds
First Division: Brigadier General James Wadsworth
Second Division: Brigadier General John Robinson
Third Division: Brigadier General Thomas Rowley

Second Corps: Major General Winfield Scott Hancock
First Division: Brigadier General John Caldwell
Second Division: Brigadier General John Gibbon
Third Division: Brigadier General Alexander Hays

Third Corps: Major General Daniel E. Sickles
First Division: Major General David Birney
Second Division: Brigadier General Andrew Humphreys

Fifth Corps: Major General George Sykes
First Division: Brigadier General James Barnes
Second Division: Brigadier General Romeyn Ayres
Third Division: Brigadier General Samuel Crawford

Sixth Corps: Major General John Sedgwick
First Division: Brigadier General Horatio Wright
Second Division: Brigadier General Albion Howe
Third Division: Major General John Newton

Ninth Corps: Major General Oliver O. Howard
First Division: Brigadier General Francis Barlow
Second Division: Brigadier General Adolph von Steinwehr
Third Division: Major General Carl Schurz

Twelfth Corps: Major General Henry W. Slocum
First Division: Major General Alpheus Williams
Second Division: Major General John Geary

Cavalry Corps: Major General Alfred Pleasonton
First Division: Brigadier General John Buford
Second Division: Brigadier General David Gregg
Third Division: Brigadier General Judson Kilpatrick

Artillery Reserve: Brigadier General Robert O. Tyler
Chief of Artillery: Brigadier General Henry J. Hunt[22]

Confederate Order of Battle
Army of Northern Virginia
General Robert E. Lee, Commanding
75,000 Men

First Corps: Lieutenant General James Longstreet
Major General Lafayette McLaw's Division
Major General George E. Pickett's Division
Major General John B. Hood's Division

Second Corps: Lieutenant General Richard S. Ewell
Major General Jubal A. Early's Division
Major General Edward Johnson's Division
Major General Robert E. Rodes's Division

Third Corps: Lieutenant General A. P. Hill
Major General R. H. Anderson's Division
Major General Henry Heth's Division
Major General William D. Pender's Division

Cavalry Division: Major General J. E. B. Stuart
Chief of Artillery: Brigadier General William N. Pendleton

---

[22] For the names of the brigade commanders and the lists of regiments in each division of both the Army of the Potomac and the Army of Northern Virginia, please see Jay Luvaas and Harold Nelson, eds., *Guide to the Battle of Gettysburg* (Lawrence: University Press of Kansas, 1994) Appendix II, or the lists in *The War of the Rebellion: Official Records of the Union and Confederate Armies*, US War Department, series 1, vol. XXVII, part 1: 926–27.

Robert E. Lee, Commanding General, Army
of Northern Virginia, 1864. Credit: Library of Congress.

The Men Who Authorized the Pennsylvania Campaign: Jefferson Davis and His Cabinet: (left to right) Judah P. Benjamin, Stephen Mallory, Alexander Stephens, Jefferson Davis, John Henninger Reagan, and Robert Toombs. Back row, standing left to right: Christopher Memminger and LeRoy Pope Walker. In 1861 Toombs was commissioned a Brigadier General and left the Cabinet. In 1862 James Seddon replaced Walker as Secretary of War and Thomas Watts was appointed Attorney General. Credit: *Harper's Weekly*.

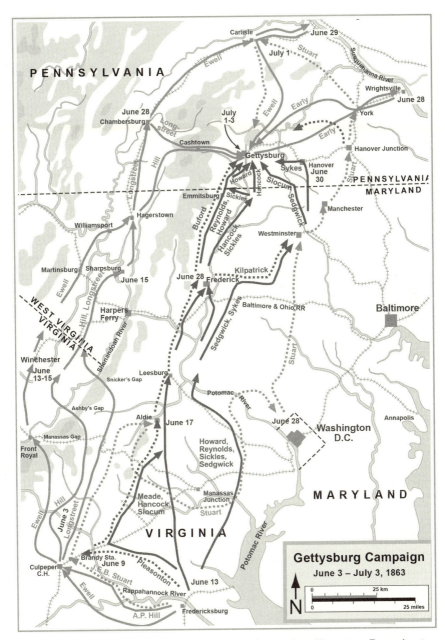

Marching Routes of the Confederate and Union Armies from Virginia to Pennsylvania.

Map by Hal Jespersen.

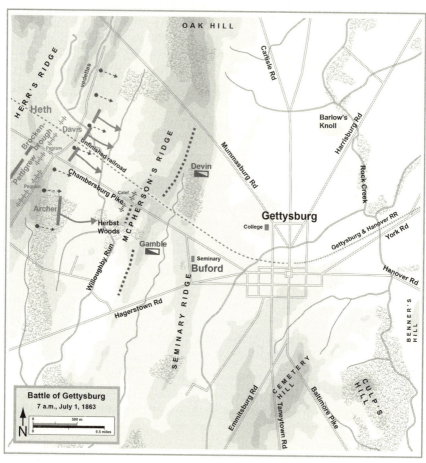

Map of Confederate attack on July 1, 1863. Map by Hal Jepersen.

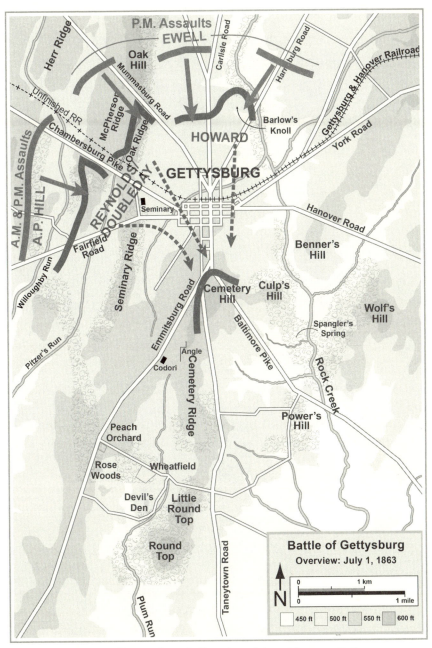

Map of Union Retreat through Gettysburg, July 1, 1863. Map by Hal Jespersen.

Lieutenant General Richard Ewell, Second Corps Commander,
Army of Northern Virginia. Credit: National Archives.

Lieutenant General James Longstreet, First Corps Commander,
Army of Northern Virginia. Credit: Library of Congress.

Brigadier General William N. Pendleton (left), West Point Class of 1830, Episcopal priest and Chief of Artillery in the Army of Northern Virginia for most of the war. Major General Isaac Trimble (right), Division Commander, Army of Northern Virginia. Credit: Wikipedia Commons.

Major General George Pickett (left), Division Commander, Army of Northern Virginia. Lieutenant General A. P. Hill (right), Third Corps Commander, Army of Northern Virginia. Credit: Library of Congress.

George G. Meade (left), Commanding General, Army of the Potomac. Credit: Photo by Matthew Brady, Library of Congress. Brigadier General Henry Hunt (right), West Point Class of 1839, Chief of Artillery for the Army of the Potomac at Gettysburg. Credit: Photo by Matthew Brady, Library of Congress.

Major General Daniel Sickles (left), Third Corps Commander, Army of the Potomac. Credit: Library of Congress. Major General Winfield S. Hancock (right), Second Corps Commander, Army of the Potomac. Credit: National Archives.

Brigadier General John Buford, Commander, First Cavalry Division, Army of the Potomac. Credit: Photo by Matthew Brady, Library of Congress.

Brigadier General Alexander Webb (left), Second Brigade Commander, Second Division, Second Corps, Army of the Potomac. General Webb received the Medal of Honor for the heroic defense of his brigade's position along the stone wall on July 3, 1863. Credit: Library of Congress. Colonel Joshua Lawrence Chamberlain (right), 20th Maine Infantry, shown in his subsequent Brigadier General's uniform. Chamberlain received the Medal of Honor for his regiment's part in the defense of Little Round Top. Credit: Photo by Matthew Brady, Library of Congress.

Sergeant Major David Johnston (left), 7th Virginia Infantry, CSA. Credit: *Story of a Confederate Boy in the Civil War*, 1914. Private Albert Davis (right), Wisconsin Iron Brigade. Credit: National Archives.

Federal cavalry on the move, 1863.

Chapter 1

The Long March:
Looking for an Opportunity in Pennsylvania

"The rain poured down in torrents and the cussing of some of the boys was fearfully serious."[1]
—Corp. Edmund Patterson, 9th Alabama Infantry

Why Gen. Robert E. Lee ordered the Army of Northern Virginia to move into Maryland and Pennsylvania in June 1863 is not hard to answer. Even though Lee had won unquestioned victories at Fredericksburg and at Chancellorsville over the previous five months, the Army of the Potomac had been reinforced to number 136,704 soldiers by the end of May, an increase of 20,000 in just three weeks.[2] Lee had been reinforced as well after his losses, but his combined strength on May 31, 1863, was just 68,352, half the number of the opposing Federal army under Maj. Gen. Joseph Hooker.[3] While Lee did not have exact strength reports, it was clear that the Union forces were immense. Moreover, after almost two years of fighting in northern Virginia, supplies for men, horses, and mules were becoming scarce. Many farms were depleted and multiple farmhouses, barns, smokehouses, and crops completely destroyed. In fact, General Lee had ordered two divisions of Longstreet's Corps to Suffolk, Virginia, in spring 1863 to collect provisions for the army.

With these challenges in mind, former Confederate States' president Jefferson Davis explained his strategy for spring 1863 in his postwar memoirs:

---

[1] As cited in John G. Barrett, *Yankee Rebel: The Civil War Journal of Edmund DeWitt Patterson* (Chapel Hill: University of North Carolina Press, 1966) 21.

[2] Major General Joseph Hooker's strength on May 1, 1863, was estimated at 133,868. The Army of the Potomac lost 17,197 in three days' fighting at Chancellorsville. Hooker's strength by the end of May was 136,704, more than making up for his casualties at Chancellorsville from April 30 through May 6. See Davis, *Rise and Fall*, vol. II, 437.

[3] Fitzhugh Lee, *General Lee* (Greenwich, CT.: Fawcett Publications, 1961) 249.

It was decided by a bold movement to attempt to transfer hostilities to the north side of the Potomac, by crossing the river and marching into Maryland and Pennsylvania, simultaneously driving the foe out of the Shenandoah Valley. Thus, it was hoped, General Hooker's army would be called from Virginia to meet our advance toward the heart of the enemy's country. In that event, the vast preparations which had been made for an advance upon Richmond would be foiled, the plan for his summer's campaign deranged, and much of the season of active operations be consumed.... If, beyond the Potomac, some opportunity should be offered so as to enable us to defeat the army on which our foe most relied, the measure of our success would be full; but, if the movement only resulted in freeing Virginia from the presence of the hostile army, it was more than could be fairly expected from awaiting the attack which was clearly indicated.[4]

Of course, there were also hopeful speculations about the benefits yet another Southern victory might bring. Brig. Gen. Fitzhugh Lee wrote later that "among other results of a decisive successful battle on Northern soil, might be a recognition of the Confederacy by foreign powers and a lasting peace."[5] Yet the notion of one great victory leading to a negotiated settlement for peace with the United States government had its skeptics.[6] What would a *decisive* victory entail? It was doubtful that anyone could have accurately predicted what was really needed to win the peace—and at what cost. Nevertheless, it seemed to President Davis that to go on the offensive was better than to remain in Virginia and face overwhelming enemy numbers and dwindling supplies. So hope prevailed.

After some discussion in Richmond during the second week in May, General Lee, President Davis, and the members of the president's cabinet agreed that the army would begin its long march toward Pennsylvania on June 3.[7] At that time the Army of Northern Virginia was positioned on the

---

[4] Davis, *Rise and Fall*, vol. II, 438.

[5] Lee, *General Lee*, 250.

[6] Among whom eventually was Lt. Gen. James Longstreet, who wrote of Gettysburg, in 1878: "The battle as it was fought would, in any result, have so crippled us that the Federals would have been able to make good their retreat, and we should soon have been obliged to retire to Virginia with nothing but victory to cover our waning cause." See J. William Jones, ed., "General James Longstreet's Account of the Campaign and Battle," *Southern Historical Society Papers* 5/6 (1878): 54–86.

[7] The vote in the Davis cabinet for General Lee to march for Pennsylvania was 5 to 1. Lee opposed proposals to send reinforcements from Virginia to Mississippi or Tennessee since that would make it even harder to oppose Hooker. See Kelly Knau-

south side of the Rappahannock River near Fredericksburg. In his report of the Gettysburg Campaign, General Lee wrote:

> The commands of Longstreet and Ewell were put into motion, and en-camped around Culpeper Courthouse on the 7th of June. As soon as their march was discovered by the enemy, he threw a force across the Rappahannock about two miles below Fredericksburg, apparently for the purpose of observation. Hill's corps was left to watch these troops, with instructions to follow the movements of the army as soon as they should retire.
>
> General Ewell left Culpeper Courthouse on the 10th of June. He crossed the branches of the Shenandoah near Front Royal and reached Cedarville on the 12th, where he was joined by General Jenkins. Detach-ing General Rodes with his division and the greater part of Jenkins' bri-gade to dislodge a force of the enemy at Berryville, General Ewell, with the rest of his command, moved upon Winchester, Johnson's division ad-vancing by the Front Royal road, Early's by the Valley turnpike....
>
> On the night of Ewell's appearance at Winchester [June 13], the enemy in front of A. P. Hill at Fredericksburg, recrossed the Rappahan-nock, and the whole army of General Hooker withdrew from the north side of the river. In order to mislead him as to our intentions, and at the same time to protect Hill's corps in its march up the Rappahannock, Longstreet left Culpeper Courthouse on the 15th, and advancing along the eastern side of the Blue Ridge, occupied Ashby's and Snicker's gaps. He had been joined while at Culpeper, by General Pickett, with three brigades of his division. General Stuart, with three brigades of cavalry, moved on Longstreet's right, and took position in front of the gaps.[8]

In these short paragraphs General Lee described a march of 88 road miles in ten days, not only for the soldiers, but also for the horses and mules and the wagons they pulled. Marching four men abreast, some corps-level

---

er, ed., *Gettysburg: A Day-by-Day Account of the Greatest Battle of the Civil War* (New York: Time Books, 2013) 14.

[8] "General Lee's Final and Full Report of the Pennsylvania Campaign and Bat-tle of Gettysburg," as cited by Rev. J. William Jones, ed., *Southern Historical Society Papers* 2/1 (1876): 35–37. Lieutenant generals James Longstreet, Richard Ewell, and A. P. Hill were Lee's corps commanders, with approximately 20,000 soldiers in each corps. Major General J. E. B. Stuart commanded the cavalry division of 9,500 troop-ers divided into six brigades plus the Stuart Horse Artillery. Brigadier General A. G. Jenkins was one of the brigade commanders in Stuart's cavalry division. Major Gen-eral Robert E. Rodes was a division commander in Ewell's Corps; Major General George E. Pickett, a division commander in Longstreet's Corps.

units stretched along the roads from 4 to 6 miles, not including the wagon trains. Usually, the infantry units began their marches at about 4:30 A.M. and continued for twelve hours, including interruptions to clear roads, fetch water, and pick apples. Even so, it took another two weeks for the army to get to Chambersburg and Carlisle in Pennsylvania.

Altogether Hill's and Longstreet's corps marched 159 miles from the Rappahannock to Gettysburg. Ewell's Corps marched 203 miles, Early's Division of Ewell's Corps some 209 miles, and Stuart's three brigades of cavalry approximately 260 miles. These troop movements were accomplished in twenty-eight days at a rate of six to nine miles a day less the time it took to fight two battles—at Brandy Station on June 9 and at Winchester from June 13 to June 15.

The chaplains who tramped or rode north with their regiments in the Army of Northern Virginia were 110 in number, supplemented by two missionaries and two ordained staff officers. Ninety of the Methodist, Presbyterian, Baptist, Episcopal, and Roman Catholic chaplains were assigned to infantry units, fourteen to cavalry regiments, and six to various artillery battalions. Eighty-five chaplains were from Virginia, North Carolina, or Georgia. The rest were from other states such as Alabama and Mississippi. Eighty-nine regiments, most in the infantry, had no chaplain with them, although many conducted their prayer meetings with their own lay leadership. Private William M. Dame from the Richmond Howitzers in Longstreet's Corps wrote in his memoirs:

> Every evening, about sunset, whenever it was at all possible, we would keep up our custom, and such of us as could get together, *wherever we might be*, should gather for prayer.... I may remark, as a notable fact, that this resolution was carried out *almost literally*. Sometimes a few of the fellows would gather in prayer, while the rest of us fought the guns. Several times...we met *under fire*...we held that prayer hour every day at sunset, during the entire campaign. And some of us thought, and *think* that the strange exemption our Battery experienced, our little loss, in the midst of unnumbered perils, and incessant service, during that awful campaign, was that, in answer to our prayers, "the God of battles covered our heads in the day of battle" and was merciful to us, because we called upon Him. If any think this is a "fond fancy" *we don't.*[9]

---

[9] As cited in Margaret E. Wagner, Gary W. Gallagher, and Paul Finkelman, eds., *The Library of Congress Civil War Desk Reference* (New York: Simon and Schuster, 2002) 481 (emphasis in original).

The Federal Response

On May 27, 1863, Major General Hooker's intelligence chief reported that "the Confederate army is under marching orders" and would probably move "around our right flank."[10] Eight days later, on June 4, Hooker was informed that some of the enemy's camps around Fredericksburg had been abandoned, and a few days later that Confederate cavalry had concentrated near Culpeper Courthouse. On June 8, Hooker sent Maj. Gen. Alfred Pleasonton's Union Cavalry Corps toward Brandy Station. Even though Pleasonton lost the eight-hour battle there, the movement of Lee's army had been confirmed.

On June 13, Hooker started the movement of seven infantry corps and one cavalry corps north toward Manassas to remain between Washington and Baltimore and Lee's army. By June 28, the Army of the Potomac had made it to Frederick, Maryland, where Hooker learned that he had been relieved of command. The remainder of the 118-mile forced march from Fredericksburg would be the responsibility of Maj. Gen. George G. Meade, who had served in every major campaign of the army since 1862 and who, like General Lee, was a veteran of the Mexican War, an experienced commanding officer, and an army engineer.

Pickett's Division, Longstreet's Corps:
   Up Close in the Confederate Ranks

Few of the lower-ranking officers or private soldiers in the Army of Northern Virginia were aware of General Lee's plans early on, for, of course, they were not involved in the strategic decision-making process. In the absence of facts, rumors abounded in the ranks. One story that buzzed through the units claimed that "more than 500 of Longstreet's men dropped out of the first day's march, some dying by the roadway."[11]

Episcopal chaplain Peter Tinsley of the 28th Virginia Infantry in Pickett's Division of Longstreet's Corps did not believe that story was true, at least not to his knowledge. Tinsley, an 1860 graduate of Virginia Theological Seminary in Alexandria, kept a detailed record of the long trek into Pennsylvania. A few pages from Tinsley's private diary, written on the march, provide a picture of hardship but also of fairly high morale among the soldiers:

---

[10] As cited in Knauer, *Gettysburg: A Day-by-Day Account*, 15.
[11] Ibid., 19.

Camp 28th Va Reg [Virginia Regiment] near Culpeper C.H.
[Courthouse]

June 16. 1863. Tu[esday].

Our Division marches to Gaines Cross Roads—(16 miles) crossing
Hazel & Thornton Rivers, which form the Rapannock.

June 17. Wed.

Our Reg. forms the advance guard & leave at 4 ½ A.M. We cross
Hedgemans Creek into Fauquier County—pass Leeds Church, a very
handsome edifice on the roadside. The country is quite mountainous & is
picturesque in the extreme. There is every indication of refinement & el-
egance, but there is an aspect of sadness about this whole region. Many
beautiful residences abandoned in whole or part by the Proprietors, the
almost entire absence of the once happy & contented laborers, of horses,
cattle, sheep & a general scarcity of almost every domestic animal are silent witness to the near residence of the invader & his frequent incur-
sions. The weather was intensely hot, & the roadside was strewn with
noble soldiers overcome by heat & fatigue. Many who had never surrendered to fatigue on their marches had to succumb today—and the rumors
of deaths by sunstroke were "legion," but I believe no genuine case (or
very few, if any) occurred in our Div[ision], & by the close of the next
day nearly all were right again. At 7 P.M. at a Brick Church 1 mile from
Piedmont. Distance 15–16 miles.[12]

Chaplain Tinsley's disclaimer may have been a bit premature, for within six days he was ill with dysentery and his friend "Griffin" left with a doctor near Shepherdstown, West Virginia.[13] Sunstroke was evidently not the
only health problem on the march. His diary resumes:

June 18—Th[ursday].

We marched to Paris about 7 or 8 miles. The Div[ision] camps a little
way from the town. Griffin and I go in & refresh ourselves with cool water
& buttermilk, he being quite unwell. Paris is a small & very unattractive village of about 150 inhabitants. There I hear of a Cavalry fight in Loudon &
see some of the prisoners. Opinions differ as to the result of the fight & the

---

[12] Peter Archer Tinsley (1833–1908), "Private Diary," in John and Joyce
Schmale Civil War Collection, Wheaton (IL) College Archives, box 1, folder 51: 1–
2. Chaplain Peter Tinsley's biography is in Appendix II of this volume.

[13] Possibly Charles R. Griffin, Company D, 8th Virginia Infantry Regiment,
detailed to help the chaplain.

conduct of our forces. A very heavy rain falls & after a lull in the storm G[riffin] and I return to Quarters. Weather previous to the rain intensely hot.

June 19—Fri[day].

We resume march at 10 ½ A.M. Instead of crossing the Mountain at Paris, we bear to the right, proceed nearly to Upperville, turn off from the stone road nearly at right angles to the left—reach Snickersville a little before sunset, meet there our friends of the 2nd Cavalry. We then cross to West Side of mountain & encamp on the other slope about dusk. A tremendous rain comes up deluging our party—On the way I meet Cousin Tinsley Pinick who is officiating in 2nd Virginia Cavalry for Chaplain Berry.[14] He tells me of Lieut[enant] Col[onel] Watts' (Cav[alry]) wound—March about 15 miles.

June 20. Sat[urday].

It continues rainy until late in the evening. We make three starts but finally get off, after having been twice been wet & muddied by leaving our tents to march. The Div[ision] wades the Shenandoah, which had become deep & rapid by the rains. Linthicum takes me over behind him.[15] We encamp about 1 ½ miles from the ford. This County Clarke is extremely fertile & picturesque...perfectly splendid indeed....[16]

A. P. Hill's Corps

On the day Pickett's Division splashed across the Shenandoah River, Ohio-born Corporal Edmund D. Patterson of the 9th Alabama Infantry in Anderson's Division, Hill's Corps, recorded an entry in his journal describing what it was like to make that river crossing in the dark the night before:

Saturday 20th [June]

Last night I felt more like "cussing" than I did like writing. Yesterday morning we marched to Front Royal, where we remained until 4 o'clock in the evening, waiting, they said until the pontoons were laid across both branches of the Shenandoah. In due time we moved forward,

---

[14] Tinsley Penick, son of Agnes Tinsley and the Reverend Daniel Penick, was Peter Tinsley's first cousin. The Reverend William W. Berry (1833–1905) was the Methodist chaplain for the 2nd Virginia Cavalry Regiment.

[15] Chaplain Charles F. Linthecum, 8th Virginia Infantry Regiment.

[16] Tinsley, "Private Diary," 3–4. Clarke County is east of Winchester; Paris is southeast at Ashby Gap.

and the head of the column commenced crossing just at dark, and about the same time it commenced raining. We found the pontoons still upon the wagons packed near the river, and as regiment after regiment came up they made sport of them, and "waded in." It was no pleasant task crossing the river at that time. I pulled off my boots, socks, pants and etc., thinking I might keep them a little dry, but by the time I had cut my feet on the sharp rocks, and fallen down a time or two, I regretted it. The bank on this side of the river is steep and by the time we crossed it had become perfectly slippery and I had to go up it on "all fours." Some of the boys would nearly reach the top and then an unlucky slip would send them "sousing" into the river again. The rain poured down in torrents and the cussing of some of the boys was fearfully serious. After reaching this side of the river, we went out into an old field, where I fell into a gully; ran over a briar patch, scratched my face and nearly broke my neck, so dark that I could see it, feel it, taste it, and smell it, and such thick darkness that a streak of lightning could not have cut through it. After wandering about in the darkness a while I ran against a fence, and taking about half a dozen rails I made me a comfortable bed, so as to keep me out of the mud, laying them side by side.[17]

Presbyterian chaplain Charles H. Dobbs, 12th Mississippi Infantry, also in Anderson's Division of Hill's Corps, was born in Louisiana in 1835. A graduate of Centre College and Danville Theological Seminary in Danville, Kentucky, Dobbs had been a chaplain just over four months when he started for Pennsylvania with his regiment. Dobbs recalled the march from Culpeper, Virginia, in detail in his postwar reminiscences:

It was a beautiful and bright morning that we broke up camp and left the spot hallowed to many of us by the blessed work of grace we had there witnessed. Our route was through Culpeper County, in sight of the famous Cedar Mountain, by way of Front Royal, over Snicker's Gap, through Winchester, Williamsport and Chambersburg to Gettysburg. This march was certainly one of the best conducted on record. Everything was arranged and executed with consummate skill.

The army was divided into three corps. Gen. Jackson's old corps, now under the command of Gen. Ewell, had gone in advance and had won a great victory at Winchester; the other two corps, under the command of Gens. A. P. Hill and Longstreet, respectively. Of these, one

---

[17] As cited in John G. Barrett, *Yankee Rebel: The Civil War Journal of Edmund DeWitt Patterson* (Chapel Hill: University of North Carolina Press, 1966) 21.

went in advance one day, the other the next. The same order was observed with the divisions, the brigades and regiments. The brigade first today was last the next day.

If one division took up the line of march at 3 o'clock, A.M., today, it went into camp at 2 o'clock, P.M., and cooked three days' rations. The last brigade would not take up the line of march until 10 o'clock, A.M., and of course did not go into camp until about 9 o'clock, P.M. The wagons were not seen by us, only every third day, we found them upon the ground when we went into camp. Usually the greatest trial to a soldier upon the march was the wagons. Something would detain one wagon, and this would bring the whole wagon train to a halt, then the men who were behind would close up, and be jammed together in the road. In a few minutes the line would stretch out again; and by the time the men would get well started, there would be another halt. Every infantryman, who has ever marched under such circumstances, will bear me out in the statement that nothing is more annoying or tiresome than these sudden halts and starts. In the march to Gettysburg there was no interruption of this kind. The wagons, I presume, went by parallel road usually, and we saw nothing of them only at regular intervals, when rations were issued. It was all like clock-work.[18]

There was only one exception to this regularity of encampment, and that [w]as at Shenandoah. We crossed just above the junction of the North and South Fork. On this day I borrowed a horse and went in advance of the army, to try and swap a gold watch and chain for a horse. In the meantime there came up a tremendous rain. The heavens were black with the thick, threatening clouds, peals of thunder followed by quick upon vivid flashes of lightening, and there I must wait. Night set in, and still my regiment came not. Soon it was pitchy dark; not an object was visible two feet off.

As I stood there upon the banks of the Shenandoah, in the rain and darkness, I called out occasionally, "What division is this?" Finally a familiar voice answered: "Bejabbers, parson, its yer own regiment, an' jist let me have the Colonel's horse if yez have him there, an' fall back into the ranks." It was Jimmy, one of an Irish company in our regiment. I remonstrated, but Jimmy took him and I fell in. After marching some half a mile more, we were filed off to the right. The darkness was oppressive, and the confusion unbounded. Men were calling out for their companies, regiments and divisions. Everywhere you could hear "Company A," "Company C," "12th Alabama," "16th Mississippi," etc. all jumbled and

---

[18] Charles Holt Dobbs, "Reminiscences of an Army Chaplain," *Presbyterian Christian Observer* (1874), as cited in Brinsfield, *Spirit Divided: The Confederacy*, 60.

mixed. At last some stentorian voice, sounding high above all the rest asked: "Where is Company Y, 799th North Carolina Tar Heels?" Then was confusion doubly confounded. In the course of time, however, we reached a fence where we were halted for camp, and the men were not long in making fires. In the meantime the rain ceased, the thousands of fires lighted up the old field, and the men lay down to sleep. I found myself among my Irish friends, drenched to the skin and hungry as a wolf. On such a night as this one place was as good as another, and amid the sons of the Emerald Isle I concluded to stay. I got a great rock, rolled it up to the fire, sat down to toast my toes, and with my head on my knees, was soon in profound slumber.[19]

Lt. William B. Taylor, in the 11th North Carolina Infantry Regiment in Heth's Division of Hill's Corps, wrote to his mother on June 22:

[W]e have been on the march since yesterday week we were 10 miles below Fredericksburg we crossed the Blue Ridge and the Rapidan Rappahannock and both branches of the Shenandoah north and south and are within 21 miles of the Potomac and I would take any amount of money for the trip the most butiful scenery I ever beheld since I have been in the army witch is some time you know.

It is suposed that we will go into Pennsylvania and I hope we may and I hope the officers will devastate the territory and give the enemy a taste of the horrors of war and that is all that will close the war soon if anything will if this invasion dont do anything but relieve Vicksburg witch will be a great thing within itself the army is in fine spirits and anxious for the trip.[20]

Finding an Objective While on the March

On June 21, 1863, at his headquarters in Paris, Virginia, General Lee did an assessment of the enemy's assumed position and concluded:

The Federal army was apparently guarding the approaches to Washington, and manifested no disposition to resume the offensive. In the meantime the progress of Ewell, who was already in Maryland, with Jenkins' cavalry advanced into Pennsylvania as far as Chambersburg, rendered it necessary that the rest of the army should be in supporting distance, and

---

[19] Ibid., 61.

[20] William B. Taylor, Letter, June 22, 1863, Gettysburg, PA: Gettysburg National Military Park Library: 1195 Baltimore Pike, Gettysburg, PA, 17325.

Hill having reached the Valley, Longstreet was withdrawn to the west side of the Shenandoah, and the two corps encamped near Berryville.[21]

General Lee then decided to direct his main effort toward Harrisburg, Pennsylvania, with Ewell moving in advance through Chambersburg and Carlisle, and Hill and Longstreet bringing their troops through Chambersburg, Gettysburg, and York. Early's lead division from Ewell's Corps, also going through Gettysburg and York, would cross the Susquehanna River over the bridge at Wrightsville and cut the railroad between Baltimore and Harrisburg.

Lee then gave Major General Stuart orders which allowed him some discretion in harassing Hooker's army, but with the stipulation that as soon as the Federals crossed the Potomac, Stuart was to position his cavalry on the right flank of Early's lead Confederate division. The first objective was to capture the bridges over the Susquehanna River as Stuart wrote in his report:

> The main army, I was advised by the Commanding General, would move in two columns for the Susquehanna—[Major General] Early commanded the advance of one of these columns to the eastward, and I was directed to communicate with him as early as practicable after crossing the Potomac, and place my command on his right flank. It was expected I would find him in York. The newspapers of the enemy, my only source of information, chronicled his arrival there and at Wrightsville, on the Susquehanna, with great particularity. I therefore moved to join him in that vicinity.[22]

General Lee did not wait idly for Stuart's report:

> It was expected that as soon as the Federal army should cross the Potomac, General Stuart would give notice of its movements, and nothing having been heard from him since our entrance into Maryland, it was inferred that the enemy had not yet left Virginia. Orders were therefore issued to move upon Harrisburg. The expedition of General Early to York was designed in part to prepare for this undertaking, by breaking the rail-

---

[21] "General Lee's Final and Full Report of the Pennsylvania Campaign and Battle of Gettysburg," as cited by Rev. J. William Jones, ed., *Southern Historical Society Papers* 2/1 (1876): 38.

[22] Ibid., "General Stuart's Report of Operations," 75.

road between Baltimore and Harrisburg and seizing the bridge over the Susquehannah at Wrightsville.[23]

Lieutenant General Hill reported that he had also received orders to move toward York:

> On the morning of the 29th of June the Third Corps, composed of the divisions of Major Generals Anderson, Heth, and Pender, and five battalions of artillery, under the command of Colonel R. L. Walker, was encamped on the road from Chambersburg to Gettysburg, near the village of Fayetteville. I was directed to move on this road in the direction of York, and to cross the Susquehanna, menacing the communications of Harrisburg with Philadelphia, and to cooperate with General Ewell, acting as circumstances might require. Accordingly, on the 29th I moved General Heth's division to Cashtown, some eight miles from Gettysburg, following on the morning of the 30th with the division of General Pender, and directing General Anderson to move in the same direction on the morning of the 1st of July.[24]

If these orders were understood as reported, Major General Stuart would not have been able to cover Early's flank at York, Pennsylvania, and simultaneously report on the march of the Union Army toward Frederick, Maryland. As Stuart reflected afterward:

> The enemy's army was moving in a direction nearly parallel to me. I was apprized of its arrival at Taneytown, when I was near Hanover, Pennsylvania, but believing from the lapse of time that our army was already in York or Harrisburg, where it could choose its battleground with the enemy, I hastened to place my command with it. It is believed that had the corps of Hill and Longstreet moved on instead of halting near Chambersburg, that York could have been the place of concentration instead of Gettysburg.[25]

---

[23] Ibid., "General Lee's Final and Full Report of the Pennsylvania Campaign and Battle of Gettysburg," 39.

[24] Ibid., "General A. P. Hill's Report of the Battle of Gettysburg," 222.

[25] Ibid., "General Stuart's Report of Operations," 75. Note: Stuart's critique may not have been well founded. Hill had already sent his lead division to Cashtown on June 29, headed toward York.

Only God Knows Where...

Even though many of the Confederate soldiers were not sure where they were going on the march, quite a few found foraging in Pennsylvania a great relief from the hunger their paltry army rations failed to satisfy. Because they were in enemy territory, no payment for provisions seemed necessary—an assumption that bothered the chaplains who accompanied them.

Francis Milton Kennedy, a Methodist chaplain assigned to the 28th North Carolina Infantry in Pender's Division of Hill's Corps, had been commissioned just five months when the Gettysburg Campaign began. He heard that there was looting by some of his men when they crossed into Pennsylvania:

> Saturday, June 27th
> Passed the Pennsylvania line about 1 mile from last night's camps. Passed through Waynesboro and purchased with Confederate money a number of things I needed. I felt like they were taking the money more as a "military necessity" then because they liked to. This country abounds in villages, in fact we seem to be passing through one continuous village all the time. The farms are in a perfect state of cultivation, and the wheat which seems to be the main crop, is vastly superior to any I have seen before.

> Sunday, June 28th
> The orders are that we remain where we are today and that the men wash their clothes and clean their guns. We learned this morning that the men committed many depredations yesterday afternoon and last night, going to houses and taking whatever they could lay their hands upon. Such practice, intrinsically wrong and indefensible will, I fear, unless promptly stopped, so demoralize the army as to bring disaster upon it. Stringent orders from Gen'l Lee have just been published which it is to be hoped will arrest the evil. Most of our men were on Picket this morning, and those left in camp were busy washing, cleaning their guns so that I could not preach until afternoon, when I addressed a pretty good congregation from I John 2nd Ch., 17th Verse. I took occasion to talk plainly to them on the subject of taking what did not belong to them from unarmed inhabitants of the country. A mail come to the Brigade today and almost everybody got a letter but me.[26]

---

[26] Chaplain Francis Milton Kennedy's diary, "Confederate Diaries of the War," Georgia State Department of Archives and History, as cited in Brinsfield, *Spirit Divided: The Confederacy*, 128–29.

Chaplain Charles H. Dobbs of the 12th Mississippi Infantry tried to refute the idea that Confederate soldiers looted Pennsylvania farms in his postwar memoirs:

> I neither saw nor heard of any plundering. I think I knew the spirit of these men. I was familiar with most of the privates in my regiment, and thought it was above the average in intellect and standing at home. I think their feelings upon this subject were common to most of the volunteers in our army. If any man had gone to plundering houses, or stealing from individuals he would have been drummed out of the regiment.[27]

Interestingly, Chaplain Dobbs went on to relate several incidents of soldiers stealing from civilians in Chambersburg, taking hats and shoes at will. These he characterized as "practical jokes," though probably not as funny for the victims as perhaps for the soldiers.[28]

Meanwhile Chaplain Tinsley and the men of the 28th Virginia Infantry, Pickett's Division, Longstreet's Corps, continued to cross rivers, battle disease, execute a deserter, and attend worship services. Tinsley recorded his thoughts for the week of June 21 through 27:

> June 21. Sun[day].
> A very pleasant day in a very pleasant camp. Bro. Perkins preaches twice for me—congregation attentive.[29] I call for the 2nd time to see Riley of the 18th Va. [Virginia Infantry] who was condemned to be shot for desertion. He is very reticent.[30]

> June 22. Mon[day].
> Our Brig[ade] is stirred before day with orders to move immediately. We again wade the Shenandoah & return to the top of the mountain & there spend the day. Hold service (P.M.)—have a good attentive congregation. About night we return to old Camp. Am attacked with dysentery in afternoon.

---

[27] Charles Holt Dobbs, "Reminiscences of an Army Chaplain," Presbyterian Christian Observer (1874), as cited in Brinsfield, *Spirit Divided: The Confederacy*, 65.

[28] Ibid., 65–66.

[29] Episcopal Chaplain Edmund T. Perkins of the Fifty-Fifth Virginia Infantry, Heth's Division, Hill's Corps.

[30] Private John Riley, Company E, Eighteenth Virginia Infantry Regiment.

June 23d. Tu[esday].
I am quite sick & stay closely in my tent.[31]

June 24. Wed[nesday].
We leave about day-break, passing through Berryville. There Griffin who had been staying there for several days sick, joins us in ambulance. I get in & go with him. At Smithfield at the house of Miss Nelson I see Gen'l Pendleton & some of his staff.[32] He introduces me to his cousin—I am kindly received & very much refreshed by a nice lunch. Thence I take the Shepherdstown road to get Griffin in good quarters at Dr. Butler's his friend, who lives about 3 miles from the town. I there meet Gen'l Pender & staff who are encamped on the grounds in front of Dr. B's house & my friend Chaplain Geo[rge] T. Williams being of his staff.[33] I am introduced to the whole party & have a very pleasant time. The General is a fine looking man, of medium statue, quiet & unassuming & every inch a gentleman. I hold service for Williams.

July 25. Th[ursday].
I leave Griffin very sick—pass through Martinsburg (I see no signs of loyalty there)—proceed Northward & cross at Williamsport. When I reached camp the Brigade had just gone out to see the execution of Riley (18th Va). I did not arrive in time to be present & officiate, so Mr. Granberry supplied my place.[34]

June 26. Fr[iday].
Weather rainy & weather & roads Terrible—We pass through Hagerstown (after a very considerable detention)—pass into Pa. [Pennsylvania]. At Middleburg & bivouac near Greencastle. Franklin [County].

[31] Tinsley, "Private Diary," 5–6.
[32] Brigadier General William Pendleton, Episcopal minister and chief of the artillery reserve.
[33] Major General William D. Pender, division commander, Hill's Corps, and Episcopal Chaplain George T. Williams, 13th North Carolina Infantry, Scales' Brigade of Pender's Division.
[34] John C. Granbery, Methodist chaplain of the 11th Virginia Infantry. Granbery lost the use of an eye and became the missionary chaplain to Longstreet's Corps. Missionary chaplains were paid by their churches, not by the government.

June 27. Sat[urday].

We move about 7 o'Clock & after a short & easy march reach
Chambersburg. While passing thro[ugh] a little village Gen'l Pickett &
aids come dashing by—A citizen touched me & asked: "Who is that?"
Gen'l P. said I.[35] To which a damsel standing by said: "O how handsome
he is!" Our Reg[iment] is left in the City as Pro[vost] Guard. The citizens generally & especially the ladies deported themselves very credita-
bly—Many were cheerful—some scared & sad. Others very mad. All
seemed to be treated better than they expected or had a right to expect.
Our men behaved very well except a few who succeeded in getting too
much liquor. I lodged at the Franklin Hotel paying my fare in Confederate bills.[36]

Ewell's Corps

While Longstreet's and Hill's corps were struggling across mountains
and rivers, Ewell's Corps was already 30 miles in advance, Maj. Gen. R. E.
Rodes's Division arriving at Chambersburg on June 24. Ewell moved his
three-division force rapidly north; one Confederate soldier wrote that in a
single day he had "breakfast in Virginia, whiskey in Maryland, and supper in
Pennsylvania."[37] With little resistance north of Winchester, General Lee
ordered Ewell to advance along a broad front. If the Pennsylvania capital of
Harrisburg "comes within your means," Lee wrote, "capture it."[38]

On June 25, Ewell drove north toward Carlisle with Rodes's Division
and two brigades of Johnson's Division. Early's Division marched east
through Gettysburg, which he entered on June 26. After capturing and pa-
roling most of the 26th Pennsylvania Militia, composed in part of students
from Pennsylvania College, Early demanded that the citizens of Gettysburg
turn over to him the equivalent of $10,000 in goods and produce, but the
town's merchants and farmers had already hidden or removed most of their
commodities. In a hurry to get to York and the bridge across the Susquehanna River at Wrightsville, Early took time for no more than a fast search
before marching east. York surrendered to Early's lead brigade on June 27.[39]

---

[35] Maj. Gen. George E. Pickett, Chaplain Tinsley's division commander.

[36] Tinsley, "Private Diary," pp. 6–9.

[37] As cited in Knauer, *Gettysburg: A Day-by-Day Account*, 20.

[38] Ibid.

[39] Ibid. Note: Pennsylvania College was renamed Gettysburg College in
1921. The 26th Pennsylvania Emergency Militia put up a brave fight but were soon
overrun by Early's troops.

One of the chaplains assigned to Ewell's Corps was Father James Sheeran, the Roman Catholic chaplain of the 14th Louisiana Infantry in Johnson's Division. Born in Ireland in 1819, Sheeran was a natural fit for the 14th Louisiana, a unit composed mainly of Irishmen from the New Orleans docks. Well known to General Lee and to General Ewell, Father Sheeran was famous for breaking up poker games and giving the winnings to Catholic charities. He chided profanity and drinking. He scolded stragglers on the march. He also kept a "War Journal" in which he described his impressions of the long march to Carlisle:

> June 13 According to previous orders all were on the way at 4 o'clock and making toward Winchester. This was the first time I had seen General Ewell since he had his leg amputated.[40] He jestingly said, "Why, Father, you have your grey horse yet." I answered, "Yes, General, we are now becoming old companions." In the course of a brief conversation he requested me to pray that God might bless our efforts in the impending struggles. Not wishing to occupy much of his time I bade him good morning, and rode to my regiment now in the front of the column. Having marched some 5 miles we came to a halt.
>
> June 16 On my way towards Winchester I heard a voice calling me by the familiar name, Father Sheeran! On turning around I found it was General Ewell's Adjutant. He told me the General wished to see me and I of course dismounted and approached the General who received me with a warm handshake. He then asked me as a favor that I would repair to Winchester and there take charge of the wounded, giving me full authority to use the sutlers' stores captured and all others which I might think necessary for the comfort of the wounded heroes.
> Having heard what the General had to say I hastened to the hospital of the 1st Louisiana Brigade where I visited all the wounded and then repaired to Winchester....
> This afternoon I heard that our whole army was on the way for Maryland.
> June 24 This morning we commenced our march in the direction of Chambersburg, passing through Middletown formerly called Smoke-

---

[40] General Ewell had suffered the loss of his leg from a wound at the battle of Groveton, August 28, 1862. In order to ride horseback he had to be lifted to the saddle and strapped there. See Joseph T. Durkin, SJ, ed., *Confederate Chaplain: A War Journal of Rev. James B. Sheeran, c.ss.r. 14th Louisiana, CSA* (Milwaukee, WI: Bruce Publishing Co., 1960) 46.

town. I was sensibly struck by the difference between the people in this part of the country and the inhabitants of Virginia. Here you find none of that grace of manners, high-toned sentiment, or intellectual culture that you find in old Virginia. Indeed, with all their wealth they appear little advanced in civilization.

June 27 We marched to within 3 miles of Carlisle and camped for the night. It was remarkable to see how orderly our men conducted themselves on this march. It is true many of them helped themselves to poultry, vegetables, milk, etc., but I saw no wonton destruction of private property. This I think redounds more to the honor of our army than a dozen victories over the enemy on the battlefield.

I perceived the people of this country were most agreeably disappointed. Knowing what their army had done to us; that they had burned our towns, laid waste our lands, driven helpless women and children from their homes, destroyed our implements of husbandry, that we might not be able to cultivate our lands, they very naturally expected that our soldiers would treat them in a similar manner. Great then was their surprise when they saw the conduct of our men. Many of these people told me that by our kindness and good treatment of the people we had made many friends among them.[41]

Chaplain Alexander D. Betts, 30th North Carolina Infantry, Rodes's Division, Ewell's Corps, was a Methodist minister and a graduate of the University of North Carolina in the Class of 1855. He was also at Carlisle on June 27.[42] Chaplain Betts's memoir is shorter, but it reveals much about the work of chaplains on the march:

June 27—Hard march. Mud! Mud! Pass through Carlisle and camp in United States Barracks. I sleep on ground. Get two letters from wife. Daughter sick June 4. God spare her!

Sunday, June 28—Bro. Lacy preaches to three North Carolina brigades in the forenoon. I preach in the afternoon and baptize five by pouring. Bro. Brooks and I baptise four each, in a pool near by. Pleasant day, but not much spirituality among the soldiers. Write to Mary at night.[43]

---

[41] Ibid., 48.

[42] The Reverend A. D. Betts was a member of the North Carolina Conference of the Methodist Episcopal Church, South. His biography can be found in Appendix II.

[43] B. Tucker Lacy, Presbyterian chaplain-at-large to the II Corps, originally appointed by Lt. Gen. T. J. "Stonewall" Jackson. Bro. Brooks was probably Baptist

June 29—Rainy. Ride into Carlisle. Call on Marshall in College grove. Meet Rev. Dr. Johnson, President of Dickinson College. Meet Rev. Grandin of Baltimore Conference, who graduated here eighteen years ago. Meet Dr. Johnson's daughter, a bright young woman, who asks me some questions. "Mr. Betts, what was your object in joining the army? Was it to help the rebellion?" I told her I could not have taken the oath of office as Chaplain if I had not been in full sympathy with the Confederate cause, but I did not think it so weak as to need my help. I told her my love for souls led me into the work. Fixing her eyes on mine, she said: "Mr. Betts, would you be willing to see the Union restored?" I quickly said: "Miss Johnson, I would rejoice to see the Union 'restored,' but you and I will never see it 'restored.'" Visit Federal prisoners at night.[44]

His confrontation with Ms. Johnson concluded, Chaplain Betts tried to be optimistic:

June 30—Division crosses Blue Ridge and camp half a mile beyond Heidleburg [Heidlersburg].[45] Dark rainy evening. I sit on a fence and write to my wife and tell her I expect to sleep on two rails on top of that fence, while soldiers sleep among the rocks around me. I add: 'Thank God! I am happy.' Happiness does not depend so much on our surroundings as some may think.[46]

---

chaplain Henry E. Brooks, Second North Carolina Battalion in Rodes's division of Ewell's corps.

[44] Baptist chaplain Asa Marshall, Twelfth Georgia Infantry in Rodes's Division, and Methodist chaplain Joshua M. Grandin, Thirty-Third Virginia Infantry, Stonewall Brigade, Johnson's Division, both in Ewell's Corps.

[45] Heidlersburg was about 10 miles northeast of Gettysburg.

[46] Alexander Davis Betts, DD, *Experience of a Confederate Chaplain 1861–1864*, ed. W. A. Betts. (Greenville, SC: Privately printed, 1904). See digital copy at http://docsouth.unc.edu/fpn/betts/betts.html, 38–39.

Chapter 2

Catching Up: The Union Army's Forced March

"Many of them dropped dead from sunstroke."[1]
—Chaplain William Corby,
88th New York Infantry
Irish Brigade

The Union Army was encamped at Falmouth, Virginia, across the Rappahannock River from Fredericksburg, when they were ordered to march north on June 13, 1863. Not all of the soldiers were sorry to leave their encampment. Some units had been there since the previous December and were tired of the long periods of boring camp life while they waited presumably to march on Richmond. Lt. Charles Francis Adams, Jr., of the 1st Massachusetts Cavalry, described Falmouth as being a combination of a "bar-room and a brothel."[2] Chaplain Joseph Twichell of the 71st New York Infantry, however, wrote on June 11, "I am sorry to leave these quarters—the most delightful I have ever had. I lived in a cool, green bower. My bed was delightful and my chair a luxury. My chapel, too, with its evergreen walls, and seats and platform, is well worth the regret I feel in leaving it."[3]

The route of the army from June 13 to June 28 was in two parallel columns. Maj. Gen. George Meade's Fifth Corps, Maj. Gen. Winfield Scott Hancock's Second Corps, and Maj. Gen. Henry Slocum's Twelfth Corps, a total of approximately 40,000 soldiers, marched from Falmouth toward Stafford Court House and Haymarket on the left or western flank. The other four infantry corps, Maj. Gen. Oliver Howard's Eleventh Corps, Maj. Gen. John Reynolds's First Corps, Maj. Gen. Daniel Sickles's Third Corps, and

---

[1] William Corby, CSC, *Memoirs of Chaplain Life: Three Years with the Irish Brigade in the Army of the Potomac*, ed. Lawrence F. Kohl (New York: Fordham University Press, 1992) xiii.

[2] As cited in Shelby Foote, *The Civil War: A Narrative*, vol. 2, *Fredericksburg to Meridian* (New York: Random House, 1958) 233. An estimated rate of six Confederates per 1,000 contracted venereal disease in 1862, down from 20 per 1,000 in 1861 (2 percent). The Union rate was 82/1000 (8 percent) for the war. Gen. Hooker became famous for allowing his men to frequent red-light districts in Washington, DC, but Richmond, Virginia, was almost as notorious.

[3] As cited in Peter Messent and Steve Courtney, eds., *The Civil War Letters of Joseph Hopkins Twichell* (Athens: University of Georgia Press, 2006) 237.

Maj. Gen. John Sedgwick's Sixth Corps, approximately 54,000 men, marched by Manassas Junction, Centreville, and Fairfax Courthouse to cross the Potomac at Edward's Ferry and Point of Rocks. Maj. Gen. Alfred Pleasonton's Cavalry Corps of 17,000 troopers rode to the west of Meade's Fifth Corps and clashed with Confederate cavalry units three times near Ashby's Gap. As usual, the horsemen generally stayed on the flank and to the front of the army.[4]

Major General Hooker crossed the Potomac on the evening of June 25 to concentrate the army at Frederick, Maryland, in accord with his orders to protect Washington and Baltimore. Hooker, however, argued with Maj. Gen. Henry Halleck, Lincoln's general-in-chief, urging that Harper's Ferry be evacuated and the 10,000 Union troops there be added to his command. When his request was refused, Hooker offered his resignation, which President Lincoln quickly accepted.

Hooker's successor, supposed to be Maj. Gen. John Reynolds, changed when Reynolds declined the position. The next candidate was Maj. Gen. George Gordon Meade.

General Meade was a graduate of West Point, a career army officer, and a civil engineer. He had served with distinction in the Second Seminole War and in the Mexican War, during which time he was promoted to brevet first lieutenant for gallant conduct at the Battle of Monterrey. When the Civil War began, Meade was promoted from captain to brigadier general of volunteers on the recommendation of Pennsylvania governor Andrew Curtin. As a brigade commander he was wounded three times during the 1862 Peninsula Campaign. After his recovery he distinguished himself with valiant leadership at South Mountain and at Antietam, where he was again wounded. During the Battle of Fredericksburg, Meade's Division made the only (temporary) breakthrough in the Confederate lines against Stonewall Jackson's Second Corps. Held in reserve during the Battle of Chancellorsville, he argued with Major General Hooker for resuming an attack on General Lee but to no avail.

In spite of Meade's reputation as a fighting general, several of his peers disliked him both personally and professionally. Among these were Hooker himself; Hooker's chief of staff, Maj. Gen. Daniel Butterfield; and Maj. Gen. Daniel Sickles, the Third Corps commander. Consequently, when a messenger from President Lincoln arrived on June 28 to inform Meade of his appointment as Hooker's replacement, Meade was taken by surprise. He

---

[4] "Army of the Potomac, June 30, 1863," War Department, *Official Records*, part 1: 151.

later wrote to his wife that when the officer entered his tent to wake him, he assumed army politics had occasioned his arrest! He had not actively sought army command and was surprised when Major General Reynolds declined the appointment. When Meade assumed command at Prospect Hall in Frederick, Maryland, he knew Lee's Army of Northern Virginia was invading Pennsylvania, but he had little knowledge of the disposition of the Army of the Potomac and nothing of Major General Hooker's plans.[5]

To General Meade's credit, he began issuing orders the day he took command. On June 28, Meade issued the order and objectives of the army's march for the next day. Maj. Gen. George Sykes became the new V Corps commander. Major General Reynolds's First Corps and Major General Howard's Eleventh Corps moved 20 miles north to Emmitsburg, Maryland, near the Pennsylvania border. Major General Sickles's Third Corps and Major General Slocum's Twelfth Corps trailed 10 miles behind at Taneytown, Maryland. Major General Pleasonton's Cavalry Corps would "guard the right and left flanks and the rear, and give the commanding General information of the movements of the enemy in front."[6] On the morning of June 29, Pleasonton ordered Brig. Gen. John Buford's Cavalry Division, minus one brigade, to move ahead of the army through Emmitsburg and on to Gettysburg, 10 miles north of the Maryland line, to communicate all information of the events rapidly and surely. Pleasonton gave Buford one day to get there.[7]

Asking God along for the Ride

Accompanying the 272 regiments of the Army of the Potomac were 128 commissioned chaplains, including two Roman Catholic priests, one rabbi, and 125 Protestant ministers, representing ten different denominations.[8] Fifteen of the chaplains were assigned to cavalry regiments, the rest to the infantry units. Most of the chaplains found a horse to ride even though

---

[5] Edwin B. Coddington, *The Gettysburg Campaign: A Study in Command* (New York: Scribner's, 1968) 37, 209.

[6] War Department, *Official Records*, part 3: 374.

[7] Ibid., 400, as cited in Michael Phipps, "Walking Point: John Buford on the Road to Gettysburg," unpublished manuscript, accessed November 2014, http://npshistory.com/series/symposia/gettysburg_seminars/10/essay3.pdf, 2–3.

[8] The denominational affiliation of 15 of the 128 Union chaplains who served at Gettysburg is unknown, but to be a commissioned chaplain one had to have the recommendation of a religious organization. See John W. Brinsfield, William C. Davis, Benedict Maryniak, and James I. Robertson, Jr., *Faith in the Fight: Civil War Chaplains* (Mechanicsburg, PA: Stackpole Books, 2003) 12.

they were not authorized one by regulations. On the long march to Gettysburg, chaplains gave encouragement to the soldiers, ate and slept with them, held religious services in the field, helped deliver and take up the mail, and tended, with ambulance drivers, to those overcome by heat exhaustion. The one duty that all chaplains encountered before the campaign was over was to minister to the wounded and dying.

Hancock's Second Corps

Father William Corby, born in Detroit, Michigan, of an Irish father and a Canadian mother, was just 30 years of age when the Gettysburg Campaign began. Educated at the fledgling University of Notre Dame in South Bend, Indiana, Corby had taken his final vows as a priest in 1860 to become pastor of St. Patrick's Parish in South Bend.[9] When the call came for Catholic chaplains to accompany Notre Dame students to war, Father Corby volunteered. On December 15, 1861, he joined the 88th New York Infantry Regiment in what became known as the Irish Brigade.

Corby wrote, in his *Memoirs of Chaplain Life*, first published in 1893, that the forced march to Gettysburg turned out to be one of the longest the Irish Brigade had yet undertaken:

> Counting the zigzag route our Second Corps had taken to Gettysburg, Pennsylvania, it was between two- and three-hundred miles in length. But we were all glad to get away from the destructive scenes of our two late campaigns. The poor soldiers, who had to carry about sixty pounds daily under the burning sun of a more southern climate than they were accustomed to, found the continued marching of from sixteen to eighteen miles per day very severe. Many of them dropped dead from sunstroke. Every day brought us farther from the Rappahannock, south of which lay, in their last sleep, between twenty-five and thirty thousand of our dear companions.[10]

In spite of the pressing time schedule for the march, Corby found time to celebrate Catholic Mass on the top of a "little mountain" and to erect a

---

[9] William Corby, CSC, *Memoirs of Chaplain Life: Three Years with the Irish Brigade in the Army of the Potomac*, ed. Lawrence F. Kohl (New York: Fordham University Press, 1992) xiii.

[10] Ibid., 171. On modern roads the distance from Fredericksburg to Gettysburg is approximately 118 miles, but Father Corby was right to point out the zigzag route from roads to river fords and back to roads again.

cross there. "During the entire march," he wrote, "Mass was celebrated as often as circumstances would permit."[11]

Near Frederick, Maryland, the soldiers caught a Confederate spy who had in his possession "a complete account of our troops, our trains, and our route," Corby recorded.[12] The man was tried, and he confessed. Corby continued:

> He was suspended from a tree and left there, and while the army passed I saw him hanging by the neck. It was rumored at the time that someone had suggested to send him to Washington and let the authorities deal with him there. If the rumor is true, Gen. Hancock swore, "No! If you send him to Washington they will promote him." There was really so much kindness shown in Washington, even to culprits, that the generals in the field decided that strict severity was necessary somewhere, to keep up discipline.[13]
>
> Passing through Maryland it was really admirable to see how careful our men were of private property. No fields, gardens, or private houses were at all injured. The men had been warned that, being in a loyal State, they had no right to molest or destroy private property. This told on the conscience of each man. Besides this, Gen. Hancock had issued a severe general order to our corps, adding a serious penalty should anyone be found in works of depredation.[14]

Corby clearly admired General Hancock, whom he described as "a polished gentleman" with a keen sense of propriety. As an example, Corby added, "Addicted merely through force of habit to the use of profane language, when excited, he would invariably stop short when he discovered the presence of a clergyman."[15]

Early in the morning of June 29, 1863, Hancock's Second Corps started from Frederick toward Gettysburg. Chaplain Corby noted that "we did not halt for the night until about 11 P.M., having made the longest march

---

[11] Ibid., 172.
[12] Ibid.
[13] Ibid., 172–73.
[14] Ibid.
[15] Ibid., 174. General Hancock, a former Baptist deacon, evidently had great respect for his chaplains. See Bruce T. Gourley, "Baptists and the American Civil War," *Baptist History and Heritage*, XLVII/2 (Summer 2013): 96.

made by infantry of any department during the war."[16] Corby slept under an apple tree in a plowed field. Without a tent or canopy, most soldiers folded their blankets about them and slept on the ground. Corby described the trials of a night march:

> Late in the evening the marching of a tired army is a sight. As a rule, not a voice is heard. Fatigue and drowsiness, added to a rather weak and faint feeling, indispose men to converse, and by silent consent each one discontinues conversation. The click of a large spur, the occasional rattle of a sword, and other mechanical movements are the only sounds heard above the slow, steady tramp of the line and the heavy tread of the few horses that carry mounted officers. Even these mounted officers frequently dismount and walk to avoid falling from the horses. Many, many times I had to do so. How men live through this is a mystery. But a kind Providence pressed many of us onward and preserved us, and for this...few of us render the thanks which God has a right to expect.[17]

At the tail end of the Second Corps marched the 145th Pennsylvania Volunteer Infantry Regiment, comprised of soldiers from northwestern Pennsylvania, principally from Erie County. Their chaplain was a German-born Lutheran pastor named John Henry Wilburn Stuckenberg, age 28. Stuckenberg immigrated to Pennsylvania with his family in 1839, graduated from Wittenburg College, and then spent two postgraduate years at the University of Halle in Germany studying theology. In 1861 he returned to Pennsylvania to accept the pastorate of three small Lutheran churches in the Erie area. On September 10, 1862, he applied for the chaplain's position in the 145th Pennsylvania Infantry and was appointed the next day. He served with the regiment at Harper's Ferry, Antietam, Fredericksburg, and Chancellorsville before commencing the march from Falmouth to Gettysburg on June 13, 1863.[18]

Being at the end of the almost infinitely long column of marching soldiers, Stuckenberg was fortunate to own a horse that he had bought himself since chaplains were not authorized government mounts. Nevertheless, his

---

[16] Corby, *Memoirs of Chaplain Life*, 176. The modern road distance from Frederick to Taneytown, Maryland, where the second corps camped on July 1, is about 20 miles, but Corby wrote that they marched 34 miles. Perhaps he meant the total distance from Frederick to Gettysburg.

[17] Ibid., 177–78.

[18] David T. Hedrick and Gordon Barry Davis, Jr., eds., *I'm Surrounded by Methodists...Diary of John H. W. Stuckenberg, Chaplain of the 145th Pennsylvania Volunteer Infantry* (Gettysburg, PA: Thomas Publications, 1995) 1, 69.

account of the foot march reflected some of the same challenges that other chaplains have described as well:

> We marched very rapidly, to join Division, and escape the enemy who might be pursuing us. Before we arrived at Stafford CH [Court-house], which we did about 10 A.M., we found trees had been felled across the road, to prevent the enemies cavalry from attacking the troops at the CH, and we afterwards learned that Genl Hancock supposed that perhaps we had been captured. For two hours we lay in the dust at Stafford CH exposed to the burning rays of the sun. I felt quite sick, sleepy and tired—and slept in the sun. My head felt dizzy—it seemed as if I was going to be very sick. The march was resumed about noon. Good water was very scarce. The heat was almost intolerable. The road was lined with those that fell out panting and exhausted. Many cases of sunstroke occurred. That night we bivouacked near Aquia creek where we arrived in the afternoon. The guns were scarcely stacked, before all the men and officers were asleep on the ground (Dumfries—old grave yard). I never saw men more tired. Sick, sleepy and weary as I was I felt more for the men who had to walk and carry heavy loads besides. It was such a march which men say they dread more than battle.[19]
>
> On the morning of the 16th we were ready by daybreak to march, but were delayed an hour or two. It was not quite as hot as the day previous, but many fell out.... I did all to help the boys along, carried their guns for them and let them ride my horse whilst I walked. It was very dusty too, so much so that at times we could scarcely see the men immediately in front of us. Great clouds of dust arose around us—I thought one might write in them, they were so thick. It was very hot again the next morning. About noon we arrived at Fairfax Station and pitched tents. I just gave out. We remained here until the afternoon of the 19th when we again struck tents and marched to Centreville where we arrived about dark. Before our tents were pitched it rained very hard wetting me to the skin.[20]

The 145th Pennsylvania Infantry Regiment passed through the Manassas-Bull Run battlefields on the way to Centreville. Chaplain Stuckenberg saw cannon balls, pieces of guns, shells, wagons, and some half-buried bones of Union soldiers, identified by blue scraps of clothing. "I never before knew

---

[19] Ibid., 69–70.
[20] Ibid.

what was meant by 'the bones bleaching on the field of battle.' It was a horrid, ghastly sight," he wrote.[21]

From Centreville the men marched to Gainsville, Haymarket, and Thoroughfare Gap, where they rested for three days enjoying some ripe cherries. Chaplain Stuckenberg wrote that he spent his time pleasantly viewing the scenery, reading, writing, and meditating. On June 26, the regiment crossed the Potomac on pontoon bridges at Edwards Ferry, and by Sunday, June 28, were 3 miles from Frederick, Maryland. At Frederick the men rested again, with a few going with Stuckenberg to worship at a Methodist church in town. Stuckenberg recalled, "Whilst at Frederick, we learned that Hooker had been superseded by Meade. To many, who had lost confidence in Hooker, this announcement was received with joy. But I felt sad that a change should be made when so near the enemy. I had learned to admire Hooker, notwithstanding his failure at Chancellorsville."[22]

From Frederick the men marched to Uniontown and Taneytown and then entered, as Stuckenberg related, into "our own beloved state—Pennsylvania—crossed the line with much pleasure" on July 1.[23]

Sickles's Third Corps

Marching behind Reynolds's First Corps and Howard's Eleventh Corps was Maj. Gen. Daniel Sickles's Third Corps, which, like the other major units, was moving toward Frederick, Maryland. Sickles's Corps contained just two divisions, the first commanded by Maj. Gen. David Birney, the second by Brig. Gen. Andrew Humphreys. In Humphreys's Division was the New York "Excelsior" Brigade that General Sickles had helped recruit in New York City in April and May 1861.[24]

Among those that Sickles personally recruited was a 23-year-old theology student named Joseph Twichell. Twichell was studying for the Congregational Church ministry at Union Theological Seminary in New York. He was a graduate of Yale College, Class of 1859, where he had rowed crew and been a member of the Scroll and Key society.[25] Sickles thought he would make a good chaplain.

---

[21] Ibid., 71.

[22] Ibid., 76.

[23] Ibid.

[24] Messent and Courtney, *Civil War Letters*, 20. Excelsior means "ever upward" and is the motto of New York State.

[25] A secret society founded at Yale in 1842. Mark Twain was elected an honorary member in 1868.

Twichell was an abolitionist, as were many of his student colleagues, and an ardent patriot. He could not stand idly by while other young men were volunteering to fill New York's quota of regiments even though he had not yet graduated from Union Theological Seminary or been ordained. On April 22, 1861, Twichell wrote to his father about serving as a chaplain in Sickles's Brigade:

> So far as I can find out, my risk of personal injury, in any event, will be slight. If my life is lost, it will be given just where it could not be refused in caring for the sick, in maintaining discipline not by violence and in the pursuit of peaceful ministrations, such as may soften in some degree the asperities of war. My Bible, tracts and a few books will constitute my weapons.
>
> I should not expect a revival, but I should expect to make some good impressions, by treating with kindness a class of men who are little used to it. Another thing. Nothing is more repugnant to a civilized sense than the burial of a man as though he were a dog. This is the privilege of the Chaplain to prevent. Where the regiment is going I know not. It will likely see tough times. Then I am the more needed.[26]

At this early date in the war, the US Congress had not yet drafted regulations requiring candidates to produce recommendations from religious leaders in order to serve as chaplains. In his quest to secure a position, Twichell had met Brigadier General Sickles who, in turn, recommended Twichell to Col. George B. Hall, a New York City politician, who was in need of a chaplain for his regiment. Hall told Twichell that he could not, as yet, pay him a salary, but he could provide rations. When Twichell agreed to serve for rations alone, Colonel Hall "retained" him as chaplain of the "Jackson," i.e., 71st New York Infantry Regiment, on July 28, 1861.[27] By early September 1861 Twichell was being paid $125 a month as a chaplain even though he did not receive his commission until December 2, 1862.[28]

---

[26] Messent and Courtney, *Civil War Letters*, 18.

[27] Rosters of New York Civil War Regiments, http://dmna.ny.gov/historic/reghist (alphabetical).

[28] Messent and Courtney, *Civil War Letters*, 20–21. Note: The purchasing power of $125 in 1861 was enough to buy a horse. One ration for a soldier, which included a pound of meat, a pound of bread, beans or peas, rice or hominy, coffee, sugar, vinegar, candles, soap, salt and pepper, potatoes, and molasses, was valued at 15 cents each. See War Department, *Revised United States Army Regulations of 1861* (Washington, DC: Government Printing Office, 1863) 244, 250.

Amazingly, given General Sickles's reputation as a corrupt politician and a hard-drinking womanizer who had barely escaped conviction for murdering his wife's alleged lover, he was able to recruit (or at least recommend to his subordinate commanders) excellent chaplains for the six regiments in his brigade. Charles H. A. Bulkley, a Congregational minister and a college friend of Sickles from New York University, became chaplain of the 70th New York Infantry Regiment; Joseph H. Twichell held the position in the 71st New York Infantry Regiment; William Eastman, another Congregationalist, was assigned to the 72nd New York Infantry Regiment; Father Joseph O'Hagan became the Roman Catholic chaplain of the 73rd New York Infantry Regiment; Protestant Chaplain Robert Sittler ministered to the 74th New York Infantry Regiment; and 56-year-old Foster Hartwell, a Baptist, became the chaplain to the 120th New York Infantry Regiment, the last of the six regiments in the Excelsior Brigade. These appointments surprised Twichell since Sickles was himself an Episcopalian and presumably would have sought at least one chaplain of his own denomination.[29]

The Excelsior Brigade spent some time in garrison duty around Washington, DC, before taking part in the Peninsula Campaign of 1862. During the Seven Days' Battles, the 71st New York lost 118 men killed, wounded, or missing. At the Second Battle of Bull Run (Second Manassas), the 71st sustained another 114 casualties. After the battles of Fredericksburg and Chancellorsville, which cost the brigade as a whole a total of 266 casualties, the Excelsior Brigade went into camp at Falmouth, Virginia, with the rest of Major General Hooker's Army of the Potomac.[30]

During these two years, at least three of the Excelsior chaplains, William Eastman, Joseph Twichell, and Father Joseph O'Hagan, became good friends. At a time when many Protestant chaplains maintained their distance from their Roman Catholic counterparts, sharing the hardships of army life seemed to overcome denominational prejudices. Chaplain Eastman recalled a story that illustrated the comradery between Chaplain Twichell and Father O'Hagan as they assisted the surgeons in a field hospital:

During the first battle of Fredericksburg, when the wounded were being brought into hospital in great numbers, they had been occupied all day

---

[29] Messent and Courtney, *Civil War Letters*, 22.

[30] Col. John N. Coyne, "History of the Excelsior Brigade," an address delivered at Gettysburg on July 2, 1893, accessed January 2016, http://www.72ndnewyork. org/excelsiorhistoryreva.htm. Coyne said that during the war, the brigade sustained a total of 3,028 casualties, or 47 percent of the 6,442 men who served in the unit from 1861 to 1864.

and far into the night in their hard and loving work. After midnight, when exhausted nature demanded an hour of rest, these two lay down to sleep. It was December and bitter cold. Presently there came a call out of O'Hagan's blanket, "Joseph," and the answer was "Well, Joseph." Their first names were alike. "I'm cold," said one and "I'm cold," said the other. "Then let's put our two blankets together." And so they did, lying close with blankets doubled. Presently there was a movement as of one struggling with suppressed laughter. "What are you laughing at?" demanded Twichell. "At this condition of things," was the reply. "What? At all this horrible distress?" "No! No! But at you and me; a Jesuit priest and a New England Puritan minister—of the worst sort—spooned close together under the same blanket. I wonder what the angels think." And a moment after, he added, "I think they like it."[31]

When Sickles's Third Corps began their march toward Frederick, Maryland, Chaplain Twichell found to his horror that his first duty would be to comfort a soldier to be executed for desertion:

> In Camp, Near Rappahannock Station
> Sunday, June 14th 1863
> The march hither I shall never forget. It will be memorable to the end of my life as the scene of an event which for importance and terrible interest surpasses nearly all of my experience hitherto. On Friday afternoon at a little after two I was called to a professional duty from which in anticipation I had always shrunk in horror, hoping that it might never befall me—which indeed I doubted my ability to perform. It was to attend and minister unto a poor wretch who was shot for desertion. His name was [John P.] Woods, a private of the 19th Indiana Vols.—1st Division—1st Corps. My being summoned to administer to his last moments was a matter of chance, or rather unusual Providence.... Still I had no thought of visiting him myself, because he was not of my own part of the army, and I felt my blood chill at the bare idea.[32]

Twichell's Brigade, marching last in the Third Corps, had mixed with the advance elements of the First Corps. The order to execute Woods was immediate, and Twichell was the only chaplain known to be in the area. In

---

[31] As cited in John W. Brinsfield, William C. Davis, Benedict Maryniak, and James I. Robertson, Jr., *Faith in the Fight: Civil War Chaplains* (Mechanicsburg, PA: Stackpole Books, 2003) 124–25.
[32] Messent and Courtney, *Civil War Letters*, 239

spite of the fact that Twichell's unit belonged to the Third Corps, he was drafted for the duty of counseling the condemned man:

Giving my horse to an officer, I got into the ambulance with the prisoner, and the sad procession started. I can never adequately tell all that passed in the ambulance—the agony of soul—the intensity of prayer—the anxious inquiry—and the black shadow of the event just at hand always present. As I never prayed before I prayed for divine guidance in what I should say to my companion, and I think I received it.

At length the ambulance stopped. He seemed to have a stronger sense of God's personal presence, and to ask for just the things as he needed—oh! how earnestly, then! The Marshall touched me on the shoulder while we were still praying. I gave the man my benediction. We rose to our feet. "Now," said I "meet it like a man!" and so he did.[33]

We buried him and I rode away from the memorable spot to rejoin my regiment. The experience was strange and providential. I hope it did me good. Next morning while riding along with Father O'Hagan, the Marshal of the day before hailed me from the roadside. He had something to tell me. While he was tying the poor fellow's arms and covering his eyes, the latter had said calmly, "You need not do this. I am ready to meet my savior." Also, "Tell that Chaplain that I thank him. I believe he has showed me the way to eternal Life, by leading me to Christ." Of course, he magnified my office, ascribing to me the work of an illuminating Holy Ghost, but my soul was greatly comforted when I heard this. Truly I had reason to praise the Lord.[34]

On the long march through Virginia, Twichell noted the days of unbroken drought, the pulverized roads to the depth of two or three inches, the moving columns of soldiers shrouded by suffocating clouds of dust, and the scorching heat that left many utterly exhausted. Twichell gave his horse to those who were weakest, but then found that he had just as hard a time on foot as did the soldiers who carried knapsacks, muskets, and ammunition. What amazed Twichell most were the women who were marching along with the men:

Nothing is so trying to a soldier's spirit as a long midsummer march. A battle does not compare with it, and the remark was frequent that to stop and fight would be a refreshment joyfully welcomed. I noticed with no small surprise that two women (wives of soldiers) kept pace with us all

---

[33] Ibid., 241.
[34] Ibid., 242.

the way, one of them actually carrying a sizable knapsack on her shoulders.... What grand times a lady might have trudging along some 60 miles beside her lord, enjoying his company, and shouldering the contents of a trunk the while![35]

By June 26, 1863, the Third Corps had reached Point of Rocks, having crossed the Potomac on pontoon bridges at Edwards Ferry. They then marched for fourteen hours to Monocacy, outside of Frederick, Maryland. Looking back at their bivouac near Gum Spring, Virginia, Twichell wrote that he was dismayed at the pillaging of the soldiers:

> I marched a large part of the way, giving my horse to the fagged-out little drummer boys, who perched on his back by twos. I stuck them up as you would fasten clothes pins on a line. One of them brought me some cherries tonight as a thank offering and another stole a sheaf of wheat for my horse. Speaking of stealing, I must, with shame, record that the conduct of our troops at Gum Spring was in that respect utterly unworthy [of] our cause. Foraging parties ranged through the country and drove in flocks of sheep and cattle or anything eatable that came in their way. To be sure we had not many luxuries and were in enemies country but to me the whole business seemed an outrage. To conquer the Confederates we must fight them, not despoil their families of food.[36]

Twichell did not know, at the time, that some of the chaplains in the Army of Northern Virginia were also witnessing the thievery of private property, but by Confederate soldiers in Pennsylvania, not Union soldiers in Virginia.[37] Nor was Twichell likely to have known of the US Congress's Confiscation Act of August 6, 1861, after he had already joined his regiment. The Confiscation Act read:

> *Be it enacted by the Senate and House of Representatives of the United States of America in Congress assembled,* That if, during the present or any future insurrection against the Government of the United States, after the President of the United States shall have declared, by proclamation, that the laws of the United States are opposed, and the execution thereof obstructed, by combinations too powerful to be suppressed by the ordinary course of judicial proceedings, or by the power vested in the marshals by

---

[35] Ibid., 243.

[36] Ibid., 244.

[37] Chaplain Milton Kennedy, 28th North Carolina Infantry, in Brinsfield et al., *Faith in the Fight*, 110.

law, any person or persons, his, her, or their agent, attorney, or employé, shall purchase or acquire, sell or give, any property of whatsoever kind or description, with intent to use or employ the same, or suffer the same to be used or employed, in aiding, abetting, or promoting such insurrection or resistance to the laws, or any person or persons engaged therein; or if any person or persons, being the owner or owners of any such property, shall knowingly use or employ, or consent to the use or employment of the same as aforesaid, all such property is hereby declared to be lawful subject of prize and capture wherever found; and it shall be the duty of the President of the United States to cause the same to be seized, confiscated, and condemned.[38]

In effect, this act by Congress gave the Union army commanders the legal right to seize, confiscate, or condemn (for destruction) any property of persons, civil or military, who might support the rebellion. Such property included but was not limited to livestock, agricultural produce such as cotton and food supplies, public buildings of use to the rebel army, private houses, churches, cemeteries, libraries, archives, college buildings, personal clothing, furniture, jewelry, railroads, wagons, and, of course, "contrabands," or slaves who sought protection from the Union armies. This policy, met by retaliation from Confederate commanders, was one of the milestones in the march of both sides toward total war.[39]

Burning the Wrightsville Bridge

After being apprised of Maj. Gen. Robert H. Milroy's defeat at Winchester, Virginia, on June 15, President Lincoln called for 100,000 men to serve for a period of six months, unless sooner discharged, from the states of Pennsylvania, Ohio, Maryland, and West Virginia. Pennsylvania's quota was 50,000 men or one-half of the total.[40] Pennsylvania governor Andrew Curtin issued an immediate proclamation calling upon all men capable of bearing

---

[38] The First Confiscation Act, August 6, 1861, accessed January 30, 2016, https://en.wikipedia.org/wiki/Confiscation_Act_of_1861, 1.

[39] As Maj. Gen. William T. Sherman remarked to some of his officers later, "A rebel has no rights, not even the right to live except by our permission." As cited in Lt. Col. Charles F. Morse, *Letters Written during the Civil War, 1861–1865* (Boston, 1898) 211, as cited in E. Merton Coulter, *The Confederate States of America* (Baton Rouge, LA: LSU Press, 1950) 370.

[40] "Pennsylvania in the Civil War: Militia Troops of 1863," accessed November 2014, http://www.pa-roots.com/pacw/1863militia, 2.

arms to enroll in the Emergency Militia for the protection of the state and country.[41]

Troops were rapidly enrolled and assembled at Harrisburg, where eight regiments were organized for the "Emergency" and mustered into the United States service. These included the 20th, 26th, 27th, 28th, 29th, 30th, 31st, and 33rd Emergency Militia Infantry regiments plus several independent companies of cavalry and artillery, all under the overall command of Maj. Gen. Darius N. Couch.

Col. William S. Jennings, a former factory owner now in command of the 26th Pennsylvania Emergency Militia Regiment, was initially ordered to march his regiment toward Chambersburg on June 24. Arriving in the neighborhood, he deployed his skirmishers, who were promptly captured before they reached their position. Jennings then withdrew to Gettysburg, where General Couch ordered him to advance his entire regiment toward the enemy on the Chambersburg Pike.

The 26th Militia Regiment consisted of 750 hastily trained farm boys, college students, and middle-aged shopkeepers sprinkled with a handful of veterans.[42] One company was from Adams County, including the group from Pennsylvania College. On June 26, they made a stand at Gettysburg.[43]

The clashes of the militiamen at Gettysburg with Maj. Gen. Jubal Early's veteran cavalry on June 26 was as might be expected. Several militiamen were shot and more than 100 rounded up as prisoners. The latter were paroled after a stern lecture from General Early himself, who told them, "You boys ought to be home with your mothers and not out in the fields where it is dangerous and you might get hurt."[44] The survivors of the 26th Pennsylvania Militia Regiment pulled back to defend Harrisburg, but they could be proud of their efforts because they had bought time for the other militia regiments to block or destroy the bridges over the Susquehanna River from Harrisburg to Wrightsville.

---

[41] Ibid.

[42] "Monument to the 26th Pennsylvania Emergency Militia Infantry at Gettysburg," accessed January 2016, http://gettysburg.stonesentinels.com/union-monuments/pennsylvania/pennsylvania-infantry/26th-emergency-militia/

[43] John A. Kirkpatrick (d. 1889) was the Presbyterian chaplain of the 26th Pennsylvania Militia. His commission was dated July 2, 1863, so it is not known if he was at Gettysburg on June 26. General Early's division had ten chaplains with his soldiers—six from Georgia, two from Louisiana, and one each from Virginia and North Carolina. See Roster of Confederate Chaplains at Gettysburg, in Appendix I.

[44] "Monument to the 26th Pennsylvania Emergency Militia," 1.

While Colonel Jennings was rounding up his survivors, Col. Jacob Frick, commanding the 27th Pennsylvania Emergency Militia Regiment, was making every effort to block the Wrightsville bridge across the river by digging as many rifle pits as possible on the western shore. Frick's command consisted of about 1,200 troops, including a company of African American soldiers who helped build trenches. In his after-action report, Frick wrote, "Justice compels me to make mention of the excellent conduct of the company of Negroes from Columbia [Pennsylvania]. After working industriously in the rifle pits all day, when the fight commenced they took their guns and stood up to their work bravely."[45]

Although Colonel Frick did not know all of the details, it was apparent that Confederate troops were attempting to cross the river at Wrightsville and at Harrisburg. In fact, that was exactly the plan: Early would cross at Wrightsville and attack Harrisburg from the south while Ewell brought the rest of the Second Corps to attack from the west. Hill and Longstreet would bring their forces along as soon as they were able.

On the way to Wrightsville, General Early had stopped at York on June 28 to issue an ultimatum to the private citizenry. In exchange for money, clothes, and shoes for his men, Early promised to spare York from destruction:

> I then made a requisition upon the authorities for 2,000 pairs of shoes, 1,000 hats, 1,000 pairs of socks, $100,000 in money, and three days' rations of all kinds. Subsequently between 1,200 and 1,500 pairs of shoes, the hats, socks, and rations were furnished, but only $28,600 in money was furnished...the mayor and other authorities protesting their inability to get any more money, as it had all been run off previously, and I was satisfied they made an honest effort to raise the amount called for.[46]

Having relieved the people of York of money and supplies, Early directed his lead brigade, commanded by Brig. Gen. John B. Gordon, to march quickly to Wrightsville, 7 miles away.

When Brig. Gen. John B. Gordon's Georgia Brigade arrived opposite Frick's entrenchments at Wrightsville, Gordon brought his artillery to bear

---

[45] Henry Louis Gates, Jr., "Did black men fight at Gettysburg?" *Nation*, July 1, 2013, accessed January 2016, as cited in http://www.theroot.com/articles/history/2013/07/did_black_men_fight_at_gettysburg.html.

[46] Mark Major, "The Wrightsville Bridge and the 27th PA Militia," http://blogs.republicanherald.com/gettysburg/index.php/2013/07/01/the-wrightsville-bridge-and-the-27th-pa-militia/, 1.

on the 27th Pennsylvania Militia regiments. Having no artillery on the west side of the river and after receiving fire for almost two hours, Colonel Frick ordered a retirement to the Lancaster side of the Susquehanna. He then ordered his men to blow up the bridge, but when that failed, he ordered them to set it on fire. As the Confederates surged forward, the bridge erupted in flames. Even though Gordon's men worked for hours to extinguish the flames, the bridge was destroyed and with it any hope of crossing the river.

On the same day Colonel Frick was firing the bridge at Wrightsville, Confederate Lt. Gen. Richard Ewell sent Brig. Gen. Albert Jenkins and the equivalent of five regiments of Virginia cavalry from Carlisle east toward Harrisburg. That night, June 28, Jenkins camped on a hill 4 miles from the Pennsylvania capital. Jenkins reported that Harrisburg looked like easy pickings, and Ewell made plans for an attack as soon as he could bring up two more infantry divisions. But then, on June 29, urgent word came from General Lee ordering Ewell's entire corps to march immediately south toward Gettysburg. The Army of the Potomac was much closer than expected. Indeed, by 11 A.M. on June 30, two brigades of Union Brig. Gen. John Buford's 1st Cavalry Division were already at Gettysburg.[47]

---

[47] The first Union cavalry force to reach Gettysburg, Brig. Gen. Joseph Copeland's brigade of four Michigan regiments arrived at 2 P.M. on June 28. However, Copeland was ordered to withdraw to Emmitsburg on June 29, where he relinquished his command to Brig. Gen. George A. Custer. Brig. Gen. John Buford's cavalry arrived at Gettysburg at 11 A.M. on June 30. Late that evening Buford reported to Major General Reynolds that A. P. Hill's Corps was at Cashtown, Ewell's Corps crossing the mountains from Carlisle, and Rebels "advancing from York." See US War Department, *Official Records*, 415.

Chapter 3

July 1, 1863: A Meeting Engagement Escalates

"Army surgeons had to treat the wounded under trees."
—Dr. Jonathan Letterman, USA

At dawn on July 1, 1863, Union Brig. Gen. John Buford deployed his two brigades of cavalry in defense of Gettysburg. Col. William Gamble's First Brigade screened to the west of the town while Col. Thomas Devin's Second Brigade moved to the north and northwest. At 7:30 A.M. Buford's advanced outpost scouts from the 8th Illinois Cavalry of Gamble's Brigade fired on advancing Confederate troops from Lt. Gen. A. P. Hill's Third Corps. General Hill was not completely surprised, for he had received word of the presence of Union cavalry on June 30:

> On arriving at Cashtown, General Heth, who had sent forward Petti-grew's brigade to Gettysburg, reported that Pettigrew had encountered the enemy at Gettysburg, principally cavalry, but in what force he could not determine. A courier was then dispatched with this information to the General Commanding [Lee]; and to start Anderson early; also to General Ewell, informing him, and that I intended to advance the next morning and discover what was in my front. On the first of July, at five o'clock, Heth took up the line of march, with Pegram's battalion of artil-lery, followed by Pender, with McIntosh's battalion of artillery, being with Anderson.[1]

In fact, General Heth had committed two of his brigades, Archer's five Alabama and Tennessee regiments and Davis's four Mississippi and North Carolina regiments, numbering about 3,000 men supported by four artillery units, to probe the Union line. Facing these two divisions at approximately 8 A.M. on July 1 were 1,600 mainly dismounted cavalrymen of Gamble's First Brigade.[2] Gamble's line, facing west, ran perpendicular to the Chambersburg

---

[1] "General A. P. Hill's Report of Battle of Gettysburg," as cited in Rev. J. William Jones, ed., *Southern Historical Society Papers*, vol. II (July to December 1876): 222.

[2] Jay Luvass and Harold W. Nelson, eds., *Guide to the Battle of Gettysburg* (Lawrence: University Press of Kansas, 1994) 5.

Pike, first along Herr Ridge, then McPherson's Ridge, and was supported by six three-inch rifled guns of Lt. John Calef's battery of horse artillery.[3]

Normally such a relatively small force of cavalry would have been swept aside by combined infantry and artillery fire, but Buford was determined to delay the Confederate advance until reinforcements could arrive. Buford had sent four dispatches on June 30 to Gen. Alfred Pleasonton, the Union Cavalry Corps commander, and to Gen. John Reynolds, the First Corps commander, detailing the positions of all of Lee's advancing columns. This was the critical battlefield intelligence General Meade needed. On July 1, Meade issued movement orders based on Buford's reports. Meade directed Reynolds's First Corps to march from Emmitsburg to support Buford, with Howard's Eleventh Corps following Reynolds. Sickles's Third Corps moved to Emmitsburg, 12 miles south of Gettysburg. Hancock's Second Corps moved to Taneytown, where Meade had his temporary headquarters. The other three corps in the Army of the Potomac took positions at Two Taverns and Hanover, Pennsylvania, and at Manchester, Maryland, covering all of the main roads from Carlisle to Baltimore and Washington, DC.

Along a creek called Willoughby Run facing Herr Ridge, Buford aligned his two cavalry brigades, Gamble's and Devin's, now numbering a combined 2,823 troopers. Still outnumbered and out-gunned, the troopers did have .52-caliber Burnside carbines which fired from two to three times faster than standard muskets and which did not require a ramrod to load. When firing in line, the cavalrymen could easily put 3,200 bullets a minute out to a range of 300 yards. With this modest but clear advantage, Buford was able to fight a successful delaying action for two hours until General Reynolds's first infantry brigades and an artillery battery arrived at 10 A.M. to reinforce the line, then along McPherson's Ridge.[4]

By 10:20 A.M. the Confederates had reached Herr Ridge and had pushed the Federal cavalrymen east to McPherson Ridge when the vanguard of the First Corps finally arrived. Major General Reynolds and his staff found Brigadier General Buford at the Lutheran seminary. When asked for his report, Buford exclaimed, "The devil's to pay!" When Reynolds asked if

---

[3] Ibid., 7, and Kelly Knauer, ed., *Gettysburg: A Day-by-Day Account of the Greatest Battle of the Civil War* (New York: Time Books, 2013) 34.

[4] Knauer, *Gettysburg: A Day-by-Day Account*, 34. For a discussion of the carbines available to Buford's cavalrymen, see "Battle of Gettysburg, First Day," accessed January 30, 2016, https://en.wikipedia.org/wiki/Battle_of_Gettysburg,_First_Day, Defense by Buford's Cavalry, 3.

he could hold out a while longer until reinforcements arrived, Buford replied simply, "I reckon I can."[5]

The first Union chaplain on the field might have been considered an unlikely candidate for a combat assignment. Chaplain John Visger Van Ingen, age 56, of the 8th New York Cavalry Regiment, was the only chaplain present in Gamble's Brigade on July 1. Van Ingen, an Episcopal priest, was from Schenectady, New York, and had been a recognized leader in his denomination for more than twenty years. In 1841 he served as a trustee for the Episcopal Diocese of Western New York; in 1854 he was the pastor of Grace Episcopal Church in Rochester, New York; and in 1857 he became a missionary to Ontario, Canada, and eventual founder of Christ Church Orphan's Home in St. Paul, Minnesota. When President Lincoln called for volunteers to put down the rebellion, Van Ingen applied for a chaplain's position and was assigned to the 8th New York Cavalry on November 18, 1861. By the time he reached Gettysburg he had been on duty for a bit more than nineteen months.

Other than a few words of encouragement and a prayer with the troopers, Van Ingen did not have much time to move down the line at McPherson's Ridge.[6] The wounded began to stack up within minutes of engaging the Confederate artillery. Although Buford had just 139 casualties all morning, there was minimal medical care available. Chaplain Van Ingen and his two colleagues from Devin's Brigade, Chaplain George Crocker and Chaplain Charles Keyes, both Baptists, found themselves doing the work of assistant surgeons by bandaging wounds and evacuating troopers back to the Gettysburg seminary building.

In his official report regarding medical support for Union soldiers at Gettysburg, Surgeon Jonathan Letterman, medical director of the Army of the Potomac, wrote of the dilemmas he experienced early in the battle:

Dr. [Jeremiah] Brinton arriving at Frederick on June 28, the day after the arrival of [Meade's] headquarters there, with twenty-five army wagon loads of such supplies as would be most required in case of a battle. The train with these supplies followed that of headquarters until we reached Taneytown.

On the 1st, it was ordered that "corps commanders and the commander of the Artillery Reserve will at once send to the rear all their

---

[5] Knauer, *Gettysburg: A Day-by-Day Account*, 34.
[6] The monument to the 8th New York Cavalry is south of the Chambersburg Pike on Gamble's left flank.

trains (excepting ammunition wagons and ambulances), parking them between Union Mills and Westminster."

On the 2d, these trains were ordered still farther to the rear, and parked near Westminster, nearly 25 miles distant from the battlefield. The effect of this order was to deprive the department almost wholly of the means for taking care of the wounded until the result of the engagement of the 2d and 3d was fully known. In most of the corps the wagons exclusively used for medicines moved with the ambulances, so that the medical officers had a sufficient supply of dressings, chloroform, and such articles until the supplies came up, but the tents and other appliances, which are as necessary, were not available until July 5.[7]

Lacking a reasonable supply of tents to set up field hospitals and enough wagons to move the wounded from temporary shelters, such as farmhouses, barns, churches, college buildings, and even the courthouse, many Army surgeons had to treat the wounded under trees or in open fields. Regimental chaplains spent the majority of their time assisting in this work for their own men, even while occasionally under artillery fire.

Buford's reinforcement came first from Brig. Gen. James Wadsworth's First Division of Reynolds's First Corps. General Reynolds had set Wadsworth's Division in motion at dawn from Emmitsburg, 12 miles away. Reynolds met the advancing column and sent two brigades directly across the fields to relieve Buford's hard-pressed cavalrymen. Brig. Gen. Solomon Meredith's Iron Brigade, composed of veterans from Wisconsin, Indiana, and Michigan, attacked Brig. Gen. James Archer's Alabama and Tennessee Brigade south of the turnpike in McPherson's Woods. Five regiments from Brig. Lysander Cutler's Second Brigade were to Meredith's right, north of the turnpike, opposing three of Brig. Gen. Joseph R. Davis's Mississippi and North Carolina regiments that were maneuvering north toward Oak Ridge on Cutler's flank.[8]

While the Iron Brigade was engaging Archer's Confederates, General Reynolds rode up to the front Union line. As he turned in the saddle to urge on the 2nd Wisconsin Infantry, a minié ball hit him in the back of the head, killing him instantly. He became the first, though not the last, corps com-

---

[7] War Department, *Official Records*, part 2: report no. 16, 195–96.

[8] Educated at Miami University in Ohio, Brig. Gen. Joseph R. Davis was a nephew of Confederate president Jefferson Davis and a former Mississippi state senator. Brig. Gen. Lysander Cutler was a former Indian fighter, businessman, and Maine state senator. Cutler's brigade fought on two fronts on July 1 and did not leave the field until 4 P.M. Cutler's casualties equaled 50 percent of his brigade.

mander to be a casualty at Gettysburg. Maj. Gen. Abner Doubleday, who had arrived on McPherson's Ridge just a few minutes before, was now the senior officer on the field.[9]

Rebels on the Right

While the fighting was raging in McPherson's Woods, General Davis's Brigade of three regiments, the 42nd Mississippi, the 2nd Mississippi, and the 55th North Carolina, met Cutler's Brigade north of the Chambersburg Pike. The 55th North Carolina, avoiding a direct frontal assault, managed to move far enough to their left to take Cutler's 76th New York and 56th Pennsylvania regiments in a flank attack. Being aware of even more Confederate troops emerging from Oak Hill on his far right, Brig. Gen. James Wadsworth ordered Cutler to retire to the next ridge. The 147th New York, protecting Hall's Second Maine Battery, did not get the order to retire, so they continued to fight, even though outnumbered.

The Mississippi infantrymen were led not only by General Davis, but also were inspired by their "fighting chaplain," Thomas Dwight Witherspoon. Chaplain Witherspoon was born in Greensboro, Alabama, and was just 27 years of age in 1863. Witherspoon was a direct descendant of the Reverend John Witherspoon, President of the College of New Jersey and a signer of the Declaration of Independence. Thomas was a graduate of the University of Mississippi, the Columbia Theological Seminary in Columbia, South Carolina, and an ordained Presbyterian clergyman.

In May 1861, Witherspoon left his pastorate in Oxford, Mississippi, and enlisted in Company G, 11th Mississippi Infantry. He accompanied this regiment to Virginia, although he was initially opposed to going farther north to invade any state outside the Confederacy:

> Let us defend our own soil and then the world will see that we cannot be subjugated. This is as it seems the only question involved in the war. We are not fighting to test the power of two nations. I am for one willing to admit that the North is more powerful. It has more wealth, more fighting men and more material out of which to make them. It can raise and

---

[9] Knauer, *Gettysburg: A Day-by-Day Account*, 35–36. Generals Reynolds and Doubleday were also at West Point at the same time: Reynolds in the Class of 1841 and Doubleday in the Class of 1842, one year ahead of Cadet Ulysses Grant.

maintain a long standing army, but can it subjugate us[?] Can it force terms of submission upon us[?] This alone we are answering.[10]

In summer 1861, at the request of officers in Witherspoon's regiment, President Jefferson Davis commissioned him a chaplain. Chaplain Witherspoon served in the 42nd Mississippi Infantry Regiment at Gettysburg. When Witherspoon picked up a musket and fought alongside his men, one observed, "He was ever found at his outpost of duty, even when that was the outpost of the army or the advance line of battle."[11]

South of the turnpike, Archer's men were expecting an easy fight against dismounted cavalrymen and were astonished to recognize the black Hardee hats worn by the Iron Brigade. As the Confederates crossed Willoughby Run and climbed the slope into Herbst Woods, they were enveloped on their right by the longer Union line, the reverse of the situation north of the pike.[12] Brig. Gen. James Archer was captured by Pvt. Patrick Moloney of Company G, 2nd Wisconsin Infantry, "a brave patriotic and fervent young Irishman." Archer resisted capture, but Moloney overpowered him. Moloney was killed later that day, but he received a posthumous Medal of Honor for his exploit. When Archer was taken to the rear, he encountered his former army colleague, Maj. Gen. Abner Doubleday, who greeted him good-naturedly, "Good morning, Archer! How are you? I am glad to see you!" Archer replied, "Well, I am not glad to see you by a damn sight!"[13]

General Archer was just one of the 200 Confederate soldiers surrounded and captured in the Herbst Woods. Lt. Col. S. G. Shepard of the 7th Tennessee Infantry, Archer's Brigade, recalled:

We had encountered the enemy but a short time, when he made his appearance suddenly on our right flank with a heavy force, and opened upon us a cross-fire. Our position was at once rendered untenable, and the right of our line was forced back. Being completely overpowered by numbers, and our support not being near enough to give us any assis-

---

[10] "Pastor Witherspoon Goes to War," New York Times, accessed November 2014, http://opinionator.blogs.nytimes.com/2011/04/29/pastor-witherspoon-goes-to-war/, 4.

[11] Ibid.

[12] Harry W. Pfanz, The Battle of Gettysburg (Washington, PA: US National Park Service, 1994) 13.

[13] Harry W. Pfanz, Gettysburg: The First Day (Chapel Hill: University of North Carolina Press, 2001) 100–101.

tance, we fell back across the field, and reformed just in the rear of the brigade that had started in as our support.[14]

According to later reports, Shepard's included, Archer's Brigade suffered 69 killed and 218 wounded, or 27 percent of the 1,048 engaged, the second highest casualty rate among Maj. Gen. Heth's four brigades.[15]

The chaplain of the 7th Tennessee Infantry was the Reverend John Henry Tomkies, a Baptist clergyman from Hanover County, Virginia. Tomkies had attended Richmond College in Virginia from 1858 to 1860. He was 24 years of age when he came to Gettysburg with his regiment. The 7th Tennessee Infantry was originally recruited in Sumner County, northeast of Nashville, and joined the Confederate service in July 1861. In their two years of service, they had been in every major battle the Army of Northern Virginia experienced.

As the wounded piled up around Willoughby Run, Chaplain Tomkies began to help carry the soldiers to the Michael Crist farmhouse, about 250 yards northeast of the Herr Tavern. The Crist stone farmhouse and large barn had been pressed into service as a Confederate hospital, and Tomkies, with Methodist Chaplain A. L. W. Stroud of the 13th Alabama and Presbyterian Chaplain Joseph D. Porter of the 5th Alabama Battalion, not only said prayers for the men but also assisted the regimental surgeons in binding up wounds as best they could.[16]

Even though the Iron Brigade had stopped the attack by Archer's Alabama and Tennessee Brigade in the woods, the cost had been heavy. The Iron Brigade casualties on July 1 totaled 1,153 casualties of 1,885 engaged, or 61 percent of the whole brigade. The 7th Wisconsin lost 52 percent of its 370 men, the 24th Michigan Infantry lost 80 percent of its regiment, and the 19th Indiana 66 percent of its 308 soldiers. Nevertheless, the Iron Brigade held fast for four hours on the south side of the Chambersburg Pike.

---

[14] "Report of Lt. Col. S. G. Shepard, CSA, Seventh Tennessee Infantry, of operations of Archer's brigade," War Department, *Official Records*, part 2: 646–48.

[15] Kelly Knauer, *Gettysburg: A Day-by-Day Account*, 44. Heth's Division lost 1,500 of 7,500 men, or 20 percent of his force.

[16] John Henry Tomkies (1839–1878) was later pastor of the First Baptist Church of Gainesville, Florida, (1873–1875) and president of the Florida Baptist Convention. His remains were buried in the Evergreen Cemetery in Gainesville. Photo credit: Alachua County Library District Heritage Collection, http://heritage.acld.lib.fl.us.

The first responders for all of these casualties were the regimental chaplains, the members of the regimental bands, who acted as stretcher-bearers, and the assistant surgeons. Chaplain Sam Eaton was assigned to the 7th Wisconsin Infantry Regiment, Chaplain William C. Way to the 24th Michigan Infantry, and Chaplain Thomas Barnett to the 19th Indiana Infantry.

Chaplain Samuel W. Eaton (1820 to 1905) was a Congregationalist minister and a direct descendant of a Mayflower passenger of the same name. He was commissioned as chaplain of the 7th Wisconsin Infantry Regiment on July 2, 1862, and served to July 3, 1865.[17] On July 1, Chaplain Eaton ministered to the wounded of his regiment at the Edward McPherson Farm, subsequently withdrawing to the Lutheran seminary. During the battle, Eaton's regimental commander, Col. W. W. Robinson, recalled that Eaton rode his horse to the front and urged the soldiers to press forward, shouting, "That's the way to do it, boys!" Robinson also wrote later that Chaplain Eaton "attends to the sick and wounded and does not hesitate to follow us to the battlefield."[18]

Chaplain William C. Way was a 39-year-old Methodist pastor from Livingston County, New York. In his early years he had worked as a printer and then as co-owner of a clothing store in Rochester. In 1857 he moved to Detroit with his wife and was licensed as a local Methodist preacher, earning about $450 a year. During his service with the 24th Michigan Infantry, Chaplain Way's wife, Eliza, accompanied him to the field. She was present with him at Gettysburg as they cared for the wounded and dying.[19]

Thomas Barnett was born July 17, 1833, in Fayette County, Ohio. He enlisted on April 10, 1863, as an ordained Methodist minister and was commissioned a chaplain on April 23, thirteen days later. He served with the 19th Indiana Infantry at the Battle of Chancellorsville and subsequently at Gettysburg, where he ministered to 119 wounded soldiers from his regi-

---

[17] Chaplain Eaton's grave is in the Hillside Cemetery, Lancaster, Wisconsin.

[18] Wisconsin Historical Society, Quiner Scrapbooks: Correspondence of the Wisconsin Volunteers, 1861–1865, v. 8, 7th Infantry, CWQ_UO080264. Accessed November 2014, http://content.wisconsinhistory.org/cdm/ref/collection/quiner/id/8818.

[19] "William Chittenden Way," http://www.oocities.org/24th_michigan/wway.html, 1. Note that Chaplain Way wore shoulder taps displaying a cross, unauthorized but evidently not unapproved. He was the only chaplain of a Michigan regiment to remain in service for the duration of the war, until June 30, 1865.

ment.[20] Chaplain Barnett wrote a letter to the *Indianapolis Journal* on July 2 summarizing the losses in his regiment the previous day.

> The Losses of the 19th Indiana.
> Gettysburg, Penn., July 2, 1863.
> Editor Journal: Permit me to drop a word of information to the many friends of officers and men of the 19th Indiana Regiment, through your valuable paper.
> I could not exaggerate the bravery of the officers and men. They, without an exception yet known, were all found at their respective posts, and although led immediately into a murderous fire, without time to adjust their pieces, yet they stood up boldly and manfully. Colonel Williams was in the thickest of the fight from the commencement and could be seen, frequently in the advance of the regiment, making observations for the success and safety of his men. He very narrowly escaped twice, a ball passing through his hat and another struck his side, and was prevented, doubtless, from killing him by a pocket map which it struck, penetrating his coat and nearly through his map, lodging in the last fold. The Colonel has never taken the ball out of the map, but keeps it as it was.
> Lt. Col. W. W. Dudley fell severely if not mortally wounded early in the day, while urging forward his men. Major John M. Lindley was severely wounded in the hand, the ball striking his hand and saber. While waving his saber over his head another ball struck him on the cheek, just grazing the skin. The Major, we hope will soon recover. Adjutant George W. Finney was slightly wounded.
> The Surgeon and First Assistant Surgeon are in the hands of the rebels.
> Fears are entertained that the Assistant Surgeon, Dr. A. B. Haines, has fallen, or is wounded. I will append to this a list of names of officers killed and wounded in the fight of the first day of July, 1863.
>
> Killed.
> Lieutenant R. Jones, Lieutenant C. G. East, and Serg. Major Blanchard.

---

[20] After the war Chaplain Barnett attended Washington University School of Medicine in St. Louis, Missouri. He practiced medicine until his death on May 19, 1904. His remains were buried at Fort Scott, Kansas. As cited by Tony Meeks, ACM genealogy, 19th Indiana Infantry Soldiers, accessed November 2014, http://boards.ancestry.com and findagrave.com.

Wounded.
Lt. Col. W. W. Dudley, severely.
Major John M. Lindley, severely.
Adjutant G. W. Finney, slightly.
Captain A. J. Makepiece, slightly.
Captain J. T. Ives, slightly.
Captain J. W. Shafer, slightly.
Captain G. W. Green, slightly.
First Lt. Wm. H. Campbell, slightly.
First Lt. S. B. Schlagal, slightly.
First Lt. J. W. Witemyre, slightly.
First Lt. A. Gisse, slightly.
Second Lt. C. V. Patrick, slightly.
Second Lt. O. Branson, slightly.
We went into the fight with about 300 men, all told, and came out
with 69, all safe.

Summary of Casualities.
Officers
Killed2
Wounded13
Missing6

Privates
Killed20
Wounded106
Missing67

Total—killed, wounded and missing204
I am your most obedient servant,
Thomas Barnett,
Chaplain 19th Reg't Indiana Vols.[21]

Chaplain Barnett's report demonstrated that he had checked on every man
in the regiment, as a good shepherd should.

---

[21] This letter appeared in the *Indianapolis Daily Journal* on July 13, 1863, on
page 2, column 1. The spelling, statistics, and punctuation are unchanged from the
original publication. As cited by Meeks, 19th Indiana Infantry Soldiers,
http://boards.ancestry.com.

All of the casualties were not on the Union side, of course. The 2nd Mississippi Infantry of Davis's Brigade got caught in an unfinished railroad cut, fifteen-feet deep in places, along the Chambersburg Pike. The 6th Wisconsin, 95th New York, and 84th New York, also known as the 14th Brooklyn, poured enfilading fire on the Confederates from both ends of the huge ditch. Some of the Mississippi soldiers were able to escape back to Herr Ridge, but the attack by Davis's Brigade was over. Of the 1,707 men in Davis's unit, 700 were killed, wounded, or captured.

Major General Howard's Eleventh Corps Arrives

At approximately 11:30 A.M. the Union Eleventh Corps reached Gettysburg. Major General Howard, the Corps Commander, discovered that General Reynolds had been killed and that he was in at least temporary command of two corps of the Union army. Howard, a West Point graduate in the Class of 1854 and a former Sunday school teacher at the academy, had lost his right arm while leading his men at Fair Oaks, Virginia, in June 1862, an action that later earned him the Medal of Honor.

The Eleventh Corps, numbering 12,096 soldiers on June 30, was composed of three divisions: the first commanded by Brig. Gen. Francis C. Barlow, the second by Brig. Gen. Adolph von Steinwehr, and the third by Maj. Gen. Carl Shurtz.[22] General Howard, surveying the field from the roof of Fahnestock's dry-goods store in Gettysburg, directed Shurtz's Division to take a position on Oak Ridge and to link up with the right flank of Major General Doubleday's First Corps. Barlow's Division then extended the Union line to the east covering the Carlisle and Harrisburg roads. Von Steinwehr's Division was placed on Cemetery Hill with two batteries of artillery in case the Union troops needed a rallying point, in accord with orders Gen. John Reynolds sent to General Howard earlier in the day.[23] Since Howard was now the overall field commander, Shurtz took over the temporary command of the Eleventh Corps and turned his division over to Prussian-born Brig. Gen. Alexander Schimmelfennig, a veteran and a participant in the retreat of the Eleventh Corps at Chancellorsville two months before.

---

[22] Harry Pfantz [*Gettysburg: The First Day* (Chapel Hill: University of North Carolina Press, 2001) 158] believed that Howard's Corps had just 8,700 effective troops on the field. The War Department [*Official Records*, part 1: 151] gives the total as 12,096 on June 30 but does not comment on the effective strength available on July 1.

[23] David G. Martin, *Gettysburg July 1* (Conshohocken, PA: Combined Publishing Co., 1996) 198–202.

Major General Doubleday, still facing Hill's Corps on the Chambersburg Pike, reorganized his line as Col. Chapman Biddle's and Col. Roy Stone's brigades from the First Corps arrived. Biddle's four regiments from Pennsylvania and New York moved to the left of the Iron Brigade, while Stone's three Pennsylvania regiments, the "Bucktail Brigade," deployed to the right along the Chambersburg Pike. Later in the afternoon Brig. Gen. John C. Robinson's reserve division moved forward, with two brigades under Brig. Gen. Gabriel Paul and Brig. Gen. Henry Baxter to support the line north of the Pike. By 2:30 P.M. six of the seven brigades in the First Corps had been positioned to the west of Gettysburg, and two of the three divisions of the Eleventh Corps to the north of the town.

Major General Meade, at Taneytown, heard of Reynolds's death about noon on July 1. Chaplain John H. W. Stuckenberg, 145th Pennsylvania Infantry, US Second Corps, was at Taneytown at the time:

> On the 1st of July we left Uniontown, marched through Taneytown...looked anxiously forward to our entering our own beloved state—Pennsylvania—crossed the line with much pleasure, heard reports of an engagement at Gettysburg and of the death of Gen Reynolds whose body was conveyed past us in an ambulance, and after dark moved into a wheat field threw out a picket as we did not know, but what enemy were in front of us, and bivouacked—glad once more to rest our weary limbs.[24]

General Meade dispatched Maj. Gen. Winfield Scott Hancock, commander of the Second Corps, to take command at Gettysburg, relieving Major General Howard of that responsibility. Howard, however, remained in command of the Eleventh Corps.

North of Gettysburg, Lt. Gen. Richard S. Ewell, a graduate of the Class of 1840 at West Point and a veteran of the Mexican War, was hastening his Second Corps toward Gettysburg.[25] On the morning of July 1, responding to orders from General Lee and reports from Lt. Gen. A. P. Hill, Ewell moved with Rodes's Division from Carlisle toward Cashtown,

---

[24] David T. Hedrick and Gordon Barry Davis, Jr., eds., *I'm Surrounded by Methodists...Diary of John H. W. Stuckenberg, Chaplain of the 145th Pennsylvania Volunteer Infantry* (Gettysburg, PA: Thomas Publications, 1995) 76.

[25] Richard S. Ewell was in the same class at West Point as future Union generals William T. Sherman and George H. Thomas. During the Mexican War, Ewell received a battlefield promotion for his courageous actions at Contreras, having accompanied Captain Robert E. Lee on a nighttime reconnaissance of enemy lines. "Richard S. Ewell," accessed November 2014, http://en.wikipedia.org/wiki/ Richard_S._Ewell, 2.

where he assumed General Lee would be. Ewell also ordered Major General Early to bring his division from the area around York to Huntersville. Lee informed Ewell that he did not want a general engagement brought on until the rest of the army came up.[26] "By the time this message [from Lee] reached me," Ewell wrote, "General A. P. Hill had already been warmly engaged with a large body of the enemy in his front, and Carter's artillery battalion, of Rodes' Division, had opened with fine effect on the flank of the same body, which was rapidly preparing to attack me, while fresh masses were moving into position in my front. It was too late to avoid an engagement without abandoning the position already taken up, and I determined to push the attack vigorously."[27]

Maj. Gen. Robert Rodes's Division of Ewell's Corps had beaten the Union troops to Oak Hill, where Confederate artillery fire forced the two divisions from Howard's US Eleventh Corps to take positions in the fields below the Oak Hill ridge. When Rodes sent two brigades, commanded by Col. Edward O'Neal and Brig. Gen. Alfred Iverson, to attack six veteran regiments of Brig. Gen. Henry Baxter's Brigade of Robinson's Division, the piecemeal attacks fared poorly and the Confederates fell back badly mauled.

General Lee's Arrival

A little after 2:00 P.M. General Lee arrived on the field with Lieutenant General Hill, just west of Gettysburg. Lee realized a general engagement was in progress, so he directed Hill to take his entire corps forward. Because Ewell was already engaged, there occurred a rare coordinated attack by almost two-thirds of the Confederate forces. Along the Chambersburg Pike, General Heth sent Pettigrew's North Carolina Brigade and Brockenbrough's Virginia Brigade forward against Doubleday's US First Corps, followed by Pender's entire division of four infantry brigades supported by Maj. William T. Poague's artillery.

The 26th North Carolina Infantry of Pettigrew's Brigade, attacking at about 2:30 P.M., was able to outflank the 19th Indiana Infantry of Brig. Gen. Solomon Meredith's Iron Brigade. Pettigrew's North Carolinians drove Meredith's Brigade back toward Seminary Ridge in some of the fiercest fighting of the war. General Meredith was downed with a head wound,

---

[26] Lt. Gen. Richard S. Ewell, "The Gettysburg Campaign," War Department, *Official Records*, part 2: ch. 39, 444.

[27] Ibid.

made worse when his horse fell on him.[28] Biddle's Pennsylvania Brigade was outflanked and decimated as well.

Baxter's Brigade, which had shattered two Confederate brigades from Rodes's Division, ran out of ammunition and was ordered to withdraw toward the seminary at about 3 P.M. Brigadier General Robinson, the Second Division commander, replaced it with Brig. Gen. Gabriel Paul's Brigade. General Paul was almost immediately shot through the head, a wound he survived but which blinded him permanently. When Rodes sent two more brigades into battle, Doubleday ordered Robinson to withdraw Paul's Brigade shortly before 5 P.M.[29] This effectively put Doubleday's entire US First Corps in retreat.

Doubleday explained his decision in his report:

> About 4 P.M. the enemy, having been strongly reinforced, advanced in large numbers, everywhere deploying into double and triple lines, over-lapping our left for a third of a mile, pressing heavily upon our right and overwhelming our center. It was evident Lee's whole army was approaching. Our tired troops had been fighting desperately, some of them for six hours. They were thoroughly exhausted, and it became necessary to retreat. All my reserves had been thrown in, and the First Corps was now fighting in a single line.[30]

Both sides had paid a high price on the western part of the battlefield. The 26th North Carolina, the largest regiment of Hill's Corps, with 839 men, ended the day with about 212 still able to fight. A bullet through the chest had fatally wounded their commander, Col. Henry K. Burgwyn. Their opposing Union regiment, the 24th Michigan, lost 399 of 496, including nine color-bearers shot down, and its commander, Col. Henry A. Morrow, wounded and captured. General Doubleday estimated the losses to the Union First Corps at 70 percent of those engaged on July 1 in his after-action report: "The First Corps only consisted of about 8,200 men when it entered the battle. It was reduced at the close of the engagement to about 2,450."[31]

---

[28] Brig. Gen. Solomon Meredith, born of Quaker parents in North Carolina, was known among the troops as "Long Sol," a reference to his 6' 7" stature. After his severe wound at Gettysburg, he was no longer eligible for field service.

[29] War Department, *Official Records*, part 1: 289–91.

[30] Ibid., 250–251.

[31] Ibid.

Among the First Corps casualties were 132 captured officers in the ranks from colonel to second lieutenant, who were transported to Libby Prison in Richmond to await exchange.[32]

Along Oak Hill, Ewell continued pressing forward with Rodes's Division just as Maj. Gen. Jubal Early arrived with four brigades down the Heidlersburg road to outflank and overwhelm Barlow's two US brigades on the Eleventh Corps flank at what became known later as Barlow's Knoll. General Lee wrote about the two-corps attack:

> General Heth pressed the enemy steadily back, breaking his first and second lines, and attacking his third with great resolution. At about 2 ½ P.M. the advance of Ewell's corps, consisting of Rodes' division, with Carter's battalion of artillery, arrived by the Middletown road, and forming on Heth's left, nearly at right angles with his line, became warmly engaged with fresh numbers of the enemy. Heth's troops having suffered heavily in their protracted contest with a superior force, were relieved by Pender's, and Early coming up by the Heidlersburg road soon afterwards took position on the left of Rodes, when a general advance was made.
>
> The enemy gave way on all sides and were driven through Gettysburg with great loss. Major-General Reynolds, who was in command, was killed. More than five thousand prisoners, exclusive of a large number of wounded, three pieces of artillery, and several colors, were captured. Among the prisoners were two Brigadier-Generals, one of whom was badly wounded.[33]

Among the Union officers wounded near Barlow's Knoll was Chaplain Ferdinand L. Sarner of the 54th New York Volunteer Infantry in Colonel Leopold von Gilsa's Brigade. Chaplain Sarner was the first clergyman of the Jewish faith to be commissioned a regimental chaplain in the US Army and became the first chaplain casualty at Gettysburg.

---

[32] "Union Officers in Richmond Prisons—A Complete Official List," *New York Tribune*, November 6, 1863, 1. The list of unwounded prisoners includes one colonel, three lieutenant colonels, four majors, forty-seven captains, thirty-one first lieutenants, and forty-six second lieutenants.

[33] Jones, "General Lee's Report of the Gettysburg Campaign," *Southern Historical Society Papers* 2/1 (1876): 40. Brig. Gen. Francis Barlow was severely wounded at Barlow's Knoll and captured on July 1. His wife, who secured permission to pass through the lines, nursed him back to health, saving his life. Brig. Gen. Charles K. Graham, commanding the First Brigade, First Division, US Third Corps, was wounded and captured on July 2.

Born in Prussia and graduated from the University of Hesse, Chaplain Sarner had been a rabbi of a congregation in Rochester, New York, when the war started. He reportedly consulted carefully with his senior rabbi before volunteering to serve as a chaplain, lest he be on the wrong side! His conscience satisfied, Sarner was commissioned on April 10, 1863, just in time to join his regiment before the Battle of Chancellorsville.

The 54th New York Infantry was a largely German-speaking regiment known for a legendary supply of lager, singing, pet dogs, and socialist views. The chaplains who had preceded Sarner in the regiment had been a peculiar collection of skeptics, heretics, and outright atheists. There has been conjecture that Sarner was worth more as a linguist than a cleric to the "freethinking Dutchmen" in his military congregation. Moreover, the 54th New York had withdrawn in haste from the battlefield at Chancellorsville, earning them another nickname, "The Flying Dutchmen."[34]

Regardless of the regiment's prior reputation, Chaplain Sarner lacked neither courage nor determination in doing his duty as the regimental chaplain. When Gen. Jubal Early's attack on Barlow's Division commenced about three o'clock, Chaplain Sarner rode his horse out to the main battle line, presumably to encourage his men. He had barely arrived just behind the ranks when he was wounded and his horse shot out from under him. As the troops began to break and run, Chaplain Sarner managed to withdraw with them. No record of his medical treatment has come to light as yet, but the regiment carried him on the rolls until October 1864. Rabbi Sarner died ten years later in a yellow-fever epidemic in Memphis, Tennessee.[35]

As Barlow's Division gave ground, Maj. Gen. Carl Schurz's Third Division, under the temporary command of Brig. Gen. Alexander Schimmelfennig, found itself in a deadly artillery crossfire from Rodes's and Early's batteries. As they deployed they were attacked by Confederate infantry from Doles's Brigade of Rodes's Division. General Early's troops were able to employ a flanking attack and roll up Schimmelfennig's Division from the right, and they fell back in confusion toward the town. A desperate counterattack by the 157th New York from Schurz's First Brigade was surrounded on three sides, causing it to suffer 307 casualties, or 75 percent of its men.

The collapse of the Eleventh Corps was completed by 4 P.M. after a fight of less than an hour. They suffered 3,200 casualties, 1,400 of them

---

[34] Benedict Maryniak, "Union Military Chaplains," in John W. Brinsfield, William C. Davis, Benedict Maryniak, and James I. Robertson, Jr., *Faith in the Fight: Civil War Chaplains* (Mechanicsburg, PA: Stackpole Books, 2003) 35.

[35] Ibid., 36.

prisoners. The losses to the two brigades from Rodes's and Early's divisions were less than 750.[36] West of Gettysburg, Col. Abner M. Perrin's South Carolina Brigade, with 1,500 fresh troops, was able to flank the left of the Union First Corps line at the Lutheran seminary. They broke through and drove the defenders north toward the Chambersburg Pike. By 4:30 P.M. the Union position was untenable. The men could see the Eleventh Corps retreating from the northern battle, pursued by masses of Confederates. General Doubleday ordered a withdrawal to Cemetery Hill, south of the town.[37]

The soldiers of the First Corps tried to retreat slowly and deliberately through Gettysburg, keeping some control. The narrow streets of the town, clogged by horse-drawn artillery and soldiers who were not sure where they were going, made defense almost impossible. General Robinson ordered Col. Charles W. Tilden to have his 16th Maine Infantry serve as a rear guard and to hold the line at any cost. The men took position behind a stone wall on the Mummasburg road and were able to help the survivors of General Paul's Brigade escape. However, the 16th Maine, which began the day with 298 men, ended their action with just 35 survivors.[38]

For the Eleventh Corps, it was a sad reminder of their retreat at Chancellorsville in May. Under heavy pursuit by Early's infantry, they clogged the streets of the town; no one in the corps had planned routes for this contingency. Parts of the corps conducted an organized fighting retreat, but the citizens of Gettysburg panicked with artillery shells bursting overhead, and fleeing refugees added to the congestion. Some soldiers tried to avoid capture by hiding in basements and in fenced backyards. Brigadier General Schimmelfennig, the temporary Third Division commander, climbed a fence and hid behind a woodpile in the garden of the Garlach family for the rest of the three-day battle. The only advantage the Eleventh Corps soldiers had was that they were familiar with the route to Cemetery Hill, having passed by there in the morning. Many of the soldiers in the First Corps, including officers, did not know where the cemetery was.[39]

By early afternoon on July 1, regimental surgeons on both sides of the battle lines realized that their aid stations and small regimental hospitals would be totally inadequate for the huge numbers of wounded that were

---

[36] Stephen W. Sears, *Gettysburg* (Boston: Houghton Mifflin, 2003) 217.

[37] Harry W. Pfanz, *Gettysburg—The First Day*, 311–17.

[38] Martin, *Gettysburg*, 389–92. Colonel Tilden held the line until he was captured. Subsequently, he was sent to Libby Prison in Richmond. "Union Officers in Richmond Prisons," *New York Tribune*, November 6, 1863, 1.

[39] Ibid., 333.

coming from the battles raging around Gettysburg. In the field, the Regimental Hospital Department was allowed two small tents for the officers and medicines, another small tent for the kitchen and supplies, and a large tent for the sick. This last, known as the hospital tent, was about fourteen feet square and was capable of containing eight cots with as many patients. There were few, if any, white sheets or pillowcases, so the assistant surgeons and male nurses made do with wool army blankets. The stock of medicines was also limited on campaign. Among them were opium, morphine, quinine, rhubarb, whiskey, castor oil, camphor, tannin, and numerous powders containing lead, copper, and iron.[40]

Soldiers from the regiment were detailed to serve on "special duty" as nurses, cooks, and ambulance drivers as well as on burial details.[41] Quite a few men served in these capacities along with surgeons, assistant surgeons, and regimental chaplains.

As the First US Corps's wounded came from the field, the surgeons set up three larger hospitals at the McPherson Farm, the Lutheran seminary, and at "the College Lutheran Church," later renamed Christ Lutheran Church on Chambersburg Street.[42] At the church, planks were placed across pews to form makeshift platforms to receive the wounded. While the men were waiting to be treated, nurses and chaplains helped apply temporary bandages, pass out cups of water, and listen to what were sometimes last requests.

The First Corps had fifteen chaplains on duty on July 1 to provide ministry for thirty-two infantry regiments. Two Presbyterian clergymen from Brig. Gen. John Robinson's Division, Chaplain Philos Cook, 94th New York Infantry, First Brigade, and Chaplain Horatio Howell of the 90th Pennsylvania, Second Brigade, covered the Lutheran seminary hospital and Christ Lutheran Church during the afternoon fighting. They were busy, as the First Brigade commander, Brig. Gen. Gabriel Paul, had been grievously wounded, and Brig. Gen. Henry Baxter's Second Brigade had been hotly engaged for three hours until it ran out of ammunition. Baxter lost almost half of his brigade and all of his personal staff in the action. Robinson's Division as a whole had sustained a loss of 1,667 of 2,500 soldiers during that time.[43]

---

[40] Charles Johnson, Union Army Medical Service, "The Regimental Hospital," accessed November 2014, http://civilwarhome.com/regimentalhospital.html, 1.
[41] Ibid., 3.
[42] Benedict Maryniak, "Union Military Chaplains," in *Faith in the Fight*, 24.
[43] War Department, *Official Records*, part 1: 289–91.

As the retreat of the First US Corps commenced about 4:30 P.M., there was neither the time nor the inclination to move the seriously wounded from either the Lutheran seminary or from Christ Lutheran Church. Some commanders ordered their surgeons to leave, but some clergy stayed behind with the wounded, as did Chaplain Howell, who seemed to pay little, if any attention, to the ebb and flow of battle.

Chaplain Horatio Howell was no stranger to combat. He had served with the 90th Pennsylvania Infantry since March 1862—through the battles of Second Manassas, Antietam, and Chancellorsville. At age 42, Howell had other credentials as well, including degrees from Lafayette College in Easton, Pennsylvania, and from Union Theological Seminary in New York City. He had served as the pastor of two Presbyterian churches and as a teacher in a boys' school as well.

Before the war, Rev. Howell had developed into a devout Unionist and a staunch abolitionist. He experienced what he called the "wickedness" of slavery firsthand while stationed in Elkton, Maryland, convincing him that the institution "would reduce to the condition of brutes those whom God had created in His own image and for whom Christ had died."[44] Upon the counsel of his fellow clergy, Howell volunteered to serve as the regimental chaplain of the 90th Pennsylvania Infantry on March 13, 1862, in Philadelphia.

Sixteen months and four campaigns later, Howell arrived at the College Lutheran Church at #44 Chambersburg Street with some of his fellow chaplains to help treat and minister to the wounded. A Gettysburg civilian recalled that 140 men were laid in the sanctuary around midday, beds being boards on top of pews. Limbs were being amputated and thrown out of the church windows, piling up on the ground below.[45]

Late in the afternoon, the Confederates began to push the Union troops back through town. Shortly after 4 o'clock, the overwhelmed First Corps soldiers fell back through the streets of Gettysburg to the heights on Cemetery Hill south of town. A chaotic scene ensued as jubilant Confederates followed closely on their heels. As the Union retreat swept toward the College Lutheran Church, Chaplain Howell was assisting members of the medical staff inside the building. After hearing shots outside, Howell turned

---

[44] "Horatio Stockton Howell," https://en.wikipedia.org/wiki/Horatio_ Stockton_Howell, 1.
[45] Ibid.

to a nearby surgeon and said, "I will step outside for a moment and see what the trouble is."[46]

Sergeant Archibald B. Snow of the 97th New York Volunteers, Second Brigade, who had just had a wound dressed at the quickly established field hospital, followed Howell out of the church. Later, Snow wrote the most detailed account of what happened:

> I had just had my wound dressed and was leaving through the front door just behind Chaplain Howell, at the same time when the advance skirmishers of the Confederates were coming up the street on a run. Howell, in addition to his shoulder straps & uniform, wore the straight dress sword prescribed in Army Regulations for chaplains.... The first skirmisher arrived at the foot of the church steps just as the chaplain and I came out. Placing one foot on the first step the soldier called on the chaplain to surrender; but Howell, instead of throwing up his hands promptly and uttering the usual "I surrender," attempted some dignified explanation to the effect that he was a noncombatant and as such was exempt from capture, when a shot from the skirmisher's rifle ended the controversy.... The man who fired the shot stood on the exact spot where the memorial tablet has since been erected, and Chaplain Howell fell upon the landing at the top of the steps.[47]

The courageous chaplain was dead at the church door. In response to charges from nearby Union soldiers that Howell was not a legitimate target, a Confederate lieutenant pointed to Chaplain Howell's maroon officer's sash and the sword belted around his body. Because there was no way to determine from his uniform that Howell was a chaplain, it was clear that the soldier, in the midst of a pursuit of the enemy through the streets, did not believe his explanation.[48]

A monument at the foot of the church steps was dedicated in 1889 to perpetuate the memory of the chaplain slain in battle. It was the first such battlefield monument ever dedicated to a chaplain killed in action.

---

[46] Ibid.

[47] Ibid., 2.

[48] Ibid., 2. By 1863, *US Army Regulations*, paragraph 1548, page 469, and paragraph 229, page 39, all line officers in uniform were directed to wear their swords unless they were under arrest. Chaplains were not directed to wear swords by paragraph 130, page 534, of the same regulations, although they were not prohibited from doing so. Prior to the twentieth century Geneva Conventions, many chaplains did wear uniforms and bear arms even though they had no authorization or encouragement in army regulations to carry weapons.

Eventide Reinforcements

In his official report of the first day's fighting, Lt. Gen. A. P. Hill characterized the battle in the west as a rout of the US First Corps:

> About half past two o'clock the right wing of Ewell's corps made its appearance on my left, and thus formed a right angle with my line. Pender's Division was then ordered forward—Thomas' brigade being retained in reserve—and the rout of the enemy was complete, Perrin's brigade taking position after position of the enemy, driving him through the town of Gettysburg. Under the impression that the enemy were entirely routed—my own two divisions exhausted by some six hours' hard fighting—prudence led me to be content with what had been gained, and not push forward troops exhausted and necessarily disordered, probably to encounter fresh troops of the enemy.[49]

From the Confederate point of view, General Hill's decision to rest was probably a mistake, as Thomas's unbloodied reserve brigade at 5 P.M. might have made a difference in the contest developing in the Cemetery Hill-Culp's Hill area. But General Hill's instinct with regard to fresh enemy troops was correct. Union Maj. Gen. Winfield Scott Hancock, commanding the US Second Corps, arrived by 5 P.M. with orders from General Meade to take command in the field. General Hancock and General Howard began to set up a determined defense of Cemetery Hill with Brigadier General Steinwehr's reserves and with the survivors of the six divisions of the First and Eleventh Corps. Before dark, Maj. Gen. Henry Slocum's US Twelfth Corps, with almost 10,000 fresh troops, began arriving.[50] Behind the Twelfth Corps were four more Union corps with 60,000 soldiers on the road to Gettysburg.[51]

If Hill's decision to rest his corps may have been a mistake, Lt. Gen. Ewell's decision on the evening of July 1 not to attack and occupy Culp's Hill, which overlooked Cemetery Hill, may have been a greater one. Certainly Ewell felt constrained to explain his pause in the waning hours of the day:

---

[49] Jones, "General A. P. Hill's Report," *Southern Historical Society Papers*, 223.

[50] Major General Hancock relinquished field command to Major General Slocum when he arrived. Major General Meade did not arrive from Taneytown until midnight. In one day the Union forces had seven overall field commanders: Brigadier General Buford and major generals Reynolds, Doubleday, Howard, Hancock, Slocum, and Meade.

[51] The Second, Third, Fifth, and Sixth Corps, not including Pleasonton's Cavalry Corps, some of whom were already there.

The enemy had fallen back to a commanding position known as Cemetery Hill, south of Gettysburg, and quickly showed a formidable front there. On entering the town, I received a message from the commanding general [Lee] to attack this hill, if I could do so to advantage. I could not bring artillery to bear on it, and all the troops with me were jaded by twelve hours' marching and fighting, and I was notified that General [Edward] Johnson's division (the only one of my corps that had not been engaged) was close to the town.

Cemetery Hill was not assailable from the town, and I determined, with Johnson's division, to take possession of a wooded hill to my left [Culp's], on a line with and commanding Cemetery Hill. Before Johnson got up, the enemy was reported moving to outflank our extreme left, and I could see what seemed to be his skirmishers in that direction. Before this report could be investigated...and Johnson placed in position, the night was far advanced.[52]

In General Ewell's defense, two of the divisions in his corps, Early's and Rodes's, had been marching and fighting all day and had prisoners to guard. Johnson's Division was still marching toward Gettysburg. Moreover, Ewell received a dispatch about midnight, intercepted from a Federal courier, that indicated the US Twelfth Corps under Major General Slocum was already present and that the US Fifth Corps, commanded by Maj. Gen. George Sykes, would arrive in not less than four hours. At daybreak Ewell received orders from General Lee to delay his attack until he heard Lieutenant General Longstreet's guns open on the right of the Confederate extended line.[53] Neither General Ewell nor General Lee could have realized that Longstreet would take almost all of the following day to get his two divisions ready to attack.

The first day at Gettysburg—more significant than simply a prelude to the bloody second and third days—ranks on its own as the twelfth most costly battle of the Civil War. About one-quarter of Meade's army (22,000 men) and one-third of Lee's army (27,000) were engaged. Total Union casualties were almost 9,000, Confederate casualties more than 6,000.[54] Perhaps more importantly were the psychological effects on Lee's troops. They had

---

[52] Report of Lieutenant General Richard Ewell, "The Gettysburg Campaign," War Department, *Official Records*, part 2: ch. 39, 445.

[53] Ibid., 446.

[54] Noah Trudeau, *Gettysburg: A Testing of Courage* (New York: HarperCollins, 2002) 272.

seen two Union corps withdraw in haste from Gettysburg just as they had seen Hooker's army break at Chancellorsville two months before. This impression produced among many, including some senior Confederate officers, the conviction that the Army of the Potomac could be beaten again if the troops just had sufficient courage and spirit. This was a mistaken belief, for as the next two days demonstrated, courage and spirit were present on both sides in at least equal measure.

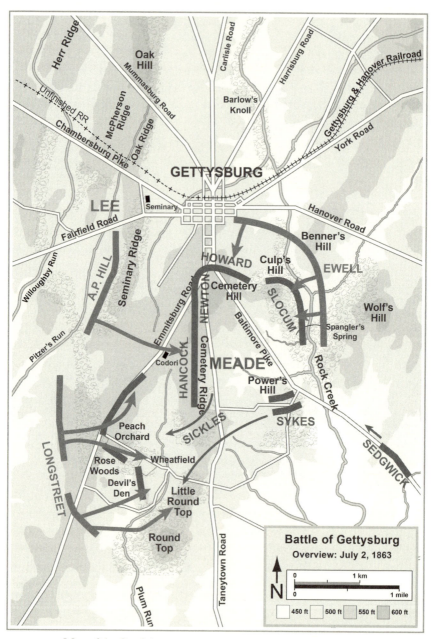

Map of the Confederate attacks on July 2, 1863. Map by Hal Jespersen.

Paul Henry Wood's *Absolution under Fire* depicting Chaplain William Corby pronouncing general absolution for the Irish Brigade at Gettysburg on July 2, 1863. Corby was later a two-term President of Notre Dame which adopted "The Fighting Irish" nickname for its athletic teams. Credit: University of Notre Dame Library.

Chaplain Francis Milton Kennedy (left), 28th North Carolina Infantry, CSA. Credit: Francis Milton Kennedy Diary, Georgia Department of Archives and History. Chaplain James B. Sheeran (right), 14th Louisiana Infantry, CSA. Credit: Patheos.com/Father James Sheeran.

Chaplain Alexander D. Betts (left), 30th North Carolina Infantry, CSA. Credit: William A. Betts, *Experience of a Confederate Chaplain*, 1904. Chaplain Thomas D. Witherspoon (right), 42nd Mississippi Infantry, CSA. Chaplain Witherspoon was a direct descendant of the Rev. John Witherspoon who signed the Declaration of Independence. Courtesy of Mr. Wayne Sparkman, Director, PCA Historical Center, St. Louis, MO.

Chaplain Charles James Oliver, Troup Artillery, Longstreet's Corps, CSA served at Gettysburg as an artilleryman—loading cannon, caring for the wounded and leading prayers. Although recognized as the informal chaplain of his artillery battalion, Oliver did not receive his commission until September 16, 1864. Credit: *Oliver Journal*, Special Collections, Woodruff Library, Emory University.

Chaplain Peter Tinsley (left), 28th Virginia Infantry, Pickett's Division. Courtesy of the Rev. Canon Carol C. Flanagan, St. John's Episcopal Church, Olney, Maryland. Chaplain John J. Renfroe (right), 10th Alabama Infantry, Wilcox's Brigade, Third Corps, Army of Northern Virginia. Chaplain Renfroe was the editor of *The Alabama Baptist* newspaper in 1875. Credit: *The Alabama Baptist*, Marion, AL, February 1875.

Chaplain William Corby (left), 88th New York Infantry, Irish Brigade. Credit: University of Notre Dame Archives. Chaplain John H. W. Stuckenberg (right), 145th Pennsylvania Infantry. Courtesy of Luther Memorial Church, Erie, Pa.

Chaplain Joseph H. Twichell (left), 71st New York Infantry. Credit: Asylum Hill Congregational Church, Hartford, Connecticut. Chaplain Ferdinand L. Sarner (right), 54th New York Infantry, Army of the Potomac. Rabbi Sarner was the first Jewish regimental chaplain to serve in the U.S. Army. He was wounded on July 1, 1863. Credit: Jewish Museum of Maryland.

Chaplain Louis Boudrye, 5th New York Cavalry Regiment, captured on July 5 and imprisoned for three months in Richmond. Credit: Chaplain Louis N. Boudrye Papers, Wheaton College [Illinois] Archives.

Chaplain Lorenzo Barber, 2nd U.S. Sharpshooters. Methodist Chaplain Lorenzo Barber was one of the best shots in his regiment. Using his own rifle and scope, he once hit a sheep grazing 400 yards away. On July 2, Barber and his men fought at the Bushman Farm, defending the high ground in front of Big Round Top. That night Barber attended the wounded at field hospitals along the Taneytown Road. Wounded while fighting at Mine Run, Virginia, later in the war, Barber was honorably discharged near Petersburg in February of 1865. He died in Troy, New York, in 1882 of a firearms accident while hunting. Credit: *History of Berdan's US Sharpshooters in the Army of the Potomac*, 1892.

Chaplain Joseph O'Hagan (left), S. J. 73rd New York Infantry. Credit: College of the Holy Cross Archives. Chaplain Samuel Eaton (right), 7th Wisconsin Infantry, Iron Brigade. Credit: Wisconsin Historical Society.

Chaplain Ezra Simons (left), 125th New York Infantry. Credit: *A Regimental History*, 1888. Chaplain John Van Ingen (right), 8th New York Cavalry, thought to be the first chaplain to arrive on the Gettysburg Battlefield, July 1, 1863. Credit: St. Paul's Episcopal Church/Central Library of Rochester, NY.

The Trostle Barn near the Peach Orchard on the Gettysburg Battlefield. Major General Sickles was wounded here on July 2, 1863. Chaplains Twichell and O'Hagan rode in the ambulance with him to the Sheaffer Farmhouse which had been converted into a hospital. Chaplain Twichell helped administer chloroform while Sickles' leg was amputated. Photo by the author.

Chapter 4

July 2, 1863: The Bloodiest Day

"The enemy was massed in my front, and extended to my right and left as far as I could see."[1]

—Maj. Gen. Lafayette McLaws, CSA

Maj. Gen. George Meade had not slept all night. He had arrived from Taneytown after 12 A.M. to receive reports from his ranking commanders at the cemetery gatekeeper's house on Cemetery Hill. Meade asked General Howard if the Union position was defensible. Howard replied in the affirmative. General Meade replied, "I am glad to hear you say so, I have already ordered the other corps to concentrate here—and it is too late to change."[2]

Major General Hancock, under orders from General Meade and in concert with Major Generals Slocum, Howard, and Doubleday, had essentially "circled the wagons," or more accurately, aligned the combined infantry and artillery units in their commands to hold the high ground on Cemetery Ridge and Culp's Hill and protect the Baltimore Pike supply route south. Slocum's Twelfth Corps commanded Culp's Hill, Howard's Eleventh Corps the northern slopes, and Doubleday's First Corps the western slopes of Cemetery Hill. As Hancock's own Second Corps, Major General Sickles's Third Corps, and Major General Sykes's Fifth Corps arrived during the night, after a 13-mile march from Taneytown, Hancock placed them along the ridge with the Second Corps in the center of the extended Union line, the Third Corps on the left flank, and the Fifth Corps in reserve on the Baltimore Pike behind Little Round Top. By the morning of July 2, 1863, six of the seven infantry corps of the Army of the Potomac had arrived on the battlefield. Maj. Gen. John Sedgwick's Sixth Corps, the largest in the army, was still 30 miles away, but it was moving north as fast as possible.[3]

General Meade inspected the positions on Cemetery Ridge, making just one personnel change: Maj. Gen. John Newton replaced General Dou-

---

[1] Maj. Gen. Lafayette McLaws, "Gettysburg," *Southern Historical Society Papers*, vol. VII (1879) 69–70.

[2] Kelly Knauer, ed., *Gettysburg: A Day-by-Day Account of the Greatest Battle of the Civil War* (New York: Time Books, 2013) 49.

[3] Harry W. Pfanz, *Gettysburg—The Second Day*. (Chapel Hill: University of North Carolina Press, 1987) 21.

bleday as the First Corps commander.[4] Doubleday then reverted to command his Third Division in the same corps.

By the end of July 2, this "fishhook" line of Union infantry and artillery units extended to Big Round Top, completing Meade's deployment of troops available that day.[5] General Sedgwick's Sixth Corps, numbering 17,625, was never totally engaged, suffering just 344 casualties in three days.[6]

Gen. Robert E. Lee did not get much sleep on the night of July 1 either.[7] Although General Ewell did not say so directly, his report implied that General Lee personally inspected the ground in front of the Second Corps position:

> I received orders after dark to draw my corps to the right, in case it could not be used to advantage where it was; that the commanding general thought from the nature of the ground that the position for attack was a good one on that side. I represented to the commanding general that the hill above [Culp's Hill] was unoccupied by the enemy...and that it commanded their position and made it untenable, so far as I could judge. He decided to let me remain, and on my return to my headquarters after twelve o'clock at night, I sent orders to [Major General] Edward Johnson by Lt. T. T. Turner, aide-de-camp, to take possession of this hill if he had not already done so.[8]

---

[4] Maj. Gen. John Newton, an army engineer, graduated second in the West Point Class of 1842. His classmates included James Longstreet and Abner Doubleday. Major General Doubleday returned to his previous division command, replacing Brig. Gen. Thomas Rowley, who was injured by falling off his horse during the fighting on July 1.

[5] Source of the Battle of Gettysburg Overview 2, accessed November 2004, https://en.wikipedia.org/wiki/Battle_of_Gettysburg.

[6] War Department, *Official Records*, part 1: 151.

[7] Local tradition in Gettysburg held that General Lee, after conferring with Lieutenant General Ewell on the night of July 1, spent the night at the Daniel Lady farm on the north side of Hanover Road in Gettysburg. The stone farmhouse was used as a hospital for Ewell's Second Corps artillerymen. See Historic Gettysburg—Adams County, *Gettysburg Civil War Field Hospital Tour* (Harrisburg, PA: The Hospital and Healthsystem Association of Pennsylvania, 2001) 31.

[8] Lt. Gen. Richard S. Ewell, "The Gettysburg Campaign," War Department, *Official Records*, part 2: ch. 39, 446. Maj. Gen. Edward Johnson was a West Point graduate (1838) and a hero of the Mexican War. His division included the famous "Stonewall Brigade." Once wounded and later captured, Johnson became a farmer after the war.

Unfortunately for General Ewell, Union soldiers from the US Twelfth Corps, some from Brig. Gen. George S. Greene's New York Brigade of five regiments, were already on Culp's Hill. They promptly captured some of the Confederate reconnoitering party from General Johnson's Division, which caused Johnson to delay his attack until he conferred with Ewell. By then it was dawn and the opportunity for Ewell and Johnson had passed. In accord with his new orders from General Lee, Ewell prepared for yet another attack as soon as Lieutenant General Longstreet could arrive and get into his attack position on the Union left flank.

At dawn on July 2, General Lee still had not heard from Major General Stuart. Two divisions of Longstreet's Corps were 5 miles west of Gettysburg, and the remaining one, Pickett's, 26 miles away at Chambersburg. While visiting Ewell's front lines, Lee had made an observation that revealed his unease. "The enemy have the advantage of us in a shorter and inside line," he said, "and we are too extended."[9] Nevertheless, Lee drew up an extensive battle plan designed to roll up the Union left from Little Round Top, which he thought rightly to be unoccupied early that morning. He needed at least two divisions of Longstreet's Corps and one from Hill's Corps to make this attack, while Ewell demonstrated on the Union right at Culp's Hill. Of course, without intelligence as to the strength or disposition of the Union forces, Lee did not know that Sickles's US Third Corps was moving to the Emmitsburg road in front of Little Round Top, or that Sykes's US Fifth Corps was in reserve behind both mountains. He also could not have known that Longstreet, instead of attacking at noon, would not be ready until almost four o'clock. By then, the Confederate attack by three divisions would encounter most of two Union corps numbering 29,000 men, supported by artillery, and occupying the high ground.

Lieutenant General Longstreet, a West Point graduate in the Class of 1842, was a Mexican War hero who had received two battlefield promotions and been wounded in the course of that conflict. During the war he had served with Lt. George Pickett in the 8th US Infantry Regiment, and afterward attended the wedding of his cousin, Julia Dent, to Ulysses S. Grant in St. Louis in 1848. Longstreet resigned from the US Army in June 1861 and reported to Richmond, where President Jefferson Davis immediately commissioned him a brigadier general.

In command of a brigade at the Battle of First Manassas and a division three months later, Longstreet soon gained the confidence of Gen. Robert

---

[9] Knauer, *Gettysburg: A Day-by-Day Account*, 68.

E. Lee, who placed him in operational command of almost half of the army during the Peninsula Campaign of 1862. Lee said of Longstreet at the time, "He was the staff in my right hand."[10]

Longstreet, however, was not immune from tragedy. In 1862 a scarlet-fever epidemic in Richmond claimed the lives of three of his children. Although his headquarters before this sad event had been noted for parties, drinking, and poker games, afterward the headquarters social life became more somber. Longstreet rarely drank any alcohol and became a devout Episcopalian.[11]

On the principal battlefields of 1862, including Second Manassas, Antietam, and Fredericksburg, Longstreet's First Corps performed well—at times brilliantly. Lee was able to coordinate both offensive and defensive operations with his three stellar commanders, Longstreet, Jackson, and Stuart. Yet by the second day at Gettysburg coordination of attacks broke down. Lee did not have an accurate picture of the battlefield and some of his subsequent orders, seemingly followed to the letter by his corps commanders, proved impossible to execute successfully.

Marching and Counter-Marching

When General Longstreet's First Corps reached Chambersburg on June 27, he gave the soldiers two days to rest. On June 29, he received orders to move two divisions and his reserve artillery to Greenwood, 7 miles east but still 20 miles from Gettysburg. On July 1, Longstreet moved again from Greenwood toward Gettysburg on the Chambersburg Pike but was delayed behind Maj. Gen. Edward Johnson's Division from Ewell's Second Corps marching south from Shippensburg. Johnson had four brigades, four batteries of artillery, and a wagon train 14 miles long. According to Major General McLaws, Longstreet's lead division commander, his troops stood by the side of the road from 8 o'clock in the morning until 4 o'clock in the afternoon—eight hours—waiting for Johnson's Division to pass.[12] In spite of the delay, Longstreet's two divisions, McLaws's, and Hood's managed to make it to the vicinity of Marsh Creek by midnight on July 1.[13]

---

[10] "James Longstreet," accessed November 2004, http:en.wikipedia.org/wiki/James_Longstreet, 4.

[11] Ibid.

[12] Maj. Gen. Lafayette McLaws, "Gettysburg," *Southern Historical Society Papers* 7/2 (1879) 67–69.

[13] War Department, *Official Records*, part 2: 358.

Pickett's Division, the last of the three divisions in Longstreet's First Corps, was still at Chambersburg on the morning of July 1. Episcopal Chaplain Peter Tinsley of the 28th Virginia Infantry in Garnett's Brigade recorded his feelings of dread in his diary on the march to Gettysburg:

July 1. Wed.
Weather cloudy & very sultry. Hold service at night. We get orders to leave at 5 A.M. & afterwards at 2 A.M.

July 2 Th[ursday].
We leave early and pass through Chambersburg & turn right at the square & go on the Baltimore Pike (macadamized)—pass through the villages of Fayetteville & c.[14] crossing the mountain at South Pass—Here in the ruins of Hon. Thad Stepens iron works, recently burned by our troops. At the door of a cottage in this pass stands a little boy with a se-cesh [secession] flag. On the way we hear various conflicting rumors of the battle of yesterday at Gettysburg. We bivouac about 5 miles from G. I hold prayers in the Regt. in anticipation of a great battle next day. Officers and men generally express great confidence of victory tomorrow. The spirit of their remarks is too boastful & seems not to recognize the hand of God in the matter. I recollect Maj. Wilson[15] made some remark of this sort: "I am a certain of the result as I am that now I live, though many of us may not live to see it." And Henry Allen[16] looking toward the setting sun said to me: "That is the last sunset that many of us poor fellows will see." I must confess that I have serious apprehensions of disaster or defeat & so much so that I took my commission from my trunk & placed it in my pocket in case I should be obliged to remain behind. Note: A day's march about 26 miles.[17]

While Pickett's Division was marching toward Gettysburg, McLaws's and Hood's divisions were trying to find their way to their attack positions in accord with General Lee's orders. Lee wanted Longstreet to attack the Union left flank across the Emmitsburg road with two divisions from the south while Hill attacked Cemetery Ridge with Anderson's Division from the west. Ewell would threaten Cemetery and Culp's hills to pin down defenders

---

[14] Caledonia, the name associated with Thaddeus Stevens's ironworks.
[15] Maj. Nathaniel Wilson, 28th Virginia Infantry.
[16] Pvt. Henry L. Allen, Company D, 28th Virginia Infantry.
[17] Peter Archer Tinsley (1833–1908), "Private Diary," in John and Joyce Schmale Civil War collection, Wheaton (IL) College Archives, box 1, folder 51:13.

there. These attacks would proceed from south to north in a series of sequential advances.[18] To accomplish this operation, which required flawless coordination, Hood and McLaws would have to march to their attack positions undetected by the Union signal station on Little Round Top.

General Lee, acting as his own chief of staff, issued his battle orders in person to General Longstreet at 10 A.M. and then rode 5 miles to confer with General Ewell. Lee intended to hear Longstreet's guns, signaling his advance, at noon. Longstreet, however, was waiting on Law's Brigade of Hood's Division to reach the field, which did not happen until noon. At that point, General McLaws, leading his division toward their assembly area, discovered that their route would take them in sight of the Union signal station on Little Round Top. When he pointed this out, General Longstreet ordered a counter-march to find a more concealed road, which took another three hours to move two divisions north and west and then south. At 4 P.M. General Longstreet was ready to attack. The Army of Northern Virginia had spent eight hours marching to get into position for what had been intended to be a surprise assault.[19]

Daniel Edgar Sickles was surely one of the most controversial of the Civil War generals. He had no military experience before the Civil War and was the only corps commander at Gettysburg without a West Point education. Sickles was a political general and a US congressman from New York whose private life had caused him to be charged with the murder of his wife's lover and escorting a known prostitute into the New York State Assembly. However, Sickles was a master at securing political support, including that of Presidents James Buchanan and Abraham Lincoln.[20]

Sickles began his military career, short though it was, by recruiting a brigade of soldiers in New York City. His brigade was named "The Excelsior Brigade" from the New York State motto "ever upward." By September 1861 he was a brigadier general of volunteers.

Sickles performed competently as a brigade commander during the Peninsula Campaign of 1862. President Lincoln nominated Sickles for the rank of major general in November 1862, although the Senate did not confirm his promotion until March 1863. Sickles was the Third Corps commander in the Battle of Chancellorsville in May 1863.

When Major General Sickles led his Third Corps on the field at Gettysburg at 3 P.M. on July 2, he had been ordered to place his troops on Cem-

---

[18] Knauer, *Gettysburg: A Day-by-Day Account*, 60–61.

[19] McLaws, "Gettysburg," *Southern Historical Society Papers* 7/2: 69.

[20] "Daniel Sickles," http://en.wikipedia.org/wiki/Daniel_Sickles, 1–2.

etery Ridge. He was to be the link between Hancock's Second Corps on his right and Little Round Top on his left. Sickles, however, moved his men almost a mile in front of Cemetery Ridge to deny the Confederates the high ground at the Peach Orchard in his front that might be used as an artillery platform.

About this time General Meade called a meeting of his corps commanders. Sickles did not appear. An aide to Brig. Gen. Gouverneur Warren, who had noticed Longstreet's troops moving to his left from the signal station on Little Round Top, soon reported the situation. Generals Meade and Warren rode to Sickles's headquarters and demanded an explanation. Though agitated, General Meade refused Sickles's offer to withdraw because he realized it was too late.[21] The Confederates would soon advance, putting a retreating force in even greater peril.

Unpleasant Surprises

Evidently even the presence of Union troops along the Emmitsburg road did not change Longstreet's determination to follow Lee's order to the letter. Longstreet told McLaws, "There is nothing in your front, you will be entirely on the flank of the enemy."[22] McLaws told Longstreet he would continue preparations for the attack.

When Major General McLaws finally arrived at his attack position, he did a quick survey of the ground to his front:

> My head of column soon reached the edge of the woods, and the enemy [in the Peach Orchard] at once opened on it with numerous artillery.... While this was going on I rode forward, and getting off my horse, went to some trees in advance and took a good look at the situation. The view presented astonished me, as the enemy was massed in my front, and extended to my right and left as far as I could see.... Thus was presented a state of affairs which was certainly not contemplated when the original plan or order of battle was given, and certainly was not known to General Longstreet a half hour previous.[23]

McLaws's Division, with Hood's Division following, found themselves under fire from Sickles's US Third Corps even as they were trying to deploy against what they had assumed was an unprotected Union left flank. Both McLaws and Hood protested to General Longstreet. They wanted to march

---

[21] Ibid., 2.

[22] McLaws, "Gettysburg," *Southern Historical Society Papers* 7/2: 69–70.

[23] Ibid.

farther south and assault the Union flank where it really existed. Three times General Longstreet denied Hood's requests and ordered his two division commanders to follow Lee's original plan—which now meant confronting the Union troops of Birney's and Humphrey's divisions head-on across the Emmitsburg road.[24] Hood was to attack first, then on order, McLaws would attack next, followed by Anderson's Division of Hill's Corps.[25]

In the end, Major General Hood faced his division eastward and launched an attack on the Devil's Den at the foot of Little Round Top, where he assumed the Union line ended. On the right was Gen. Evander Law's Alabama Brigade supported by a Georgia brigade commanded by Brig. Gen. Henry Benning. To the left was Hood's old Texas brigade, now commanded by Brig. Gen. J. B. Robertson, backed up by another Georgia brigade under Brig. Gen. George T. Anderson.[26]

On Hood's left flank was McLaws's Division of four more brigades from South Carolina, Mississippi, and Georgia, whose mission was to cross the Emmitsburg road and attack east toward Cemetery Ridge. McLaws, however, would not advance with Hood, but would wait for orders to move forward. Hood's Division of 5,500 men, supported by four batteries of artillery, was expected to take their objective first and then support McLaws's advance through the Peach Orchard and the Wheatfield toward Cemetery Ridge.

Reinforcements: A Matter of Minutes

After reviewing Sickles's extended line with General Meade about 3 o'clock P.M., Brig. Gen. Gouverneur K. Warren, Meade's chief of engineers, rode to the crest of Little Round Top. He realized that the hill was "the key to the Union position," unoccupied except by a signal station.[27] Warren was told by the signalmen that they believed there were Confederate troops in the woods a mile to their front. Warren ordered Smith's New York battery

---

[24] Knauer, *Gettysburg: A Day-by-Day Account*, 65.

[25] Brig. Gen. E. M. Law, who commanded a brigade in Hood's division, concluded twenty years after the war that the Battle of Gettysburg was lost when General Hood's requests to maneuver were repeatedly denied. See Jay Luvass and Harold W. Nelson, *Guide to the Battle of Gettysburg* (Lawrence: University of Kansas Press, 1994) 68.

[26] Knauer, *Gettysburg: A Day-by-Day Account*, 65.

[27] http://en.wikipedia.org/wiki/Gouverneur_K._Warren, 2. General Warren was an 1850 graduate of West Point. He entered the academy at age 16 and graduated second in his class. He served the army as both an engineer and as an infantry brigade commander at Second Manassas and at Fredericksburg.

at the Devil's Den to fire a shot into the woods. The missile caused a stir of Confederates, "which by the gleam of the sunlight on their bayonets, revealed their long lines outflanking the position."[28]

Warren rode back to Cemetery Ridge where he intercepted two brigades of General Sykes's Fifth Corps and urged the commanders to deploy their troops on the crest of Little Round Top. Col. Strong Vincent, a 26-year-old Harvard graduate and lawyer, sent his four infantry regiments, the 16th Michigan, the 44th New York, the 83rd Pennsylvania, and the 20th Maine, racing to the top. Brig. Gen. Stephen H. Weed followed with four more New York and Pennsylvania regiments that immediately encountered the attacking Confederate infantry from Robertson's Texas Brigade climbing the western slope. Weed's Brigade had beaten the Texans to the top by a matter of minutes.

First Lieutenant Charles E. Hazlett, commanding a battery from the Third Division, Fifth Corps Artillery, managed to have his crew manhandle six three-inch Parrot rifled guns to the top of the hill. Confederate sharpshooters at the Devil's Den immediately targeted the gunners and the officers. General Weed, Lieutenant Hazlett, and Col. Patrick O'Rorke, commander of the 140th New York Infantry, were killed and General Warren wounded in the neck.[29]

The Confederate attack, however, was slowly coming apart. Shortly after he rose in his stirrups to order his men forward, General Hood was hit by shrapnel from an artillery shell. His left arm was permanently disabled, and command of the division passed to Brig. Gen. Evander Law, a former professor of history from South Carolina and a veteran of the Second Manassas and Antietam campaigns.

General Law did not issue any new orders to his brigade commanders, so each of the four brigades simply moved forward in what they believed to be their proper avenue of approach. Brigadier General Benning's Brigade, which was supposed to support Law's own Alabama Brigade in assaulting the extreme left of the Union line where the 20th Maine was strung thin, became engaged in the Devil's Den and never made it to their attack point. Law's Alabama Brigade fought their way up Big Round Top and then back

---

[28] Henry Hird III, ed., *Gettysburg National Military Park Handbook* (St. Augustine, FL: Historic Print and Map Co., 2011) 34.

[29] Colonel Patrick O'Rorke was a native of Ireland who graduated number one in the West Point Class of 1861, whose members included Charles E. Hazlett and George Armstrong Custer. O'Rorke was a veteran of both the Battle of Fredericksburg and the Battle of Chancellorsville.

down again. After four unsuccessful charges by the 15th Alabama, the 386 men of the 20th Maine, commanded by Col. Joshua Lawrence Chamberlain, ran out of ammunition. In spite of this crippling shortage, Chamberlain ordered a bayonet charge which routed the surviving Alabama troops. Col. William C. Oates, commander of the 15th Alabama Infantry and later governor of Alabama, wrote after the war that his men "ran like a herd of wild cattle."[30] Colonel Chamberlain lost 130 of his men, one in three, but he held his position and secured the flank that Hood and Longstreet had so desperately sought.

After an hour and a half of fruitless assaults against Little Round Top, General Longstreet ordered General McLaws to move forward with his division across the Emmitsburg road. It was about 5:30 P.M.[31] However, before McLaws's attack began, General Meade, anticipating such a maneuver, ordered General Hancock to send Brig. Gen. John Caldwell's Division forward from the Second US Corps to support Major General Sickles's exposed Third Corps units.[32] Sickles had two divisions deployed already—Birney's and Humphreys's—and support from three brigades of Brig. Gen. James Barnes's Division of the Fifth Corps, but the right flank of the Union line at the Wheatfield was being pushed back.

Caldwell's Division was comprised of four brigades commanded by Col. Edward E. Cross, Col. Patrick Kelly, Col. John Brooke, and Brig. Gen. Samuel Zook and supported by three brigades from the Fifth Corps. Kelly's Irish Brigade, which numbered just 532 men, formed the center of the attacking Union reinforcements. It was the largest combined Union assault of the three-day battle.[33]

Challenges for Chaplains

At about four o'clock in the afternoon of July 2, 1863, Father William Corby, Roman Catholic chaplain of the Irish Brigade, heard what he esti-

---

[30] Knauer, *Gettysburg: A Day-by-Day Account*, 66.

[31] Ibid., 69.

[32] Ibid.

[33] Brig. Gen. John Caldwell had been a schoolteacher and headmaster in Maine before he joined the army. Col. Edward Cross was a newspaperman in New Hampshire and an army scout in Arizona in his early years. Col. Patrick Kelly, from County Galway in Ireland, commanded the 88th New York Infantry Regiment before he became a brigade commander. Col. John Brooke from Pottstown, Pennsylvania, was just 24 years of age in 1863, and Brig. Gen. Samuel Zook, from a Pennsylvania Mennonite family, was a telegraph operator. All were veterans of the battles of Fredericksburg and Chancellorsville.

mated to be a hundred-and-twenty cannon open with shot and shell directed toward the Union lines in the Peach Orchard and in front of Little Round Top.[34] Corby recalled that Union Maj. Gen. Daniel Sickles's Third Corps, composed of two divisions, occupied a slight ridge along the Emmitsburg road, which included the areas under attack from two divisions of Longstreet's Corps, Army of Northern Virginia. Sickles's 14,000 veterans fought hard, but they were attacked from the front and on both flanks and soon began to give way.

Father Corby wrote later that during that critical hour, Major General Hancock, in support of Sickles's retreating units, ordered Brigadier John Caldwell's Division from the Second Corps to attack the charging Confederates. Colonel St. Clair Mulholland, commanding the 116th Pennsylvania Infantry Regiment of the Irish Brigade, described the preparation for the advance:

> Now (as the Third Corps is being pressed back), help is called for, and Hancock tells Caldwell to have his men ready. "Fall in!" and the men run to their places. "Take arms!" and the four brigades of Zook, Cross, Brooke, and Kelly are ready for the fray. There are yet a few minutes to spare before starting, and the time is occupied by one of the most impressive religious ceremonies I have ever witnessed. The [Irish] brigade stood in column of regiments, closed in mass. As a large majority of its members were Catholics, the Chaplain of the brigade, Rev. William Corby, proposed to give a general absolution to all the men before going into the fight. Father Corby stood on a large rock in front of the brigade. Addressing the men, he explained what he was about to do, saying that each one could receive the benefit of the absolution by making a sincere Act of Contrition and firmly resolving to embrace the first opportunity of confessing his sins, urging them to do their duty, and reminding them of the high and sacred nature of their trust as soldiers and the noble object for which they fought.[35]

---

[34] William Corby, CSC, *Memoirs of Chaplain Life: Three Years with the Irish Brigade in the Army of the Potomac*, ed. Lawrence F. Kohl (New York: Fordham University Press, 1992) 181–84. The Irish Brigade was technically the Second Brigade in Brig. Gen. John C. Caldwell's division of Hancock's Corps. Also, though perhaps a minor point, Corby was not an Irishman; he had been born in Detroit, Michigan, on October 2, 1833, to an Irish-born father and a Canadian mother. Corby, *Memoirs of Chaplain Life*, xi.

[35] Ibid.

As Father Corby raised his right hand toward the brigade, the soldiers knelt on the ground to receive absolution. Corby spoke the Latin words, "Dominus noster Jesus Christus vos absolvat, et ego, auctoritate ipsius, vos absolvo ab omni vinculo."[36] Mulholland continued, "The scene was more than impressive; it was awe-inspiring. Near by stood a brilliant throng of officers who had gathered to witness this very unusual occurrence, and while there was profound silence in the ranks of the Second Corps, yet over to the left, out by the peach orchard and Little Round Top...the roar of the battle rose and swelled and re-echoed through the woods...."[37]

As Corby himself described the scene in his 1893 memoirs, he intended the absolution to be for all the soldiers on the battlefield, friend and foe alike:

> In performing this ceremony I faced the army. My eye covered thousands of officers and men. I noticed that all, Catholic and non-Catholic, officers and private soldiers showed a profound respect, wishing at this fatal crisis to receive every benefit of divine grace that could be imparted through the instrumentality of the Church ministry. Even Major General Hancock removed his hat, and as far as compatible with the situation, bowed in reverential devotion. That general absolution was intended for all...not only for our brigade, but for all, North or South, who were susceptible of it and who were about to appear before their Judge.[38]

After the war, Corby served twice as president of the University of Notre Dame in South Bend, Indiana, and then, beginning in 1886, as provincial general of the Congregation of Holy Cross for the entire United States. In 1910, thirteen years after Father Corby's death, grateful friends and veterans raised a statue of him at Gettysburg, the only statue of a chaplain to stand on an American battlefield.

Father Corby was not the sole chaplain in Caldwell's Division, although he was the only one in the Second (Irish) Brigade. There were seven other chaplains and eighteen surgeons supporting Caldwell's troops in their

---

[36] "Our Lord Jesus Christ absolves you, and I, by his authority, absolve you of all bonds [of sin]."

[37] Corby, *Memoirs of Chaplain Life*, 183.

[38] Ibid., 184. Corby may have been impressed with Major General Hancock's attendance, not only because Hancock was his Corps commander, but also because Hancock was once a Baptist deacon.

preparation for the attack.[39] One was Lutheran chaplain John Stuckenberg, who liked to be as close to the battle as possible.

Chaplain John H. W. Stuckenberg of the 145th Pennsylvania Infantry had traveled more than 100 miles with his regiment over the course of seventeen days before reaching Gettysburg on the morning of July 2. He recorded in his memoirs, "Turning to the right we halted in the woods. The occasional firing near us assured us that another battle was imminent. Col Brooke summoned all the officers of the Brigade before him, and said that General Meade had requested all the Commanders to exhort those under them to do their duty faithfully, and that here perhaps the impending battle might end the war. Col Brown also exhorted the regt to do their duty."[40]

Stuckenberg noted that the Second Corps formed part of the center of the Union line to the left of the cemetery. Skirmishing was going on briskly with a general engagement expected at any moment when he noticed some soldiers kneeling: "Seeing the Irish Brigade bowed in prayer and feeling deeply impressed with the idea that many might enter the battle never to return, I asked permission of Col Brown to hold worship before entering the battle. He willingly acquiesced. 'Attention' was called. After a few remarks we joined in prayer. The occasion was a very solemn one—it was the last prayer in which some of our regt joined."[41]

After a brief visit to the Division hospital, Stuckenberg heard the heavy thunder of cannon on the front. He grabbed his canteen and some bandages and went to join the regiment:

> But coming to the top of a hill the shells fell rapidly between the regt and myself, and I thought it folly to expose myself. I remained on this hill for a while, attending to some wounded men, watching the prisoners who came in and the fight generally as much as possible. But soon my position became too much exposed. The shells came nearer and nearer, some exploding just in front of me, others passing over my head and pieces falling far and near around me. One struck the ground a short distance

---

[39] The chaplains were from the 148th Pennsylvania Infantry, the 61st New York Infantry, the 81st Pennsylvania Infantry, the 52nd New York Infantry, the 2nd Delaware Infantry, the 64th New York Infantry, and the 145th Pennsylvania Infantry—Methodists, Lutherans, a Baptist, and a Presbyterian by denomination.

[40] David T. Hedrick and Gordon Barry Davis Jr., eds., *I'm Surrounded by Methodists...Diary of John H. W. Stuckenberg, Chaplain of the 145th Pennsylvania Volunteer Infantry* (Gettysburg, PA: Thomas Publications, 1995) 77. Col. Hiram L. Brown was the commander of the 145th Pennsylvania Infantry Regiment.

[41] Ibid.

before me and threw its pieces and earth and rocks high in the air. Some shells fell near the place where my horse was. The hospital was moved hastily. I moved my horse, took him farther back to the side of a hill under cover of some high rocks. Leaving my horse there in charge of some of our regt. I went to assist the wounded.[42]

For the remainder of the day Chaplain Stuckenberg ministered to the wounded and dying at the brigade hospital just behind Cemetery Ridge.[43] Among the wounded he found his regimental commander, Col. Hiram Brown, and Brig. Gen. Samuel Zook, who was shot through the abdomen and died at the hospital the next day. Stuckenberg remained with the wounded while the doctors probed for bullets, asked the dying if they had any messages for their families, prayed for the agonizing soldiers, and accepted some of their personal effects to be sent home to their parents. At one point the chaplain began directing the transport of some of the men farther back to the corps hospital. There were so many disabled soldiers that they could not all be carried off the field. Stuckenberg returned to the battlefield: "It was very evident that our regiment had again suffered severely, though the extent of our loss was not yet known—many of our men wounded being still missing. I soon started to the front to see the regt. It was very small—66 men and officers, commanded by Captain [Moses] Oliver. Though saddened by their heavy loss, they were in good spirits because they had driven the rebels and taken 75 or 100 prisoners."[44]

Across the field from the Peach Orchard, Confederate private Charles Oliver was serving as a crew member in the Troup Artillery of Cabell's Artillery Battalion.[45] Born in Warwick, England, in 1831, Oliver at age nine had immigrated with his parents to Athens, Georgia. Before the war started, Charles Oliver had begun his studies for ordination as a Methodist minister. He enlisted in the Troup Artillery at Athens in August 1862. Because he was a local Methodist preacher, though not yet ordained, his unit recognized him as their unofficial chaplain. Oliver finally received his chaplain's commission with the help of Brig. Gen. William N. Pendleton, an Episcopal minister and Lee's chief of Reserve Artillery, in September 1864.[46]

---

[42] Ibid., 77–78.

[43] There were eight Union army hospitals located along the Taneytown Road including those at the Patterson and Weikert farms.

[44] Ibid., 79.

[45] Named for Georgia governor George Troup (1780–1856).

[46] John Wesley Brinsfield, *The Spirit Divided: Memoirs of Civil War Chaplains—The Confederacy* (Macon, GA: Mercer University Press, 2005) 160.

Oliver's journal, which he carried and annotated throughout the war, contained his observations of the fight on July 2 around the Peach Orchard:

The battalion was along the crest of a hill. The firing was very warm. N. Hemphill was badly wounded he staggered down toward the limber[47] with his life clasped in his hands poor fellow. I hope he will recover but don't expect it.

Late in the afternoon our division charged the battery. I was anxious to see it but could not. They drove the enemy from his position and took three guns in the orchard to our left Hood also took three guns. I do not know if any others were taken having been separated from the guns when they moved. I wandered down the pike conversing with our wounded men—went to Kershaws hospital...then went up to the position of the yankee batteries. axcessioned a forsaken limber, counted a half dozen dead Yankees lying round found one poor fellow, number one at his piece, who had been shot in the back while spunging out his gun. The air bubbled thro the wound with every inspiration of his breath. I gave him some water, picked up some blankets and made him a bed and pillow. Poor fellow blessed me and I gave him some good advice (I believe many of these poor fellows perished from neglect between the armies).[48]

Three Final Attacks

With three of McLaws's brigades in the fight, Brig. Gen. William Barksdale, a 41-year-old former US congressman from Mississippi, pleaded with General Longstreet to let him lead his brigade forward. Finally at about 6:30 P.M. Longstreet ordered Barksdale to attack. Barksdale rode on horseback to the front of the 13th Mississippi Infantry Regiment and from there led his 1,600 Mississippi troops toward the apex of the Peach Orchard.

The first Union troops, six Pennsylvania regiments led by Brig. Gen. Charles Graham, began to fall back when their supporting artillery batteries withdrew. Fighting to the last, Graham was wounded and captured. His brigade lost 740 of its 1,516 men. But one company of Union soldiers as a group targeted General Barksdale and wounded him nine times in one vol-

---

[47] A limber was a two-wheeled cart that carried artillery ammunition. A cannon was attached to the limber and both pulled by six horses.

[48] As cited in John W. Brinsfield, William C. Davis, Benedict Maryniak, and James I. Robertson, Jr., *Faith in the Fight: Civil War Chaplains* (Mechanicsburg, PA: Stackpole Books, 2003) 106.

ley. He was knocked off his horse and captured, to die at the Second US Corps hospital at the Hummelbaugh Farm the next day.

As the fight for the Peach Orchard was raging, Maj. Gen. Daniel Sickles, the US Third Corps Commander, also on horseback, was hit by a solid shot that took off most of his right leg. One of General Sickles's chaplains, Joseph Twichell, had taken shelter from the artillery fire in a barn owned by farmer Abraham Trostle, not far from General Sickles's headquarters. He recorded his actions in a letter to his sister:

> At a little before sunset the sad intelligence spread that Gen. Sickles was wounded. He had been the master spirit of the day and by his courage, coolness, and skill had averted a threatened defeat. All felt that his loss was a calamity. I met the ambulance in which he had been placed, accompanied it, helped lift him out, and administered the chloroform at the amputation. His right leg was torn to shreds, just below the knee—so low that it was impossible to save the knee. His bearing and words were of the noblest character. "If I die," said he, "let me die on the field," "God bless our noble cause," "In a war like this, one man isn't much," "My trust is in God," were some of the things he said. I loved him then, as I never did before. He has been removed, but we are informed that he is doing well. That night I was so exhausted that I had to sleep. The next day the enemy made another desperate attempt to turn our left but failed. Again and again they hurled their masses against our batteries, only to be slaughtered and recoil. Since the first I have, of course, been among the wounded.[49]

As the US Third Corps recoiled under the attacks from four brigades of McLaws's Division, Major General Hancock was busy sending reinforcements to bolster the Union line along Cemetery Ridge. It was a matter of finding anyone available to plug the gaps. From the US Second Corps he sent Brig. Gen. George Willard's Brigade of four New York regiments, and the 1st Minnesota Infantry Regiment from Brig. Gen. William Harrow's Brigade. From the US Fifth Corps he borrowed Brig. Gen. James Barnes's Division of Massachusetts, Michigan and Pennsylvania troops, and the Pennsylvania Reserve regiments from Brig. Gen. Samuel Crawford's Division. As General Lee had predicted on the first day of the battle, the Union

---

[49] As cited in Peter Messent and Steve Courtney, eds., *The Civil War Letters of Joseph Hopkins Twichell: A Chaplain's Story* (Athens: University of Georgia Press, 2006) 249. Note: For his service at Gettysburg, which cost him a leg, General Sickles received the Medal of Honor in 1897.

JOHN W. BRINSFIELD, JR.

had more soldiers and shorter interior lines, which enabled them to move units quickly to meet threats.

With all of General Longstreet's available divisions engaged, the second phase of General Lee's echelon sequence fell to Lieutenant General Hill's Corps—specifically to Maj. Gen. R. H. Anderson's Division. Anderson ordered his four brigades forward toward the center of Cemetery Ridge shortly after Barksdale swept into the Peach Orchard. The 1,413 Confederates under Brig. Gen. Ambrose Wright, who commanded the center brigade in the attack, made significant progress.

Wright's four Georgia regiments penetrated almost to the crest of Cemetery Hill, the farthest advance of any Confederate brigade that day. Brig. Gen. Cadmus Wilcox's Alabama Brigade, to the right of Wright's troops, however, were met with a heroic attack by the 1st Minnesota Infantry, numbering just 262 men, who drove into the startled Confederates and forced them to halt their attack. At most the 1st Minnesota bought time, for 82 percent of their regiment was killed or wounded. Just 47 Minnesota soldiers were left at the end of the day, but they still held the field.

In his official report, General Wright did not mention the attack by the 1st Minnesota, but he did complain that both the brigade on his right, Wilcox's, and the one on his left, Posey's Mississippi Brigade, failed to move up and cover his flanks. Brig. Gen. Carnot Posey evidently thought his brigade was in reserve, so he never attacked. As a result, after about thirty minutes, Wright withdrew, abandoning twenty pieces of artillery that his men had captured on Cemetery Ridge.[50] That he had made good progress in the center of the line with just one brigade was noted by General Hill and by General Lee, who were observing both Longstreet's and Hill's attacks that Thursday afternoon.

Chaplain Charles Dobbs, 12th Mississippi Infantry, was with Posey's Brigade:

> As the men advanced to the front, I rode along with them. A greater number came to me and gave me a finger ring, a locket, a purse, or some other memento or keepsake, with the invariable request, "Parson, if I am killed, send this to my mother, wife, sister, or to the person whose name you will find in the package." In the latter case usually accompanied with a knowing look, "You understand, Parson." Soon I had in trust about thirteen thousand dollars in Southern money. Thus, with the rings, the pocket books, etc. filled a large haversack. They caused me a great deal of uneasiness and several sleepless nights. Finally I rolled them up in an oil

---

[50] *Official Records of the War of the Rebellion*, part 2: 623–24.

cloth and put them in the medicine chest. The surgeon was now one of my warmest friends, and did all in his power to make me comfortable.[51]

It would seem that the Mississippi troops were ready to go into battle but may have been relieved that they did not have to charge the enemy's artillery that day.

While Anderson's brigades were trying to coordinate their attack on Cemetery Ridge, fighting continued on or around Little Round Top. Sgt. Valerius Giles, 4th Texas Infantry, Robertson's Brigade, was pinned down among the boulders at the foot of the mountain. After fighting for two and a half hours, Giles was angry at almost everything and everyone:

Minie balls were poured down upon us from the crest above us.... By this time order and discipline were gone. Every fellow was his own general. Private soldiers gave commands as loud as the officers. Nobody paid any attention to either. To add to this confusion, our artillery on the hill to our rear was cutting its fuse too short. Their shells were bursting behind us, in the treetops, over our heads, and all around us.

Nothing demoralizes troops quicker than to be fired into by their friends. I saw it occur twice during the war. The first time we ran, but at Gettysburg we couldn't. This mistake was soon corrected and the shells burst high on the mountain or went over it.

Major Rogers, then in command of the Fifth Texas Regiment, mounted an old log near my boulder and began a Fourth of July speech. He was a little ahead of time, for that was about six thirty on the evening of July 2nd. Of course nobody was paying any attention to the oration as he appealed to the men to "stand fast."

From behind my boulder I saw a ragged line of battle strung out along the side of Cemetery Ridge and in front of Little Round Top. Night began settling around us, but the carnage went on. There seemed to be a viciousness in the very air we breathed.... Officers were cross to the men, and the men were equally cross to the officers. It was the same way with our enemies. We could hear the Yankee officer on the crest of the ridge in front of us cursing the men by platoons, and the men telling him to go to a country not very far away from us just at that time....

The advance lines of the two armies in many places were not more than fifty yards apart. Everything was on the shoot. No favors asked, and none offered. My gun was so dirty that the ramrod hung in the barrel, and I could neither get it down nor out.... It was no trouble to get another gun there. The mountain side was covered with them.

---

[51] Brinsfield, *The Spirit Divided: The Confederacy*, 67–68.

Our spiritual advisers, chaplains of regiments, were in the rear, caring for the wounded and dying soldiers. With seven devils to each man, it was no place for preachers, anyhow. A little red paint and a few eagle feathers were all that was necessary to make that crowd on both sides into the most veritable savages on earth. White-winged peace didn't roost at Little Round Top that night! There was not a man there that cared a snap for the golden rule, or that could have remembered one line of the Lord's Prayer. Both sides were whipped and we were furious about it.[52]

Corporal Henry Myer, 148th Pennsylvania Infantry, who fought with Caldwell's Division in the Wheatfield, recalled a very different scene:

We were the first troops to cross the field, and the yellow grain was still standing. I noticed how the ears of wheat flew in the air all over the field as they were cut off by the enemy's bullets.

Men in battle will act very differently; some become greatly excited, others remain perfectly cool. One of the boys in my rear was sitting flat on the ground and discharging his piece in the air at an angle of forty-five degrees, as fast as he could load. "Why are you shooting in the air?" I asked. "To scare 'em," he replied.

He was a pious young man, and the true reason why he did not shoot at the enemy direct, was because of his conscientious scruples on the subject. What struck me as being peculiar was that some of the boys swore energetically, who never before were heard to utter an oath.[53]

The third and last major attack of the day came against the Union lines on Cemetery Ridge and Culp's Hill. General Lee had ordered Lieutenant General Ewell to demonstrate against Cemetery Hill in order to prevent the shift of Union troops toward Little Round Top. Ewell's demonstration was to start when he heard Longstreet's artillery begin firing.

General Ewell followed Lee's orders, but Longstreet was late, so Ewell's men waited for ten hours for the attack to begin, some even taking a nap. Finally at 4 P.M. Ewell began a two-hour artillery barrage. He had told General Lee that his artillery was not able to be as effective as he liked against the higher, steep hills where the Union troops had spent all day building log barricades and trenches, but he tried anyway.

---

[52] Henry Woodhead, ed., *Voices of the Civil War—Gettysburg* (Richmond, VA: Time-Life Books, 1995) 81.

[53] Ibid., 89.

Instead of demonstrating against the Union positions, Ewell ordered a full-scale assault by two divisions, Early's and Johnson's, beginning about 7 P.M. Only two of Major General Early's brigades, Louisiana troops led by Brig. Gen. Harry Hayes and three North Carolina regiments led by Col. Isaac Avery, made any headway on the extreme right of the Union position on East Cemetery Hill. When General Hancock responded by sending Col. Samuel Carroll's Brigade from the US Second Corps to reinforce the Union line, the Confederates fell back.

At Culp's Hill Confederate Maj. Gen. Edward Johnson's Division had better luck. Federal troops led by Brig. Gen. George S. Greene, a master engineer, greeted the attacks from behind their strong fortifications on Culp's Hill, but on the southern slope of the hill the Union works were thinly manned. An hour earlier two US Twelfth Corps divisions had been called from these fortifications to reinforce the Union center. Johnson, finding the works weakly defended, took possession of them but did not press the attack further. Only a few hundred yards away on the Baltimore Pike lay the Union supply trains. Failure of Confederate reconnaissance was again critically important.[54] At about 10:30 P.M., with darkness covering the fields and ammunition running low, the second day's battles ended with two exhausted armies clinging to precious ground.

Blessed Nightfall

At the end of the six hours of conflict, the Army of Northern Virginia had lost 6,500 soldiers, killed, wounded, or missing. The Army of the Potomac had lost 9,000, slightly more than the total of both armies' losses on July 1. These six hours on July 2, 1863, from 4 to 10 P.M., marked the largest casualty accumulation in American military history. Lee's carefully constructed but poorly executed echelon attacks had broken down completely. Generals Lee and Hill had been little more than spectators during Longstreet's assaults. One staff officer reported that Lee sent only one dispatch, and received only one, during the entire day. As a member of Lee's staff said later, "The whole affair was disjointed. There was an utter absence of accord in the movements of the several commands."[55] Lee's confidence in his corps commanders had been misplaced, for they had followed his orders to the letter even when circumstances changed.

---

[54] Henry Hird III, ed., *Gettysburg National Military Park Handbook* (St. Augustine, FL: Historic Print and Map Co., 2011), 45.

[55] As cited in Knauer, *Gettysburg: A Day-by-Day Account*, 75.

Chaplains on both sides were appalled at the casualties. Regimental bands that had tried to inspire the troops earlier that morning were silent because the band members were now serving as stretcher-bearers. Sadly, not all of the wounded could be rescued because they lay between the lines. Chaplain Twichell of the 71st New York Infantry wrote:

> The rear was one vast hospital. The wounded were everywhere, and scenes of sickening horror were presented on every side. The fortunes of the day were of varied aspect. At times we were forced back, but generally the appearance was hopeful. Both sides fought with the utmost desperation. At nightfall it was plain that our arms had gained an essential victory. The plan of the enemy—to turn our left flank—was foiled, although he held portions of the field—the more deplorable because we could not get at our wounded.[56]

Chaplain Stuckenberg of the 145th Pennsylvania Infantry tried to give medical attention to the wounded in a house behind the Wheatfield but he had neither a candle to use in the dark nor adequate dressings. He managed to find some whiskey, which he administered to hopefully keep the fallen heroes alive:

> I left the many wounded at their house (no physician to attend them, no candle even, though they were taken away as fast as the ambulances could carry them) and went further to the front. Back of the house we saw the first corpse. Scarcely had we passed it when a bullet from the rebels whistled past us and warned us to proceed no further. Nor could we have gone much further, for our picket line was but a short distance in front of us.
>
> In passing from the field we learned that a wounded man was lying all alone in the woods. We carried him to a place where he could easily be found, and sent a stretcher for him. We went back to the hospital, where I found quite a number of our wounded. I then went to bed. Seldom had I been so tired.[57]

Chaplain Milton Kennedy, 28th North Carolina Infantry, in Pender's Division, was more analytical:

> About three o'clock or four the most fearful cannonading of which I ever conceived commenced. The earth fairly shook with explosions of the guns. The enemy occupied a position of great strength. Longstreet at-

---

[56] Messent and Courtney, *Civil War Letters*, 249.
[57] Hedrick and Davis, *Diary of John H. W. Stuckenberg*, 79.

tacked their left about four o'clock and Ewell their right. Hill attacked them in the center. The fighting has been fearful, and we have no means of ascertaining tonight the result of the conflict, but we all feel confident of success. Gen'l Pender was disabled this afternoon by a shell wound on the thigh, not serious. Gen'l Lane is now commanding Pender's Division, and Col. Avery our brigade.[58]

Friday, July 3, 1863
We learned this morning that our success would have been complete but for the bad conduct of Posey's Brigade last night, which gave way, causing a panic, which resulted in the falling back of the whole line.[59]

Chaplain William Corby of the 88th New York Infantry had a theological outlook on the result of the day's fighting as he recalled pronouncing the general absolution for the Irish Brigade:

The Irish Brigade had a very many advantages over other organizations, as it was at no time during the war without a chaplain; but I was the only one at the battle of Gettysburg. Often in camp and sometimes on the march we held very impressive religious services, but the one at Gettysburg was more public, and was witnessed by many who had not, perhaps, seen the others. The surroundings there too, made a vast difference, for really the situation reminded one of the day of judgment, when shall be seen "men withering away for fear and expectation of what shall come upon the whole world," so great were the whirlwinds of war then in motion.[60]

Chaplain John H. W. Stuckenberg, writing two months after the battle, thought that in addition to chaplain support, the band had made a great difference in encouraging soldiers to do their duty:

In the brass band you have a variety of tunes, the old and familiar patriotic and sentimental and the new and beautiful ones. The rich mellow tunes floating on the air thrill the heart and awaken thoughts. "How Beautiful" we often exclaimed, when language could not express the emotions awakened—which were themselves perhaps indefinite. The 2nd of July, just before we entered the field of battle at Gett[ysburg] a

[58] Brinsfield, *The Spirit Divided: The Confederacy*, 130. General Pender died of his wound on July 18th in Staunton, Virginia.
[59] Ibid., 131.
[60] Corby, *Memoirs of Chaplains Life*, 185.

band struck up near us, as if to prepare us for the terrible ordeal through which we were to pass. "Never did music affect me more than that," said an officer to me the other day; and surely "Hail Columbia" and the "Star Spangled Banner" were never more opportunely played.[61]

Whatever the explanation, the Union troops from Big Round Top to Culp's Hill had turned back successive attacks by five of General Lee's nine divisions in six hours. When the sun went down, the soldiers of the Army of Northern Virginia held the Devil's Den, the Peach Orchard, part of the Wheatfield, and a few trenches on the southern part of Culp's Hill. The Army of the Potomac, however, occupied all of the high ground.

---

[61] Hedrick and Davis, *Dairy of John H. W. Stuckenberg*, 110.

Chapter 5

July 3, 1863
The Last Desperate Gamble

"Had Hell itself broken its boundaries, it would not have presented a more terrifying spectacle."[1]
— Chaplain James Sheeran, 14th Louisiana Infantry

After the largely unsuccessful attacks of July 2, there seemed few options for General Lee to gain the great victory at Gettysburg he so clearly desired. Assaults against the Little Round Top and the Cemetery Hill-Culp's Hill lines had cost too much and were too difficult to renew in force. He could order a withdrawal and then move the army south for a defensive battle as Generals Hood and Longstreet had suggested, but this would involve moving 60,000 troops still able to fight and at least a 17-mile train of supply wagons parallel to Meade's army. Lee thought this would be a dangerous move, inviting an attack during a long and probably slow march in a narrow corridor.[2] Moreover, four brigades of Stuart's Cavalry Division, decremented by their long march and insufficient supplies of food and forage, had not arrived until noon on July 2. Robertson's and Jones's brigades of cavalry did not arrive until July 3.[3] The cavalry was, therefore, unavailable to do the reconnaissance that Lee needed.

The other option was much more to General Lee's liking. Wright's Georgia Brigade had advanced to the crest of Cemetery Ridge the day before and would have gone farther had the supporting brigades arrived. The impression was that the Union center was weak, with a much easier avenue of approach than on either of the flanks. An attack on the center of the Union line might work.

---

[1] Pat McNamara, "Father James Sheeran: Immigrant Priest and Confederate," *Patheos* (April 4, 2011) 2, as cited at http://www.patheos.com/Resources/ Additional-Resources/Father-James-Sheeran-Immigrant-Priest-and-Confederate-Pat-McNamara-04-05-2011.

[2] Maj. Gen. Jubal Early's recollection as cited in Chaplain J. William Jones, *Personal Reminiscences, Anecdotes, and Letters of General Robert E. Lee* (New York: D. Appleton and Co., 1875) 34.

[3] "General Lee's Report of the Gettysburg Campaign," as cited in J. William Jones, ed., *Southern Historical Society Papers*, 2/1 (1876): 45.

Since he generally preferred the offense to the defense, General Lee decided to follow up the partial success of Wright's Brigade on July 2 with a more deliberate assault: "The result of this day's operations induced the belief that with proper concert of action, and with the increased support that the positions gained on the right would enable the artillery to render the assaulting columns, we should ultimately succeed, and it was accordingly determined to continue the attack."[4]

The overall plan, distributed in orders to Lee's three corps commanders, was for Lieutenant General Longstreet to begin the attack early on the morning of July 3. Adjutant James Crocker of the 9th Virginia Infantry in Armistead's Brigade, described the attack order as he recalled it:

> It was to be made in the morning—presumably in the early morning—with the whole of Longstreet's corps, composed of the divisions of Pickett, McLaws, and Hood, together with Heth's Division, two brigades of Pender and Wilcox's brigade, and that the assaulting column was to advance under the cover of the combined artillery of three corps, and that the assault was to be the combined assault of infantry and artillery—batteries to be pushed forward as the infantry progressed, to protect their flanks and support their attack closely.[5]

This order, coupled with direction to Lieutenant General Ewell to demonstrate against the Union right flank at Cemetery Hill at the same time Longstreet attacked, theoretically involved eight of Lee's nine divisions. But, as Adjutant Crocker noted cryptically, "The attack was not made as here ordered."[6]

General Longstreet did not believe the attack would work and asked Lee to reconsider ordering Hood's and McLaws's divisions forward. Longstreet thought that his right flank would be open to attack from Little Round Top. He wanted two divisions to remain on the right flank. Lee conceded and directed a smaller attack at the center, two divisions instead of four, supported by four additional brigades. Pickett and Pettigrew would take their divisions toward the center of the line. Two brigades from Anderson's Division would protect Pickett's right flank, while two brigades from Pender's Division, commanded by Maj. Gen. Isaac Trimble, would follow Pettigrew. Lee later wrote, "General Hill was directed to hold his line with the rest of his command, afford General Longstreet further assistance if re-

---

[4] Ibid., 43.

[5] As cited in Richard Rollins, ed., *Pickett's Charge: Eyewitness Accounts* (Torrance, CA: Rank and File Publications, 1994) xxii.

[6] Ibid.

quested, and avail himself of any success that might be gained."[7] Maj. Gen. J. E. B. Stuart took four brigades of cavalry—6,300 men—3 miles east of Gettysburg in an attempt to reach the rear of the Union army and to exploit any success that Pickett and Pettigrew might achieve.[8]

The Union Defense

At 8 P.M. on the evening of July 2, Maj. Gen. George Meade sent a telegram to Washington informing Maj. Gen. Halleck—and President Lincoln—that "I shall remain in my present position tomorrow."[9] Three hours later Meade met with his senior commanders at his Leister Farm headquarters just off the Taneytown Road. His corps commanders, led by General Slocum, were of the opinion that the army should stay on their favorable ground for at least another day and fight it out. General Meade made the decision formal—the Army of the Potomac would remain in place and await Lee's attack.

As his staff meeting concluded, Meade turned to Brig. Gen. John Gibbon, division commander in Hancock's Second Corps. "If Lee attacks tomorrow," he said, "it will be on your front." When Gibbon asked why General Meade thought so, Meade replied with a prophetic reading of Robert E. Lee's mind: "Because he has made attacks on both our flanks and failed, and if he concludes to try it again, it will be on our center."[10]

Brig. Gen. John Gibbon was a Pennsylvania native, born in Philadelphia and graduated from the US Military Academy in the Class of 1847. He was commissioned a brevet second lieutenant in the 3rd US Artillery. After service in the Mexican War and a posting to south Florida, he returned to West Point to teach artillery tactics. He wrote *The Artillerist's Manual* in 1859, a highly scientific treatise on gunnery used by both Union and Confederate artillery officers during the war. Gibbon's subsequent assignments included serving as captain of Battery B, 4th US Artillery, and, in 1862, as the brigade commander of the Wisconsin Iron Brigade. As a veteran of the battles of Second Manassas and Antietam, Gibbon knew that the battle at Gettysburg would depend as much on firepower as on manpower. He was very well versed in both.

---

[7] Jones, "General Lee's Report," *Southern Historical Society Papers*, 44.

[8] Kelly Knauer, ed., *Gettysburg: A Day-by-Day Account of the Greatest Battle of the Civil War* (New York: Time Books, 2013), 103.

[9] Ibid., 76.

[10] Ibid., 77.

Brigadier General Gibbon commanded the Second Division in Hancock's US Second Corps. The division was composed of units from six states ranging from Maine to Michigan, but with one brigade—Webb's—made up entirely of Pennsylvania regiments. Six batteries of artillery were formally in support of Gibbon's Division and Brig. Gen. Alexander Hays's adjacent Third Division at the center of the Union line, including Battery A of the 4th United States Artillery commanded by Lt. Alonzo Cushing.

In addition to Gibbon's and Hayes's divisions, Doubleday's Division from the US First Corps, Caldwell's Division from the US Second Corps, and Birney's Division from the US Third Corps completed the line from Ziegler's Grove to approximately the Peach Orchard. Brig. Gen. John C. Robinson's Division was also posted on the southern slope of Cemetery Hill on the Taneytown Road. In all, the Union line consisted of six under-strength divisions, but not more than 5,750 Union soldiers were stretched along the half-mile front that was the aiming point for Pickett's and Pettigrew's Confederates.[11]

The defensive line for the Union, however, was not comprised of infantry alone. Gen. Henry J. Hunt, chief of artillery for the Army of the Potomac, had posted seventy-seven guns along the crest of Cemetery Ridge, with twenty-five additional guns at the crucial center. Another fifty guns were posted on Cemetery Hill and Little Round Top to support the Federal flanks.[12]

The range of the Union artillery was such that part of the Confederate line, 1,400 yards away, could be hit before any charge began. Solid shot could hit a target at 1,700 yards. The preferred range for explosive shells was 1,300 yards or less; that of canister, filled with twenty-four one-inch balls, inside 400 yards. A well-trained crew could fire two spherical rounds or three rounds of canister per minute.[13] Coupled with the infantryman's ability to fire two .58-calibre minié balls per minute, the firepower of the Union line was extraordinary.[14] If only half of the Union infantrymen and half of the Union guns in the crucial center of the line fired at once, in one minute more than 5,700 bullets and fifty artillery shells could be delivered downrange. In ten minutes the impact would be ten times as much: 57,000 bullets and 100 artillery shells or canister projectiles. The Civil War generals were

---

[11] Ibid., 92.

[12] Ibid.

[13] Jay Luvaas and Harold W. Nelson, eds., *Guide to the Battle of Gettysburg* (Lawrence: University Press of Kansas, 1994) 206–207.

[14] Ibid., 204.

well aware of the risks of a frontal attack. As a rule of thumb they estimated a successful attack against a fortified position would require three times more attackers than defenders. Although the Union defenders did not know it, the Confederate attack would not meet that 3:1 ratio on July 3.

The Federals on Cemetery Ridge that morning sought whatever shade they could find. They tied their horses, if they had any, to trees and dozed in the heat that was climbing to 87 degrees by afternoon.[15] As usual, some soldiers took a nap.

At about 9 A.M. General Meade rode over to confer with General Hancock. With fighting going on around Culp's Hill, Meade decided that Lee would not attack the center of the line, as he had predicted, but would attack again at Little Round Top. Accordingly, Meade left the Fifth Corps, the survivors of the Third Corps, and the Sixth Corps on the left flank. The Eleventh Corps and the Twelfth Corps and most of the First Corps were still positioned on the right flank. That left the center to General Hancock's two divisions plus part of Doubleday's Division from the First Corps.[16] Except for artillery, the center was, in fact, the least defended section per mile of the Union line.

Pickett's Division: Anxious Waiting

Pickett's Division had marched 26 miles from Chambersburg on Thursday, July 2, camping that evening along the "Baltimore road" about 5 miles from Gettysburg.[17] Rising early on July 3, Pickett marched the division south to Marsh Creek and Black Horse Tavern, then a mile farther to the battlefield. Composed of approximately 5,500 men in fifteen infantry regiments and four artillery batteries, all from Virginia, the division was well supplied for battle, with sixty rounds of ammunition per soldier. But there was anxiety in the ranks early in the day. Chaplain Peter Tinsley, in Garnett's Brigade, recorded his impressions:

---

[15] Dr. Michael Jacobs of Pennsylvania College at Gettysburg measured the temperature at 87 degrees F at 2 P.M. on July 3, 1863. See http://www.accuweather.com/en/weather-news/battle-of-gettysburg-150th-ann/14824506, accessed November 2014.

[16] Knauer, *Gettysburg: A Day-by-Day Account*, 92.

[17] Peter Archer Tinsley (1833–1908), "Private Diary," in John and Joyce Schmale Civil War Collection, Wheaton (IL) College Archives, box 1, folder 51: 14. Chaplain Tinsley was referring to the Chambersburg Pike. Evidently he thought the road ran to Baltimore.

We are now come to the battlefield & here halt to await preparations along the line. Our men on yesterday evening & particularly this morning had gotten some hint of the sort of work they are called upon to do. It was hinted that the position was something of a Malvern Hill, that our men yesterday had driven the enemy to it, but had to halt or fall back a little.[18] Nevertheless Gen'l Lee regards the possession of that point as highly important to us, because we would thus be masters of the positions of the Yankee Army also.

I think there is a feeling of solemnity throughout the Division. They are veterans & know what it is to fight. They know what victory is—but they know too what it is to lose friends, comrades, kinsmen by experience or observation, the horrors of imprisonment & the agonies of wounds. None—not the bravest can purchase any exemption from these. They all know the bloody price of victory. "Maybe my life will be part of that price"—Then some thoughts of home—of eternity—which even the veteran cannot wholly banish from his mind at such a time.

The fury of battle—the rattling musketry—the deep mouthed artillery, the bursting of shells—the impetuous charge & the cheers of the moving host—the stern words of command, the fiery passions—will soon banish these troublesome thoughts—these intrusive visitors.[19]

Chaplain Tinsley then turned his attention to describing what was happening around him, including passing a weeping girl—an omen of a future not yet fully understood:

How dreadful is the suspense of this moment. Every movement of aids, couriers, & Generals is closely watched. Every passer-by who can be stopped, is closely interrogated. It seemed to me that as they meet each other, they seem to interrogate every man. The tone—the countenances of his friend, to ascertain if possible what he thinks or hopes or fears. I must confess for myself that I was possessed by sad forebodings.

When I was coming to the field this morning I saw a young lady weeping bitterly and occasionally turning her head toward the passing army. She would in a moment weep again as before. Was she weeping for her countrymen as she saw our host going to meet them in deadly conflict? Or did one alone, a brother—a husband—a lover in arms fill her

[18] Ibid., 15. Malvern Hill was a battle in the Peninsula Campaign. Fought on July 1, 1862, it was very similar to Pickett's Charge at Gettysburg a year later, with a loss of more than 5,000 Confederate soldiers in a fruitless charge.
[19] Ibid., 16–17.

mind? Some said: "She is Secesh"—Maybe she wept as she saw our army going to battle in a holy cause against the myriads that opposed—I know not. But it was a sad sight, that weeping girl. I can never forget it—It is present now with a sort of superstitious import. It seems an Omen boding sorrow to some one, but the future is the only interpreter of its meaning.[20]

At some time in the morning, General Lee visited Pickett's Division, but Chaplain Tinsley was not specific as to the time:

At a little distance from us was Gen'l Lee, sitting on a stump with a small map spread out before him. He is calm, thoughtful, determined. Near him is his Adj[utant] Gen'l [R. H.] Chilton & a few couriers standing around. Presently Gen'l A. P. Hill with a portion of his staff comes up— Longstreet from our front soon joins them. All of them seem to wear a serious aspect—they converse very little & after a while each moves off in a different direction to his position.[21]

Interestingly, Tinsley does not record any seeming disagreement between Lee and Longstreet. He did realize that time for an attack was probably close:

I had been watching for some good opportunity of having prayers at the head of my Regt & I determined to seize this last opportunity. Not only my own Reg't but a large portion of the brigade & many bystanders gathered around me. It is a solemn moment, I offer a short prayer—the congregation then sang the long metre doxolog[y] : Praise God from whom all blessings flow & are dismissed with the Apostolic benediction [2 Corinthians 13:14]. How sincere and fervent must have been that prayer. Everyone knows that in probability it is his last!!

In a few moments the Division marched on and took their position in rear of the artillery on the hill. I retired about the same distance to the rear, as neither duty nor prudence nor inclination bad me to the charge. I take my place with the field Surgeon. From the top of the hill which the charge was made there is an open plain extending about 3/4 mile to the front, interspersed with orchards, barns, fences & the "abodes of man scattered at intervals." More than 200 pieces of our artillery are on the hill & just behind them, a little sheltered by the slope of the hill is our line of battle.

---

[20] Ibid., 17–18.
[21] Ibid., 19.

On the other side of this plain, on an elevated ridge commanding the whole field, the enemy Infantry and artillery are strongly posted behind breastworks of stone fences strengthened by earth thrown upon and against it. In some places there are double lines of works. The ground in their rear also is quite strong & well suited to rallying a broken column or for holding reserves.[22]

Lee's Plans Begin to Go Awry

Originally General Lee had envisioned an attack on July 3 that would be a rerun of the one he had ordered on July 2, but with fresh troops. Instead of having Longstreet assault Little Round Top, Longstreet would attack the center of the Union line. Ewell would synchronize an attack on the Cemetery Hill-Culp's Hill sector with Longstreet's advance, as signaled (again) by the sound of Longstreet's artillery. Hill's Corps would furnish eight brigades to join Pickett's three brigades in the main effort.

Ewell's support, however, was thrown off by an early morning counterattack at Culp's Hill by troops from two Union divisions of the US Twelfth Corps, Brig. Gen. Alexander Shaler's Brigade from the Sixth Corps, and six regiments from the First and Eleventh corps seeking to reclaim the trenches lost the night before. Maj. Gen. Henry Slocum, commander of the US Twelfth Corps, directed Brig. Gen. John Geary and Brig. Gen. Thomas Ruger to commit their divisions to the attack at about 3:30 A.M. The fighting raged for seven hours with more than 1,200 Confederates killed and 277,000 rounds of ammunition expended by Union soldiers.[23]

Behind the Union lines on East Cemetery Hill, Major General Slocum was satisfied with the conduct of the battle. Ewell's Confederate infantry had been forced to retreat in face of the Union counterattack. Chaplain John H. W. Stuckenberg rode over from the Second Corps hospital to observe the fighting around Cemetery Hill:

On our extreme right were three batteries, each one occupying a commanding position, which were almost incessantly throwing shells at the rebels. The rebels had fired no cannon at our right. I ascended a rocky hill—it was composed of large masses of rocks—to the middle one of the three batteries. Gen Slocum was here, in person directing the firing. A

---

[22] Ibid., 21.

[23] "Report of Brigadier General John W. Geary, USA," War Department, *Official Records*, part 1: 826–33 as cited in Jay Luvass and Harold W, Nelson, *Guide to the Battle of Gettysburg*, 156–58.

short distance before us was a round hill, covered with trees. On the side of the hill nearest us, the smoke was seen rising in columns from the forest—there the fighting took place. The rattling of musketry was constant, rapid and terrific. The columns of smoke indicated the progress of the fight. It also served to indicate the position of the rebels to the artillerists. The shelling was rapid and must have produced terrible havoc in the rebel ranks. Our men were victorious here. The rebels were repulsed, our rifle pits regained, the field covered with heaps of slain and wounded rebels whilst our loss was comparatively small.[24]

The battle for Culp's Hill was over two hours before Longstreet's artillery signaled his advance. Incredibly, Longstreet was not informed that Ewell would no longer be able to cooperate with Pickett's attack.[25]

Father James Sheeran was the Roman Catholic chaplain for the 14th Louisiana Infantry Regiment, part of Nicholl's Brigade, Johnson's Division. Nicholl's Brigade was in support of Walker's "Stonewall Brigade" on the east side of Culp's Hill on the morning of July 3.

Father Sheeran had been commissioned as a chaplain in September 1861 and had accompanied the Army of Northern Virginia on all of its major campaigns for almost two years. He had witnessed the battles of Second Manassas, Fredericksburg, and Chancellorsville, where he ministered to both the Confederate and Union wounded.[26] Still, Father Sheeran admitted that "I was never yet on a battlefield that I was not afraid."[27] Further,

I had seen hundreds of thousands of my fellowmen drawn up in battle array, heard the thundering of artillery and felt the earth quake beneath its powerful voice. I had heard the loud shouts of victorious triumph as well as the groans and lamentations of our wounded and dying. I had seen the worst passions of the human heart displayed under the names of liberty

---

[24] David T. Hedrick and Gordon Barry Davis, Jr., eds., *I'm Surrounded by Methodists...Diary of John H. W. Stuckenberg, Chaplain of the 145th Pennsylvania Volunteer Infantry* (Gettysburg, PA: Thomas Publications, 1995) 80.

[25] James Longstreet, *From Manassas to Appomattox: Memoirs of the Civil War in America* (Philadelphia: J. B. Lippencott, 1896) 390.

[26] John Wesley Brinsfield, Jr., *The Spirit Divided: Memoirs of Civil War Chaplains—The Confederacy* (Macon, GA: Mercer University Press, 2005) 158–59.

[27] Pat McNamara, "Father James Sheeran: Immigrant Priest and Confederate," *Patheos* (April 4, 2011) 2, as cited at http://www.patheos.com/Resources/ Additional-Resources/Father-James-Sheeran-Immigrant-Priest-and-Confederate-Pat-McNamara-04-05-2011.

and humanity. I had seen displayed a patriotism more noble, more elevated, more brave and chivalrous than any recorded in the world's history.[28]

The fighting at Gettysburg, however, was another matter. Father Sheeran, busy ministering to the wounded of five Louisiana regiments, wrote later in his war journal, "Had Hell itself broken its boundaries, it would not have presented a more terrifying spectacle."[29]

One of the Confederate soldiers wounded at East Cemetery Hill was Pvt. Charles F. Lutz of the 8th Louisiana Infantry. Lutz was an African American. It is not known if there were other African American soldiers on the fields of Gettysburg, but there were hundreds of other African Americans who served as teamsters and even as musicians and band members in the Army of Northern Virginia; there was also an armed African American company of soldiers who supported Col. Jacob Frick's Union troops earlier at Wrightsville.[30] For Father Sheeran, regardless of the color of the skin, the blood shed by soldiers was uniformly red and uniformly sacrificial.

By noon it was hoped that if General Lee's assault plans worked perfectly, then the Pickett-Pettigrew-Trimble charge would push through the center of the Union line. General Ewell's three divisions would attack the Union forces on Cemetery and Culp's hills, and Maj. Gen. J. E. B. Stuart's Cavalry division would block the road to York and, if successful, cut across the main Union supply line, the Baltimore Pike. In essence, the concept was a four-pronged offensive that depended upon coordinated infantry and cavalry assaults by three commanders, Longstreet, Ewell, and Stuart, with Hill's Third Corps in support or reserve. The vital fourth prong was the effect of the Confederate artillery against the Union guns and the partially entrenched Union lines. The Army of the Potomac might then be split into

[28] Joseph T. Durkin, SJ, ed., *Confederate Chaplain: A War Journal of Rev. James B. Sheeran, c.ss.r, 14th Louisiana, CSA* (Milwaukee WI: Bruce Publishing Co., 1960) 28.

[29] McNamara, "Father James Sheeran," 2.

[30] Henry Louis Gates, Jr., "Did black men fight at Gettysburg?" *Nation*, July 1, 2013, accessed January 2016, as cited in http://www.theroot.com/articles/history/2013/07/did_black_men_fight_at_gettysburg.html, 3. According to the Appomattox roster of surrendered Confederate soldiers, Longstreet's Artillery Battalion employed sixteen negro slaves, and the 18th Georgia Battalion, also in Longstreet's First Corps, included eight enlisted colored men, four cooks and four musicians. R. A. Brock, ed., "Paroles of the Army of Northern Virginia," as cited in the *Southern Historical Society Papers*, vol. XV (1887).

two parts and the victory won. By the time Pickett advanced, at about 3 o'clock, three of the four attacks by Confederate infantry, cavalry, and artillery units had failed to achieve their objectives. Somewhat surprisingly, it would also seem that neither General Lee nor General Longstreet were aware of these developments in time to consider a change in orders for Pickett's, Pettigrew's, and Trimble's infantry. Time, again, was on the side of the Union.

The Artillery Duel

According to Brig. Gen. William Pendleton, a graduate of West Point, an Episcopal minister, and Lee's chief of artillery, almost 150 Confederate cannon were to prepare the way for Pickett's Charge early on the morning of July 3: "By direction of the commanding general, the artillery along our entire line was to be prepared for opening, as early as possible on the morning of the 3d, a concentrated and destructive fire, consequent upon which a general advance was to be made. The right, especially, was, if practicable, to sweep the enemy from his stronghold on that flank."[31]

Pendleton had made an early inspection tour that Friday morning of five artillery battalions containing twenty-two batteries of cannon in Longstreet's Corps, a total of sixty guns. These batteries had been placed under the command of Col. E. P. Alexander by General Longstreet. Pendleton cautioned the battalion and battery commanders to waste as little ammunition as possible.

Then Pendleton checked the positioning of the artillery from Hill's Third Corps and Ewell's Second Corps, "each group having specific instructions from its chief."[32] He also checked the position of ordnance trains that held ammunition for resupplying the guns. All this was necessary because General Lee had ordered the artillery to move forward to support the infantry attack after the initial bombardment of the Union lines.

At about 1 P.M. on the signal of a gun from the Washington Artillery, the whole line opened fire.[33] General Pendleton wrote that the guns fired from right to left:

> Salvos by battery being much practiced, as directed, to secure greater deliberation and power. The enemy replied with their full force.... The av-

---

[31] War Department, *Official Records*, part 2: 351–53.

[32] Ibid.

[33] The Washington Artillery of New Orleans was part of the First Corps. Their 17-year-old Methodist chaplain, Marcus Boatner Chapman, was the youngest chaplain in either army.

erage distance between contestants was about 1,400 yards, and the effect was necessarily serious on both sides. With the enemy, there was advantage of elevation and protection from earthworks; but his fire was unavoidably more or less divergent, while ours was convergent. His troops were massed, ours diffused. We therefore, suffered apparently much less.[34]

On the Union side of the field, as early as 11 o'clock in the morning, Brig. Gen. Henry Hunt had observed a line of Confederate artillery, estimated at 160 guns, stretching almost 2 miles across his front. As General Meade's chief of artillery, Hunt had operational control of about 100 pieces of artillery.[35] At 1 P.M. these guns replied immediately, sending shells toward the Confederate lines. Hunt, like his counterpart on the other side, was concerned about the placement of the artillery and the amount of ammunition quickly available. Hunt, however, remained in overall command of his guns while Pendleton yielded to Longstreet's choice of Colonel Alexander to direct the Confederate artillery effort.[36]

Most of the shells from the massed Confederate artillery went over the Federal infantry, but some found their targets farther back. General Meade's headquarters at the Leister farmhouse was hit twice, wounding Major General Butterfield, Meade's chief of staff. Sixteen horses outside the headquarters were killed. General Meade moved back beyond the Taneytown Road.

Union batteries on Cemetery Ridge came under terrific fire. Rorty's New York battery, on the southern end of Brigadier Gibbon's Division, had guns dismounted, caissons blown up, and their commander killed. At the other end of Gibbon's line, three ammunition chests were hit and exploded, wrecking the limbers of Cushing's Battery A, 4th US Artillery. A gun in the same area belonging to Brown's Rhode Island battery was hit in the muzzle while being loaded, killing one soldier and mortally wounding another. A few minutes later Brown's battery, with all of its officers killed or wounded,

---

[34] As cited in Rollins, *Pickett's Charge*, 28.

[35] Historian Stephen Sears put the number of Confederate cannon at 163, stretching in an arc from the Peach Orchard to the town of Gettysburg. Sears's estimate of Union guns was 119 from Cemetery Hill to Little Round Top. Knauer, *Gettysburg: A Day-by-Day Account*, 93.

[36] According to official reports from the Army of the Potomac, on June 30, 1863, a total of 352 guns were available, 110 of which were in the artillery reserve. The Army of Northern Virginia counted a total of 240 guns in their units. War Department, *Official Records*, part 1: 151 ff.

withdrew behind the ridge. Major Thomas Osborn, who commanded nearly fifty guns on Cemetery Hill, estimated the rate of fire to be 1,500 shots a minute passing between the armies.[37]

Brigadier General Hunt wrote later,

> The losses of the artillery...were very large. The destruction of materiel was large. The enemy's cannonade, in which he must have almost exhausted his ammunition, was well sustained, and cost us a great many horses and the explosion of an unusually large number of caissons and limbers. The whole slope behind our crest, although concealed from the enemy, was swept by his shot, and offered no protection to horses or carriages.[38]

Meanwhile Major General Hancock and one orderly, carrying the Second Corps flag, rode up and down the firing line on horseback to encourage the men to remain in position. When a brigadier scolded him for risking his life so glibly, Hancock replied, "There are times when a corps commander's life does not count."[39]

In the Confederate lines the Union shells were finding their marks randomly but fairly well. General Lee had advised Pickett's and Pettigrew's divisions to lie down in the woods behind their artillery. Even so, shells from the Federals seemed to Colonel Alexander to be winning the duel. One Confederate soldier wrote that "there were to be seen at almost every moment of time guns, swords, haversacks, human flesh flying above the earth, which now trembled beneath us as shaken by an earthquake."[40]

In Kemper's Brigade, Sergeant Major David Johnston remembered lying on the ground with the other members of the 7th Virginia Infantry:

> Overconfidence pervaded the Confederate army, from the commanding general down to the shakiest private in the ranks. Too much overconfidence was the bane of our battle. For more than six long hours the men were waiting, listening for the sound of the signal guns. The stillness was at last broken: the shot was fired: down, according to program, went the men on their faces.[41]

> I began to breathe a little more freely and raised my head off the ground and looked around, whereupon Lt. Brown said to me, "you had

---

[37] Rollins, *Pickett's Charge*, 112.

[38] War Department, *Official Records*, part 2: 238–41.

[39] Knauer, *Gettysburg: A Day-by-Day Account*, 94.

[40] Ibid., 95–96.

[41] Rollins, *Pickett's Charge*, 69.

better put your head down or you may get it blown off." I replied, "well, Lt., a man had about as well die that way as to suffocate for want of air." I had barely spoken these words when a terrific explosion occurred, which for a moment deprived me of my breath and of sensibility, but it was momentary, for in a moment or so I found myself lying off from my former position and gasping for breath. Around me were brains, blood and skull bones; my first thought was that my Colonel's head had blown off, but this was dispelled the next moment by his asking me if I was badly hurt, to which I replied I thought I was and called for that which a wounded soldier always first wants, a drink of water. By this time I had turned about and discovered that the heads of the two men who lay on my left side had been blown off just over the ears, and that the shell had exploded almost directly over me, a little below my left shoulder blade, breaking sever[al] of my ribs loose from my backbone, bruising severely my left lung and cutting my grey jacket almost into shreds....[42]

By some estimates, Longstreet's Corps lost at least 500 soldiers to the Union bombardment. Sergeant Major Johnston wrote that due to the losses occasioned by the shelling, just 4,400 men of Pickett's Division of 5,500 were able to form in ranks by 2:50 P.M.[43] If the latter number was true, perhaps 10 percent of the total Confederate infantry force was disabled before the charge.

While there are no known examples of regimental bands playing during the artillery duel, there were chaplains and commanders attempting to keep up the spirits of the men. Lt. Francis W. Dawson on Longstreet's staff recalled seeing prayers offered up "in front of Armistead's brigade and Garnett's brigade before the advance began."[44] Chaplain John J. D. Renfroe of the 10th Alabama Infantry in Wilcox's Brigade tried to encourage his soldiers by offering a short sermon in front of the regiment. This was nothing new for the Baptist chaplain, for he declared afterward that he preached thirteen sermons on the Gettysburg Campaign, several on the line of battle. "I have several times preached when shot and shell were flying over our heads," he wrote, "and also several times I had minnie-balls to strike in my

---

[42] As cited in Henry Woodhead, ed., *Voices of the Civil War: Gettysburg* (Richmond, VA: Time-Life Books, 1995) 117. Johnston survived the Civil War to serve in West Virginia as a lawyer, judge, and congressman.

[43] Rollins, *Pickett's Charge*, 69.

[44] As cited in Woodhead, *Voices of the Civil War*, 115.

congregation while preaching."[45] But the third day at Gettysburg was so punctuated by shot and shell that even Chaplain Renfroe eventually had to take cover.

Acting chaplain Charles James Oliver of the Troup Artillery, positioned in front of General Longstreet's headquarters, recorded his memories of loading the guns during the morning:

> Fri 3rd This is a day long to be remembered. Early in the misty morning we went into position a mile to the front and left our former position. We were not fired upon in going in, but in shifting position shortly afterwards, they either fired upon us or a battery going in behind us, tearing those to pieces, killing Hop Adams and stunning McConnell.
>
> Detail was digging the grave for poor Adams. All the morning the drivers were digging them pits.... In the afternoon pickets division came in and formed in line of battle. Just below our guns soon afterward the batteries opened. There was in round numbers 100 guns in each side, and firing was terrific. Probably there never was such firing of field artillery before in the world's history of war.
>
> It seems strange that such a storm should leave a single survivor, but by God's grace most of us escaped. I was knocked down at the caisson together with Hill Swan, but I was able immediately to resume my work. The shell cut of[f] a horses leg near the caisson and I had to shoot him. Our ammunition was nearly exhausted. I had to get out the damaged shell from our rear chest. Then strip the second caisson, transfer what remained in it to ours and then send it to the rear for more.[46]

Chaplain Charles H. Dobbs of the 12th Mississippi Infantry, in General A. P. Hill's Corps, also watched the battle develop:

> The battle progressed fearfully. We could hear the booming of the guns, the bursting of shells and roar of artillery for miles to the right and left. I advanced toward the front, and by chance saw Gen. Lee, his staff and

---

[45] Rev. J. William Jones, *Christ in the Camp: Or Religion in the Confederate Army* (Harrisonburg, VA: Sprinkle Publications, 1986) 510–11.

[46] As cited in John W. Brinsfield, William C. Davis, Benedict Maryniak, and James I. Robertson, Jr., *Faith in the Fight: Civil War Chaplains* (Mechanicsburg, PA: Stackpole Books, 2003) 106–107. In a sketch Chaplain Oliver included in his journal, it appears that most of the wagon drivers were African American. Evidently when the drivers were not busy with their wagons, they were digging graves or trenches. Oliver's journal is on microfilm, mss #444, Special Collections, Robert W. Woodruff Library, Emory University, Atlanta.

several generals in a prominent position, evidently viewing the field of battle. Going forward I took my position near them, and there the grandest scene I ever witnessed burst upon my view. The central lines of both armies were in full view, the enemy upon an elevation beyond, and our lines upon the great flat, with rising ground here and there. The roar of artillery and musketry was almost incessant. Soon, however, I could only distinguish the lines by the denser clouds of smoke and bright flashes of fire.[47]

The Critical Deception

At approximately 2:30 P.M., after ninety minutes of continuous artillery bombardment, the Federals made a decision that proved to be a turning point in the battle. Major Thomas W. Osborn, the commander of the Eleventh Corps batteries, suggested to Brigadier General Hunt that if the Union batteries temporarily stopped firing, it might lure the Confederates into an early assault. Hunt had already decided that it was time to conserve ammunition, for it was obvious that an infantry attack from across the field was immanent. Accordingly, Hunt's cease-fire order was passed down the line, and one by one the Union batteries fell silent.

Major General Winfield Hancock objected at first to this tactic, for he believed that the artillery helped encourage the Union infantrymen to hold their ground. However, most of Hunt's artillerymen obeyed their chief of artillery because they did need to replenish their supplies of shell and canister.

While this discussion was going on in the Union lines, Confederate Brigadier General Pendleton, Lee's chief of artillery, had made two other fateful decisions that seemed reasonable at the time but which would have terrible consequences for Lee's army. First, he ordered the reserve artillery ammunition in the First Corps ordnance train to be moved further to the rear, out of range of the Union guns.[48] This move made it impossible later for the gun crews to resupply their caissons in a timely manner. Second, he detached the batteries that were to move forward with Pickett and Pettigrew, presumably to protect them as well. Lee had specifically ordered that Longstreet's, Hill's, and part of Ewell's artillery would "be pushed forward as the infantry progressed, protecting their flanks, and support their attacks

---

[47] Charles Holt Dobbs, "Reminiscences of an Army Chaplain," *The Presbyterian Christian Observer* (1874) as cited in Brinsfield, *The Spirit Divided: The Confederacy*, 67.

[48] War Department, *Official Records*, part 2: 351–53.

closely."[49] Moreover, the Confederate batteries that had been firing for almost two hours were now out, or almost out, of ammunition and would be useless in an attack.

When General Longstreet sensed that something was wrong, he rode to Colonel Alexander's position: "I mounted and spurred for Alexander's post. He reported that the batteries he had reserved for the charge with the infantry had been spirited away by General Lee's chief of artillery; that the ammunition of the batteries of position was so reduced that he could not use them in proper support of the infantry. He was ordered to stop the march at once and fill up his ammunition chests. But, alas! There was no more ammunition to be had."[50]

It would appear from General Lee's own report of the battle that none of his subordinate commanders reported a shortage of ammunition to him before Pickett's and Pettigrew's divisions were well into the attack.[51] By then, it was too late. In General Longstreet's memoirs he blamed Lee for not giving him more discretion over the battle: "General Lee and myself never had any deliberate conversation about Gettysburg. The subject was never broached by either of us to the other. On one occasion it came up casually and he said to me (alluding to the charge of Pickett on the 3d) 'General, why didn't you stop all that thing that day?' I replied that I could not under the circumstances assume such a responsibility, as no discretion had been left me."[52]

It was no secret among some of the commanders that General Longstreet did not believe a frontal attack against an entrenched, superior force would prove successful. Longstreet wanted to move around the Union army and force them to attack his well-placed troops, but his arguments were in vain.

Longstreet wrote that no less than 30,000 men would be needed to penetrate the Union lines, "that the conditions were different from those in the days of Napoleon when field batteries had a range of six hundred yards and musketry about sixty yards."[53] In retrospect, Longstreet wrote of Lee,

---

[49] Ibid., 320–21.

[50] Lt. Gen. James Longstreet, *From Manassas to Appomattox: Memoirs of the Civil War in America* (Philadelphia: J. B. Lippencott, 1896) as cited in Rollins, *Pickett's Charge*, 22.

[51] Jones, "General Lee's Report," *Southern Historical Society Papers*, 44.

[52] Lt. Gen. James Longstreet, *From Manassas to Appomattox: Memoirs of the Civil War in America* (Philadelphia: J. B. Lippencott, 1896) as cited in Rollins, *Pickett's Charge*, 16.

[53] Ibid., 18.

"Knowing my want of confidence, he should have given the benefit of his presence and his assistance in getting the troops up, posting them, and arranging the batteries; but he gave no orders or suggestions after his early designation of the point for which the column should march. Fitzhugh Lee claims evidence that General Lee did not even appear on that part of the field while the troops were being assigned to position."[54]

It is not clear what General Longstreet meant by his last comment. General Lee had ridden down the entire Confederate line starting with a 3 A.M. meeting with Brig. John B. Gordon opposite Cemetery Hill, concluding with a consultation later that morning with Generals Longstreet, Hill, and Heth at or near Longstreet's headquarters opposite Little Round Top. There were many witnesses to these meetings including Chaplain Peter Tinsley, Col. A. L. Long, Lee's secretary, and Maj. C. S. Venable, Lee's aide-de-camp.[55]

In spite of these afterthoughts, it was still clear by midafternoon on July 3 that Lee's subordinate commanders had not kept him informed. They had responsibilities as a corps commander, as a chief of artillery, and as an operational artillery commander to keep the commanding general aware of changing circumstances. It was not Lee's job to relieve Longstreet or Pendleton or Alexander of their accountability for details such as a critical shortage of ammunition. In the meanwhile, the division commanders waited for someone to give them an order to advance.

Behind the Union lines, Brig. Gen. Henry Hunt made detailed preparations to meet the Confederate attack. At 10 A.M. he inspected the whole Union line, making sure all of the batteries were in good condition and well supplied with ammunition. He directed his subordinate artillery commanders to concentrate their fire on one enemy battery at a time until it was silenced and to "husband their ammunition as much as possible."[56]

At 2:30 P.M., "finding our ammunition running low and that it was very unsafe to bring up loads of it," Hunt directed the fire to be stopped.[57] When the Confederate artillery fire ceased as well, he brought up new batteries of guns, twenty-four cannon in all, in the center of the Union line, and one battery on the flank of the expected Confederate advance. "It required

---

[54] Ibid., 19.

[55] Colonel A. L. Long, *Memoirs of Robert E. Lee*, (London: Sampson Low, Marston, Searle and Rivington, 1886) 287–88 as cited in Rollins, *Pickett's Charge*, 25.

[56] War Department, *Official Records*, part 2: 238–41.

[57] Ibid.

but a few minutes, as the batteries, as fast as withdrawn from any point, were sent to the Artillery Reserve, replenished with ammunition, reorganized, returned to the rear of the lines, and there waited assignment."[58] Any attack on the Union line would be met by both direct and enfilading fire. Hunt had constructed an artillery machine, constantly resupplied and stretching 2 miles, that would provide an iron curtain for the Army of the Potomac. The Union defense, engineered by Hunt and Hancock, was an ambush just waiting to happen.

Pickett's Charge: Theirs Not to Reason Why[59]

Col. Porter Alexander, who had been directing the Confederate artillery fire for almost two hours, noticed that the Union guns had largely stopped firing and that some batteries appeared to be withdrawing from their lines. Porter then sent a message to General Pickett, "For God's sake, come quick, or we cannot support you. Ammunition nearly out."[60] Pickett, in turn, found General Longstreet and asked if he should advance. Longstreet, knowing that it had to be, but unwilling to give the order, turned his face away. Pickett saluted and said, "I am going to move forward, Sir," and galloped off to his division.[61]

General Pickett's three brigade commanders, Brigadier Generals James L. Kemper, Richard B. Garnett, and Lewis A. Armistead, commanding a total of fifteen Virginia regiments, formed up for battle as if on parade. Garnett's Brigade, upon which the others would dress, was on the left front. Kemper's Brigade would move on Garnett's right, and Armistead's Brigade would follow behind the other two. At a steady pace of about 100 yards per minute, Pickett's Division should reach the Union front line in not more than 20 minutes, allowing for a change in direction to join the right flank of Heth's Division, commanded by Brig. Gen. James Pettigrew. For the first 1,200 yards, Pickett's men would undertake, in effect, a long bayonet attack against Federal guns.

---

[58] Ibid.

[59] Alfred Lord Tennyson, "The Charge of the Light Brigade": Stanzas 1, 2, and 3: "Someone had blundered, Theirs not to make reply, Theirs not to reason why, Theirs but to do and die. Cannon to the right of them, Cannon to the left of them, Cannon in front of them, Into the mouth of hell, Rode the six hundred." John Bartlett, *Bartlett's Familiar Quotations* (New York: Permabooks, 1957) 395.

[60] As cited in Woodhead, *Voices of the Civil War*, 96.

[61] E. Porter Alexander, "The Great Charge and Artillery Fighting at Gettysburg," as cited in Ned Bradford, ed., *Battles and Leaders of the Civil War* (New York: Appleton-Century-Crofts, 1956) 395–96.

On Pickett's left, and about a quarter-mile away, General Pettigrew placed his four brigades in line, supported by two more brigades under the command of Maj. Gen. Isaac Trimble. On Pickett's right, two brigades from Anderson's Division, commanded by Brig. Gen. Cadmus Wilcox, and Perry's Brigade, by Col. David Lang, were to provide a supporting attack over almost the same route Wilcox had attempted the day before.

Before the men stepped off, the issue of horses arose. The previous day Longstreet's officers had received notice that no one under the rank of brigadier general could ride a horse during the attack, "because of the fact that the government had a great deal of difficulty in replacing the horses killed."[62]

Two of the senior officers who insisted on riding into battle, Maj. Gen. John B. Hood and Brig. Gen. William Barksdale, had both been shot off their horses, one wounded and one killed. On July 3, the order came down for officers in the attack to go in dismounted. Generals Kemper, Garnett, Pickett, and Trimble, as well as Col. J. K. Marshall, commanding the first brigade in Pettigrew's Division, were allowed to remain mounted. General Armistead led his men on foot with his hat on the end of his sword.[63]

The soldiers in Pickett's Division had been ordered to march in silence so they could hear commands. They were neither to fire their weapons until ordered nor to give their rebel yell.[64] In the absence of other morale supports, it was important for the men to see their colors and their commanders, who were expected to lead from the front. As it turned out, these measures were inadequate if the commander were killed or the color-bearer fell, for then confusion would pass down the ranks as to what the soldiers should do.

Finally, at 3 P.M., perhaps nine hours behind General Lee's original schedule, Pickett gave the order to advance: "Charge the enemy and remember old Virginia!" "Forward! Guide center! March!"[65] As Pickett's men came into view near the woods, Pettigrew and Trimble also gave their men the order to move forward.

---

[62] Maj. George B. Gerald, 18th Mississippi Infantry, as cited in Woodhead, *Voices of the Civil War*, 90.

[63] Captain Robert Bright, Pickett's Staff, "Pickett's Charge at Gettysburg," *Confederate Veteran* 38/7 (1930) as cited in Rollins, *Pickett's Charge*, 140–41.

[64] Knauer, *Gettysburg: A Day-by-Day Account*, 96.

[65] Col. Joseph Mayo, Third Virginia Infantry, as cited in Rollins, *Pickett's Charge*, 157, and Knauer, *Gettysburg: A Day-by-Day Account*, 96.

Pickett advanced his three brigades ahead and then moved at a 45-degree angle to the left en echelon to close on Pettigrew's flank. The Confederate infantry presented an orderly line of nine brigades in double ranks, about 11,500 men, stretching almost a mile. As was the custom, brigade and regimental commanders led from the front, followed by their color-bearers, blue Virginia state colors and red Confederate battle flags intermingled.

Behind the Union front lines Maj. Gen. Winfield Scott Hancock marveled at the discipline and courage of the Confederate infantry:

> Their lines were formed with precision and steadiness that exhorted the admiration of the witnesses of that memorable scene. The left of the enemy extended slightly beyond the right of Gen. Alexander Hays' Division, their right being about opposite the left of General Gibbon's. Their line of battle thus covered a front of not more than two of the small and incomplete divisions of the corps. The whole attacking force is estimated to have exceeded 15,000 men.[66]

When Pickett's and Pettigrew's divisions came within 1,000 yards, the massed guns of the Union artillery opened with a fusillade of shot and shell. Col. Freeman McGilvery of the 1st Maine Light Artillery trained his thirty-nine guns on the flank of Kemper's Brigade, which passed within easy range. New York and New Jersey batteries, coupled with six 12-pounder cannon from the 5th US Artillery, pounded the center of the Confederate line, each shell tearing holes ten men wide in the front ranks. No longer obscured by smoke, the rebel soldiers were in plain view.[67] Gen. Henry Hunt commented, "The enemy advanced magnificently, unshaken by the shot and shell which tore through his ranks from his front and from our left. The batteries of the Second Corps on our right, having nearly exhausted their supply of

---

[66] "Report of Maj. Gen. Winfield S. Hancock, USA, Commanding Second Army Corps," War Department, *Official Records*, part 1: 373–74. This was perhaps an overestimation of the size of the attack and an underestimation of the infantrymen that would eventually be present to repulse it.

[67] Rollins, *Pickett's Charge*, 162–63 and "Report of Major Charles S. Peyton, CSA, 19th Virginia Infantry," War Department, *Official Records*, part 2: 385–87. Much speculation has been given as to why the Confederate artillery was not more effective before Pickett's charge. Some blame has been attached to faulty fuses, but some must be charged to the inability of the artillerymen to see their targets and adjust their fire from Seminary Ridge as they had done the day before against the Union lines on Little Round Top.

ammunition, except canister, were compelled to withhold their fire until the enemy, who approached in three lines, came within range."[68]

If Pickett's Division was having a bad day on the right, Pettigrew's and Trimble's soldiers were having a worse day on the left of the long gray line. Col. John Brockenbrough, a Virginia Military Institute graduate and a veteran of the battles of Fredericksburg and Chancellorsville, was in command of the Second Brigade of Pettigrew's Division, positioned on the left flank. There is no record that Brockenbrough marched with his men toward Cemetery Ridge that day, however, and Col. Robert M. Mayo of the 47th Virginia Infantry was in temporary command. It is possible that the death of Brockenbrough's brother during the battle on July 1 left him distraught and unable to step up to his responsibilities. Assigned to the far left flank of Pettigrew's divisional line, the brigade was subjected to heavy shelling from Union artillery on Cemetery Hill. When the 8th Ohio Infantry and the 125th New York State Volunteers from Hays' Division came up on their left flank and opened an enfilading fire, the Virginians turned and retreated.[69] Some, caught in a crossfire, were the first to surrender.

Twenty-three-year-old Chaplain Ezra D. Simons, the Baptist chaplain for the 125th New York, recorded the events that caused the Confederate flank to crumble:

> Captain Samuel C. Armstrong was in charge of the brigade pickets. During the morning the men hugged the ground, for the firing was hot, the rebels pouring in a flank fire on the picket line from the houses in Gettysburg, killing and wounding some of our men. Noticing a lull in the cannonading, Captain Armstrong looked around and saw the Confederate lines marching grandly down the slope towards our men.
>
> He immediately ordered the entire picket reserve and all he could muster—about seventy-five all told—to fall in, and led them on the "double-quick" about three hundred yards down the Emmettsburg road, to get at the enemy in flank. Finding a rail fence at right angle to their advancing line, some sixty or seventy yards from their extreme left, he posted his men along the rail fence. They took position unflinchingly; and, resting their rifles on the top of the fence, took deliberate aim and

---

[68] "Report of Gen. Henry J. Hunt, USA, Chief of Artillery, Army of the Potomac," War Department, *Official Records*, part 2: 240.

[69] As cited in https://en.wikipedia.org/wiki/John_M._Brockenbrough, 1–2, accessed November 2014.

poured a murderous fire into the rebel flank, comprising Pettigrew's men.[70]

Meanwhile the 8th Ohio Infantry, approximately 160 men, took cover behind a board fence and poured more fire into the Confederate flank. Private T. S. Potter of Company H recorded: "The slaughter among them was fearful. They struggled and fought bravely, but it was of no avail. We had captured three battle flags and a large number of prisoners, but we had lost fearfully—107 killed and wounded."[71]

Chaplain Simons was even more descriptive in his regimental history:

From Captain Armstrong's position [with the 125th New York] the Confederate dead could be seen lying in heaps. Hundreds of the charging line prostrated themselves on their backs in the Emmitsburg Road, and waved their hats and handkerchiefs in token of surrender. Some of the bravest rushed close to the main Union line and fell a few yards away. The Confederate leader afterwards confessed surprise that this part of the charging line should have been the first to break. Of the five officers who served with Captain Armstrong in his brave action, which aided in the great victory secured, he was the only survivor.[72]

Sixty-one-year-old Maj. Gen. Isaac Trimble led two North Carolina brigades from Pender's Division forward to support Pettigrew's men. Neither brigade was under its original commander, and many of the men were wearing bandages, still recovering from wounds received on July 1. Trimble, who lost a leg in the attack, left his recollection of the events along with a suggestion regarding the attack itself:

We marched 3/4 mile under a terrible fire, passed the first line & reached a point some 200 yards from the breastworks—here the men broke down from exhaustion & fatal fire & went no further but walked sullenly back to their entrenchments. It was a mistake to charge batteries & lines over so great a distance, every yard exposed to a hot fire. Had we marched at night to 1/2 mile of the works it is I think certain we should have carried them...the enemy admit they "Shook in their shoes." I was shot through

---

[70] Ezra D. Simons, *A Regimental History: The One Hundred and Twenty-Fifth New York State Volunteers* (New York: Ezra D. Simons, 1888) 136–38.

[71] Rollins, *Pickett's Charge*, 298–300.

[72] Simons, *A Regimental History*, 136–38.

the left leg on horseback near the close of the fight, my fine mare after taking me off the field died of the same shot....[73]

Twenty-four-year-old Col. James K. Marshall commanded the First Brigade in Pettigrew's Division. A grandson of Chief Justice John Marshall, James had graduated from Virginia Military Institute in 1860. His brigade, which had lost 1,100 of its 2,500 soldiers during the first day's fighting, rested on July 2. Colonel Marshall had the band play music that day to raise morale.[74]

On July 3, Marshall's Brigade was at the center of Pettigrew's Division. His men made the 1,100-yard march in good order, though like the rest of the division, there were high casualties from Union artillery. As his brigade climbed over a five-foot fence and neared the wall, Colonel Marshall was killed instantly by two bullets in the forehead while cheering his men on.[75] One of his regiments, the 26th North Carolina Infantry, made it to the stone wall before it was forced to retire. In this charge the 26th North Carolina had eight color-bearers shot down and suffered 120 casualties out of its contingent of 212 men. A small monument at Gettysburg marks their farthest advance.

On Colonel Marshall's left, Brig. Gen. Joseph Davis's Mississippi Brigade was so decimated by the time they reached the stone wall that marked the Union line that Davis decided "any further effort to carry the position was hopeless." Davis's survivors made it back to Seminary Ridge about 4 P.M., an hour after they had initially moved forward.[76]

On the right flank of Pettigrew's Division, Col. Birkett Fry's Brigade also made it to the wall, but there Colonel Fry was wounded and captured. Fry wrote later, "All of the five regimental colors of my command reached the line of the enemy's works, and many of my men and officers were killed or wounded after passing over it. I believe that the Federal troops—probably blinded by the smoke—continued a rapid fire for some minutes after none but dead and wounded remained in their front."[77]

---

[73] Isaac R. Trimble, "Civil War Diary of I. R. Trimble," *Maryland Historical Magazine* 17/1 (March 1922): 1–2.

[74] As cited in http://en.wikipedia.org/wiki/James_K._Marshall, 2, accessed November 2014.

[75] Ibid.

[76] Rollins, *Pickett's Charge*, 255–56.

[77] B. D. Fry, "Pettigrew's Charge at Gettysburg," *Southern Historical Society Papers* 7/2 (1879): 93.

More than 1,600 rounds of artillery were fired at Pettigrew's men during the assault. Portions of the assault never advanced much farther than the sturdy fence at the Emmitsburg road. By this time, the Confederates were close enough to be fired on by artillery using canister, and Alexander Hays's Division unleashed very effective musketry fire from behind 260 yards of stone wall, with every rifleman of the division lined up as many as four deep, exchanging places in line as they fired and then falling back to reload.[78]

At this point in the battle, at about 3:45 P.M., six of the nine Confederate brigades in the main attack were already halted under fire or in retreat back toward Seminary Ridge. Pickett's Division of three brigades would last a few minutes more.

Chaplain Alexander Betts of the 30th North Carolina Infantry had spent the afternoon visiting one hospital after another behind the Confederate lines and was eventually overcome by exhaustion. He fell from his horse, and remained unconscious for an hour. He wrote later that day, "God could take a man out of this world without his knowing anything of it."[79]

The Last Hurrah

On the right flank, Pickett's Virginians crossed the Emmitsburg road and wheeled partially to their left to face northeast. They marched in two lines, led by the brigades of Brig. Gen. James L. Kemper on the right and Brig. Gen. Richard B. Garnett on the left. Brig. Gen. Lewis A. Armistead's Brigade followed closely behind. As the division wheeled to the left, its right flank was exposed to McGilvery's guns and the front of Doubleday's Union Division on Cemetery Ridge. Stannard's Vermont Brigade marched forward, faced north, and delivered withering fire into the rear of Kemper's Brigade.

General Kemper, on horseback, was wounded and captured, only to be recaptured and returned to the Seminary Ridge line. He was the only brigade commander to survive the assault. His brigade, caught in an L-shaped ambush, "almost entirely disappeared," wrote Lt. Wyatt Whitman of the 53rd Virginia Infantry, "for they received the brunt of the enemy's merciless

[78] Stephen W. Sears, *Gettysburg* (Boston: Houghton Mifflin, 2003) 429–31.

[79] Alexander Davis Betts, DD, *Experience of a Confederate Chaplain 1861–1864*, ed. W. A. Betts (Greenville, SC: Privately printed, 1904). See digital copy at http://docsouth.unc.edu/fpn/betts/betts.html, 22, accessed November 2014.

fire and were lying wounded and dead upon the valley across which we had come."[80]

General Garnett, also on horseback, led his men to within 20 feet of the wall when he was shot off his horse by canister. Private James Clay of the 18th Virginia Infantry described what happened next:

During the next fifteen minutes the contending forces were engaged in a life and death struggle, our men using the butts of their rifles. At this time a number of Federals threw down their arms and started across the field to our rear. Two of them came to the clump of rocks where Capt. Campbell and I were and asked to be allowed to assist us to our rear, obviously for mutual safety, and the kind offer was accepted. These men told us that our brigade general had been killed, having been shot through the body at the waist by a grapeshot. Just before these men reached us Gen. Garnett's horse came galloping toward us with a huge gash in his right shoulder, evidently struck by a piece of shell.[81]

Garnett's Brigade, like Kemper's, was reduced to a handful of survivors.

Leadership in Blue

Like their Confederate opponents, the Union generals along the front were conspicuous by their leadership under fire to encourage the men and to rush reinforcements to the line. Brig. Gen. Alexander Hays, commander of the Third Division, a graduate of West Point in the Class of 1844 with Winfield Scott Hancock and a close friend of Gen. U. S. Grant, was said by his men to be "as brave as a lion."[82] During Pettigrew's attack, Hays rode up and down his line yelling, "Hurrah! Boys, we're giving them hell."[83] In spite of having two horses shot out from under him, Hays was unwounded as the gray lines in his front melted away.

At about this time, Union general Hancock, who had been prominent in displaying himself on horseback to his men during the Confederate artillery bombardment, was wounded by a bullet striking the pommel of his saddle, entering his inner right thigh along with wood fragments and a large

[80] Wyatt Whitman as quoted in Maud Carter Clement, *The History of Pittsylvania County Virginia* (Baltimore, MD: Regional/Genealogical Publishing Company, 1937) 248–50.

[81] James Clay, "About the Death of General Garnett," as cited in Rollins, *Pickett's Charge*, 150.

[82] Larry Tagg, *The Generals of Gettysburg* (Campbell, CA: Savas Publishing Co., 1998) 53.

[83] Rollins, *Pickett's Charge*, 301.

bent nail. He refused evacuation to the rear until the battle was settled. Not far away, Brig. Gen. John Gibbon, Second Division commander, was wounded in the left shoulder and turned over his division to Brig. Gen. William Harrow, his First Brigade commander.

As Pickett's men advanced, they withstood the defensive fire of first Stannard's Brigade, then Harrow's, and then Hall's, before approaching a minor salient in the Union center, a low stone wall taking an 80-yard right-angle turn known afterward as "The Angle." It was defended by Brig. Gen. Alexander S. Webb's Philadelphia Brigade. Webb placed the two remaining guns of Lt. Alonzo Cushing's Battery A, 4th US Artillery, at the front of his line at the stone fence, with the 69th and 71st Pennsylvania regiments of his brigade to defend the fence and the guns. The two guns and 940 men could not match the massive firepower that Hays's Division, to their right, had been able to unleash.

Two gaps opened up in the Union line. The commander of the 71st Pennsylvania ordered his men to retreat when the Confederates came too close to the Angle, and south of the copse of trees, the men of the 59th New York in Hall's Brigade inexplicably bolted for the rear. In the latter case, this left Captain Andrew Cowan and his 1st New York Independent Artillery Battery to face the oncoming infantry. Assisted personally by Artillery Chief Henry Hunt, Cowan ordered five guns to fire double canister simultaneously. The entire Confederate line to his front disappeared. The gap vacated by most of the 71st Pennsylvania, however, was more serious, leaving only a handful of the 71st, 268 men of the 69th Pennsylvania, and Lt. Alonzo Cushing's two three-inch rifled guns to receive the 2,500 to 3,000 men of Garnett's and Armistead's brigades as they began to cross the stone wall. The Irishmen of the 69th Pennsylvania resisted fiercely in a melee of rifle fire, bayonets, and fists. Webb, mortified that the 71st had retreated, attempted to bring the 72nd Pennsylvania (a Zouave regiment) forward, but they did not immediately obey the order. Instead, the veteran regiment formed a line of battle approximately 80 yards up the ridge. Two other regiments, the 19th and 20th Massachusetts infantry from Hall's Brigade, had to fill the gap. During the fight, Lt. Alonzo Cushing was killed, three bullets striking him as he fired his last gun alone.

As General Webb struggled to hold his part of the line, he personally led his reserve regiments forward:

I ordered my few guns to fire and we opened great gaps in them and steadily they advanced in four solid lines right up to my works and fences, and shot my men with their muskets touching their breasts; seeing two companies driven out, all my artillery in their hands, I ordered up my reserve right and led it up myself. General Armistead, an old army officer, led his men, came over my fences and passed me with four of his men. He fell mortally wounded. I got but one shot, grazing my thigh. I stood but thirty-nine paces from them. Their officers pointed me out, but God preserved me. As soon as I got my regiment up to the wall, the enemy was whipped for good and all. When they came over the fences, the army of the Potomac was nearer being whipped than it was at any time of the battle. When my men fell back I almost wished to get killed. I was almost disgraced but [Colonel Norman] Hall on my left saw it all and brought up two regiments to help me.[84]

The Confederates seized his two guns and turned them to face the Union troops, but they had no ammunition to fire. As more Union reinforcements arrived and charged into the breach, the defensive line became impregnable and the Confederates began to slip away individually, with no senior officers remaining to call a formal retreat.[85]

The Pickett-Pettigrew infantry assault lasted about an hour. The supporting attack by Wilcox's and Perry's brigades on Pickett's right was of little help. They did not approach the Union line until after Pickett was defeated, and their advance was quickly broken up by McGilvery's guns and by

---

[84] Letter of Brigadier General Webb to his wife, July 6, 1863, as cited in Rollins, *Pickett's Charge*, 317. Webb received the Medal of Honor on September 28, 1891, for "distinguished personal gallantry in leading his men forward at a critical period in the contest" at Gettysburg on July 3, 1863. President Lincoln nominated Webb for appointment to the brevet grade of major general of volunteers for his service at Gettysburg, to rank from August 1, 1864, and the US Senate confirmed the appointment on February 14, 1865, accessed November 2014, https://en.wikipedia.org/wiki/Alexander_S._Webb5.

[85] The nine infantry regiments reinforcing Webb's Brigade included the 72nd Pennsylvania, the 19th, and 20th Massachusetts, the 42nd New York, the 7th Michigan, the 19th Maine, the 15th Massachusetts, the 82nd New York, and the 1st Minnesota, as cited in Rollins, *Pickett's Charge*, 333–34. For more information about the 72nd Pennsylvania Infantry and their role in stopping Armistead's advance, see Stephen W. Sears, *Gettysburg* (New York: Houghton Mifflin Co., 2004) 451 and Brig. Gen. Alexander Webb's testimony in Rollins, *Pickett's Charge*, 317.

Stannard's Vermont Brigade, which once again fired into the flank of the Confederate infantry.[86]

As the survivors of what became the most famous charge of the Civil War straggled back to their Seminary Ridge line, many to wash their wounds in a creek that turned red from their blood, General Lee rode up to speak to General Pickett. Just then General Kemper, the sole surviving brigade commander, was carried back from the field on a litter. Private Charles T. Loehr of the First Virginia recorded the scene:

General Pickett broke out into tears, while General Lee rode up to him and they shook hands. General Lee spoke to General Pickett in a slow and distinct manner. Anyone could see that he, too, felt the repulse and slaughter of the division, whose remains he viewed. Of the remarks made to General Pickett by General Lee, we distinctly heard him say: "General Pickett, your men have done all that men could do; the fault is entirely my own." These words will never be forgotten.[87]

Across the field the rebel yell had been supplanted by cheers from the Union soldiers, who realized that the battle was over, "Hurrah! Hurrah! Hurrah!" On the Confederate side, a regimental band began to play "Nearer My God to Thee" as the ambulances arrived.[88]

From a stone house on the edge of the battlefield, Chaplain Sheeran with the 14th Louisiana Infantry in Ewell's Corps, reflected:

We now discover but too late that our line of battle is too extended, being some six miles, and consequently we were without reserves where they were most needed. At every charge our men drove the enemy from their guns, but for want of sufficient support were unable to keep them. The enemy on the contrary had their lines contracted, and their army concentrated so that they could throw a powerful force on any point and very quickly. By this arrangement of the enemy's forces they suffered, it is true, terribly from the shells of our batteries, but they were enabled to throw an immense force on any advance of our weak, because too extended, lines. General Lee seeming now to despair of carrying the enemy's works reforms and contracts his line. His left is drawn in and his right

---

[86] https://en.wikipedia.org/wiki/Pickett%27s_Charge, 9, accessed January 30, 2016.

[87] Charles T. Loehr, "The 'Old First' Virginia at Gettysburg," *Southern Historical Society Papers*, vol. XXXII (January–December 1904) 37.

[88] Michael Lanning, *The Civil War 100* (Napierville, IL: Sourcebooks, Inc., 2007) 244.

and centre made more compact. In this position he defies the enemy to come out of his works and try the fate of a fair and open battle.[89]

Gen. George G. Meade

When the fighting died down, General Meade, who was behind the crest of Cemetery Hill and had not seen the events along the stone wall, arrived on horseback to view the Union line. Lt. Frank Haskell, a staff officer in Gibbon's Division, informed the commanding general of the victory:

> As he arrived near me, coming up the hill, he asked in a sharp, eager voice: "How is it going here?" "I believe, General, the enemy's attack is repulsed," I answered. Still approaching, and a new light began to come in his face, of gratified surprise, with a touch of incredulity, of which his voice was also the medium, he further asked: "What? Is the assault entirely repulsed?"—his voice quicker and more eager than before. "It is, Sir:" I replied. By this time he was on the crest; and when his eye had for an instant swept over the field, taking in just a glance of the whole—the masses of prisoners—the numerous captured flags, which the men were derisively flaunting about—the fugitives of the routed enemy, disappearing with the speed of terror in the woods, partly at what I had told him, partly at what he saw, he said impassively, and his face was lighted: "*Thank God.*"[90]

According to the Union count, some 792 unwounded Confederate soldiers, largely from Pettigrew's and Pickett's divisions, surrendered along the Emmitsburg road. While the Union lost about 2,500 killed and wounded, total Confederate losses during the attack were approximately 6,840, of which at least 1,123 Confederates were killed on the battlefield, 4,019 were wounded, and a good number of the injured were also captured.[91] Pickett's Division alone suffered 2,655 casualties: 498 killed, 643 wounded, 833 wounded and captured, and 681 captured unwounded. Every one of his fifteen regimental commanders had fallen, as had sixteen of seventeen field officers under them. Two brigadier generals and six colonels were among the division's dead.[92]

---

[89] Joseph T. Durkin, SJ, ed., *Confederate Chaplain: A War Journal of Rev. James B. Sheeran, c.ss.r., 14th Louisiana, CSA* (Milwaukee, WI: Bruce Publishing Co., 1960) 48–49.

[90] As cited in Rollins, *Pickett's Charge*, 371–72.

[91] "Pickett's Charge," accessed November 2014, http://en.wikipedia.org/wiki/Pickett%27s_Charge, 12.

[92] Knauer, *Gettysburg: A Day-by-Day Account*, 103.

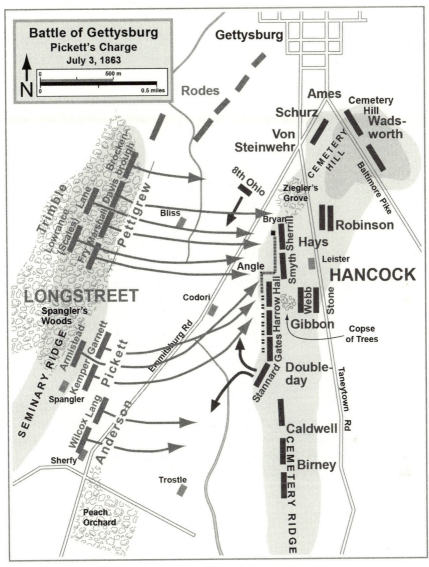

Map of the Pettigrew-Pickett Charge, July 3, 1863. Map by Hal Jespersen.

Major General Winfield S. Hancock at Gettysburg. Courtesy of Henry Hird III, photographer of the Gettysburg Cyclorama and editor of the *Gettysburg National Military Park Handbook*, 2011.

Union soldiers marching through Centreville, Virginia, June 20, 1863.
Credit: Library of Congress.

Some of the 12,000 or so Confederate prisoners who were wounded or captured at Gettysburg start their long journey to prison camps in Maryland, Ohio, or New York. Many who survived were not freed until the winter of 1865. Credit: Library of Congress.

Brigadier General Armistead leading his brigade against the Union lines near a copse of trees on July 3, 1863. Armistead died from his wounds at the Spangler Farm two days later.
Credit: Library of Congress.

North Carolina Monument on Confederate Avenue, Gettysburg. Photo by the author.

Lieutenant General A. P. Hill's artillery along Confederate Avenue. Photo by Justine Hill.

Brigadier General Lewis Armistead CSA and Captain Henry Bingham USA. Friend to Friend Masonic Memorial, Gettysburg. Photo by the author.

Major General Meade's statue on Cemetery Ridge facing west
toward his main battle line. Photo by the author.

Detail of figure of Union soldier atop the 72nd Pennsylvania
Infantry Monument. Credit: National Park Service.

Maryland Monument at Gettysburg showing a Union soldier helping a wounded Confederate counterpart. Credit: National Park Service.

Lieutenant Sanford Branch, 8th Georgia Infantry, on cot at right, recuperates in a Federal field hospital after being left for dead on the field. Credit: Atlanta History Center, DuBose Collection.

Christ Lutheran Church in Gettysburg served as a military hospital during the battle. Chaplain Horatio Howell, 90th Pennsylvania Infantry, was shot and killed on the front steps. There is a memorial to him placed there by the veterans of his regiment in 1889. Photo by the author.

Nurse Georgeanna Woolsey, U.S. Sanitary Commission.
Credit: *The US Sanitary Commission*, 1863.

Dr. Jonathan Letterman, Medical Director of the Army of the Potomac.
Credit: US Army Medical Department Museum, Ft. Sam Houston, TX.

Confederate Dead from the 2nd South Carolina Infantry at Gettysburg.
Credit: Library of Congress.

Gettysburg National Cemetery. Credit: Photo by the author.

Tombstone for Chaplain and Mrs. John Stuckenberg
in the Gettysburg National Cemetery. Photo by the author.

President Abraham Lincoln arrived at Gettysburg by train on November 18, 1863 to dedicate the National Cemetery the next day. The next week, on November 25, the nation celebrated Thanksgiving Day, decreed by Lincoln after the victories at Vicksburg and Gettysburg. That same day, November 25, 1863, General Grant relayed the news of yet another triumph for the Union—the victorious Battle of Missionary Ridge south of Chattanooga.

Chapter 6

July 4, 1863
Prisoners of Hope:

The Quick, the Dead, and the Exhausted

The Quick, the Dead, and the Exhausted[1]
"I thanked God that we had been spared."[2]
—Chaplain John H. W. Stuckenberg,
145th Pennsylvania Infantry

Somehow the Confederate artillery found enough reserve ammunition at the end of the day to begin firing a few more rounds at the Union lines. Acting chaplain Charles J. Oliver from the Troup Artillery seemed jubilant over the part his guns played:

> Late in the afternoon when the firing was slack Capt Carlton was knocked down by something too much spent to hurt the flesh, but it did break his arm above the elbow.... I mounted a horse and went in search of some spirits.[3] The first surgeon I found gave it to me grudgingly, and I rode back a mile through the dying and wounded of Pickets division a ghastly procession.... The pieces had moved forwarded. I believe it was the proudest moment of my life. I realized the danger—thought it doubtful I should live to recross the hill, but commending my soul to God I ascended the hill at an easy trot, and when I reached the crest and saw the flash of the guns on the other hill, I sang and shouted with delight. If I was ever proud of being a member of the Troop Artillery, it was then.

---

[1] Zechariah 9:12 (RSV): "Return to your stronghold, O prisoners of hope...."

[2] As cited in David T. Hedrick and Gordon Barry Davis, Jr., eds., *I'm Surrounded by Methodists...Diary of John H. W. Stuckenberg, Chaplain of the 145th Pennsylvania Volunteer Infantry* (Gettysburg, PA: Thomas Publications, 1995) 83.

[3] Captain H. H. Carleton, commander of the Troup Artillery. See Richard Rollins, ed., *Pickett's Charge: Eyewitness Accounts* (Torrance, CA: Rank and File Publications, 1994), Appendix A, 383 ff for a list of the regimental and battery commanders in both armies.

Our guns had ceased firing when I reached them, and the enemy fired only occasionally. By order of Gen. Lee we remained there until after nightfall and some skirmishers were advanced to our line.[4]

Chaplain Peter Tinsley, with Pickett's Division, was very busy on the evening of July 3 recording his observations, comforting the wounded, and helping to bury the dead in hasty and shallow graves:

Poor Col Allen falls fighting valliantly & now lies unknelled & uncoffined in an unknown grave.[5] Gen'L Armistead mounts the breastworks & putting his hat upon his sabre cheers on his brave men—but falls wounded & is captured.[6] Like him hundreds fall in the embrace of death to sleep in a stranger land & in an unknown grave or are destined to pine and suffer, perhaps die in a gloomy hospital. Poor Maj Wilson is brought from the field by four of his men. A gallant youth! He frequently inquires for me as his men bear him from the field.

The scene at our field hospital stand is horrid beyond description & by far the worst I have ever seen. Friend after friend comes in & gives the most dreadful account of the slaughter of his comrades so that, that which we hear of is worse almost than what we see.

After all the men are sent off to Division Hosp. at Breams Mill, I go there also & attend the wounded, taking with me the body of Maj. Wilson to bury it.[7] Besides those I had already seen, I find at the Hosp. Gen'l Kemper, mortally wounded, as is supposed.[8] Mr. John T. Currens,

---

[4] As cited in John W. Brinsfield, William C. Davis, Benedict Maryniak, and James I. Robertson, Jr., *Faith in the Fight: Civil War Chaplains* (Mechanicsburg, PA: Stackpole Books, 2003) 107.

[5] Colonel R. C. Allen of the 28th Virginia Infantry, Chaplain Tinsley's regimental commander.

[6] Brig. Gen. Lewis Armistead died on July 5, 1863, at the George Spangler farm on Blacksmith Shop Road.

[7] Bream's Mill was about 400 feet from the John Currens farmhouse on the north side of Plank Road. Major Nathaniel Wilson was buried on July 4 under a walnut tree in front of John Currens's house. He was buried wrapped in a blanket with his sword.

[8] Brig. Gen. James Kemper did not die from his wound but was left behind and captured. He was exchanged two months later but did not recover from his wound in time to take another field command. He was elected the thirty-seventh governor of Virginia during Reconstruction.

at whose house our quarters are, seems very polite & professes peace sentiments.[9]

Behind the Union lines, Chaplain Ezra Simons of the 125th New York Infantry described the challenges the surgeons faced as a rainstorm arrived during the night:

At the rear were the dead, and the dying, and the suffering wounded. Barns and houses were crowded with wounded men. The outlying grounds were covered. On rude benches the surgeons wrought their needful, merciful work. The barn—on the Taneytown road, on the very battlefield—that served as a hospital for the One Hundred and Twenty-Fifth and of other regiments...was full of the wounded. The stalls were full of them; the loft was full, the yard in front and rear was full.

That night, given to the care of hundreds of suffering men—Confederates and Union men mingled—remains a dark, dread memory. But, over against the darkness of the suffering was the brightness of victory: and the price paid in blood was none too great for the fruitage to the Nation and the world. Some things are evermore costly; and they are the more prized because their price is paid in blood and death. Rock Creek, in that night of storm, overflowed its banks, and the ground where the wounded were lying was flooded. The men were hastily moved, some being taken from a foot depth of water.[10]

Chaplain John H. W. Stuckenberg, 145th Pennsylvania Infantry, spent his time on the evening of July 3 and 4 conducting a worship service in Caldwell's Division and tending to the wounded who were not yet under shelter:

I was requested by the Major of the 64th N.Y. to hold services in his regt.[11] I did so immediately after leaving our dead. The men were behind their breastworks, I stood in front of them. Brisk skirmishing was going on all the time, rebels and our men and rebels as well as our men could be seen running and firing. A rebel flag was also seen at the edge of the woods. Worship at such a place, at such a time, with fearful scenes

---

[9] Peter Archer Tinsley (1833–1908), "Private Diary," in John and Joyce Schmale Civil War Collection, Wheaton (IL) College Archives, box 1, folder 51: item 28, p. 23.

[10] Ezra D. Simons, *A Regimental History: The One Hundred and Twenty-Fifth New York State Volunteers* (New York: Ezra D. Simons, 1888) 146.

[11] Major L. W. Bradley, commanding the 64th New York Volunteer Infantry in Chaplain Stuckenberg's brigade.

just enacted and being enacted, was very solemn. I thanked God that we had been spared, prayed for the many wounded and remembered the relatives and friends of the killed. The soldiers felt deeply and many were moved to tears.

In the afternoon it rained very hard. There was not a hospital tent at our hospital. Some of the wounded were in shelter tents which sheltered them poorly, others lay in the rain and mud, covered with a woolen or rubber blanket—or nothing at all. I labored to shelter them till I was wet through, and returned to my tent very weary and sick. After the rain I got some hay and placed under the wounded. I gave my rubber blanket to one of our men, my woolen one to Wm Brown, and tore another woolen one...and divided it between E. Allen and H. Mann Co. I.[12]

What a hospital on or near the field of battle is can only be known by those that have seen one. There were between 2000 and 3000 wounded in our 2nd Corps hospital. In 1st Division there were two operating stands, where the Surgeons were constantly consulting about operations and performing amputations. Heaps of amputated foot and hands, arms and legs were seen under the tables and by their sides.[13]

The Rolling Chaplain

About 8 P.M. on July 3 the guns on both sides had fallen silent. Chaplain William Eastman of the 72nd New York Infantry rode into the Wheatfield near Little Round Top looking for wounded soldiers he might be able to help. An artillery round went off nearby, and Eastman's horse shied, stumbled, and then pitched over on Eastman's leg. Chaplain Eastman was able to extricate his leg from under the horse, but he couldn't bear to stand on it. He could hear the moans and cries of the wounded around him, and he still had canteens of water. His solution was to roll across the ground to the nearest wounded soldier, give him some water, then roll to the next. This went on for some time until two Union soldiers found him and constructed a makeshift litter to carry the chaplain around the field. Eventually more stretcher-bearers arrived, and Chaplain Eastman agreed to go back to the Third Corps hospital.

---

[12] Corporal Horace Mann, Company I, was wounded in the thigh but recovered from his wound.

[13] As cited in David T. Hedrick and Gordon Barry Davis, Jr., eds., *I'm Surrounded by Methodists...Diary of John H. W. Stuckenberg, Chaplain of the 145th Pennsylvania Volunteer Infantry* (Gettysburg, PA: Thomas Publications, 1995) 83.

When Maj. Gen. O. O. Howard, the Eleventh Corps commander, heard the story of "the Rolling Chaplain," he included Eastman among the unsung heroes of the Battle of Gettysburg in a pamphlet he published afterwards.[14] Eastman, however, never completely recovered from his injury, though he remained on duty until he was discharged with his unit in June 1864. Eastman was the third Union chaplain to become a casualty on the fields of Gettysburg.

Chaplain Joseph Twichell, Eastman's friend and colleague in the neighboring 71st New York Infantry, spoke of the stench of the battlefield but also of the importance of cause and faith:

> I got away awhile to bury our dead on the field and look up the wounded that had been left to the enemy. The Confederate line had been withdrawn a little so that this was possible. In a pouring rain we performed the last sad offices for the fallen and left them in soldiers' graves. We found five of our wounded. They had lain two nights on the ground—three of them with broken legs—suffering God alone knows how much.
>
> It was the most terrible battle field I ever beheld. The stench was almost unendurable and the dead lay everywhere. In one place more than 30 were gathered together and the look of their bloated, blakened corpses was a thing to murder sleep.
>
> We sent but 13 line officers into the field—of them 6 were wounded and one killed. The Adjutant also was wounded.... The Army of the Union has fought as if appreciating its Cause. The accidents of war are dreadful, but the fruits of such a war as this amply pay the cost. As Gen. Sickles said "a man isn't much," weighed against Faith. We have undoubtedly gained a victory. God be praised![15]

Back to Old Virginia

At approximately 4 P.M. on July 4, 1863, General Lee's Army of Northern Virginia began its retreat back to Hagerstown and Williamsport. With wagon trains stretching as long as 17 miles, the procession moved very

---

[14] Oliver O. Howard, "Sketches about Private Charles McDonald, Captain William Duncan, 1st Lieutenant William McIntyre, and Chaplain W. R. Eastman," in the O. O. Howard Papers, Special Collections, Bowdoin [College] Library, catalog number M 91.8, item 43, number 19.

[15] As cited in Peter Messent and Steve Courtney, eds., *The Civil War Letters of Joseph Hopkins Twichell* (Athens: University of Georgia Press, 2006) 249, 252.

slowly through rain and mud.[16] Longstreet's Corps led the way, with Ewell's Corps not leaving Gettysburg until July 5. According to the official reports, Lee had lost 20,451 soldiers, killed, wounded, and missing, although later estimates reached 28,000, or 37 percent of his effective fighting force.[17] Although numbers are often hard to authenticate, the Union forces documented 12,227 Confederate soldiers captured during the three-day battle; 5,425 of them were unwounded.[18]

Three of the Confederate chaplains recorded their memories of the preparations and conduct of the retreat. Chaplain Milton Kennedy of the 28th North Carolina Infantry had watched Pickett's Charge from "an eminence upon which Gen'l Lee was stationed," and thought the scene was "terribly sublime."[19] Yet Kennedy also noted on July 3 that his brigade had "suffered very heavily, my Regiment losing a great many in killed and wounded," and that "the Medical Department was badly managed today causing a good deal of unnecessary pain and trouble to the wounded."[20]

Kennedy went on to write that Pickett's Charge "is *the mistake* of the campaign and will be well for us if our repulse does not grow into our disaster."[21]

On July 4, in the rain, Kennedy recorded the evacuation of his wounded soldiers:

> Our wounded were all moved 3 miles back and, while there was no fighting, everything looked like a retrograde movement. This afternoon all the slightly wounded, and such others as transportation could be provided were started back in the direction of Cashtown.... I had my feelings sorely tried when telling the officers and other men good-bye who were so seriously wounded as to disqualify them for traveling. About sundown we received orders to start with the medical train in an hour by another road.[22]

---

[16] Kelly Knauer, ed., *Gettysburg: A Day-by-Day Account of the Greatest Battle of the Civil War* (New York: Time Books, 2013), 112.

[17] Jay Luvass and Harold W, Nelson, *Guide to the Battle of Gettysburg*, 231.

[18] War Department, *Official Records*, part 1: 151.

[19] As cited in John W. Brinsfield et al., *Faith in the Fight*, 111.

[20] Ibid., 112. The 28th North Carolina Infantry was part of Lane's Brigade in Pender's Division, Gen. A. P. Hill's Corps.

[21] Ibid.

[22] Ibid.

The sad fact for both armies was that many of the wounded were not able to be moved immediately from the battlefield. Dr. Jonathan Letterman, medical director for the Army of the Potomac, reported 6,802 Confederate wounded left on the fields or in the hospitals in Gettysburg.[23]

They joined the Union wounded that numbered 14,529. On July 4, the total number of wounded soldiers from both armies was not less than 21,331.[24] Of the 650 medical officers in the Union army, one had been killed, 13 wounded, and 106 left behind to provide medical care to the 21,000 wounded men, a ratio of one surgeon to 200 patients.[25]

Of course, not all the casualties were numbered among the killed or wounded. On July 4, there were 5,365 Union soldiers who had been captured or were missing and 5,150 Confederate soldiers unaccounted for.[26] Chaplain Charles Holt Dobbs of the 12th Mississippi Infantry reported some soldiers just walking away:

> I met numbers of men who had been slightly wounded and were sent to this hospital [at the Lutheran seminary] and were not returning, determined to walk to Staunton, rather than be captured. Many of them I knew, and they tried to persuade me to return, as I would be captured. I was bent, however, on the work of ministering to these poor fellows, so on I went. I hastened back to the hospital, where I found everything packed, preparatory to a backward movement. There was no haste, however, no undue confusion, and nothing like a panic. As we fell slowly back, requisitions of horses, medicines, and clothing were made on the various towns. The army moved with great, good order, considering the disastrous results.[27]

The last Union chaplain to be listed as a casualty at Gettysburg was a Methodist, Chaplain Louis Napoleon Boudrye of the 5th New York Cavalry Regiment. The 30-year-old clergyman had been a chaplain for just over five months when he accompanied his regiment, part of Brig. Gen. Elon J. Farnsworth's Brigade, Kilpatrick's Cavalry Division, to Gettysburg. Boudrye

---

[23] War Department, *Official Records*, part 2: 198, 346.

[24] Ibid., and report in Jay Luvass and Harold W. Nelson (eds.) *Guide to the Battle of Gettysburg*, 231.

[25] War Department, *Official Records*, part 2: 197–98.

[26] As cited in Jay Luvass and Harold W. Nelson (eds.) *Guide to the Battle of Gettysburg*, 231.

[27] As cited in John Wesley Brinsfield, Jr., *The Spirit Divided: Memoirs of Civil War Chaplains—The Confederacy* (Macon, GA: Mercer University Press, 2005), 68. The 12th Mississippi Infantry was in Posey's Brigade of General A. P. Hill's Corps.

was a witness to numerous cavalry skirmishes, including the one on July 3 in which his brigade commander was killed.[28]

During a pursuit of Confederate wagon trains on July 5, a very dark night, Boudrye was captured at Monterey Springs at the southern end of South Mountain. He was marched for two weeks to Libby Prison in Richmond, where he remained until his exchange on October 7, 1863. Boudrye survived his time as a prisoner, but he contracted malaria, which eventually entitled him to an army pension. Boudrye was the fourth Union army chaplain to be killed, wounded, injured in combat, or captured during the Gettysburg Campaign.[29]

In Chaplain Boudrye's account of the cavalry pursuit of Lee's army, he suggested that there was confusion and sometimes panic in the Confederate ranks. Not everyone agreed with that assessment. Father James Sheeran, riding half asleep with the men of the 14th Louisiana Infantry, noted his feelings on the retreat south:

> How agreeably did these men disappoint me! They had fought hard at Gettysburg, but failed to drive the enemy from their stronghold, and were now falling back and wading to their knees in mud and mire. These circumstances, calculated to depress the spirits of even the bravest men, had no such effect on these Confederate heroes. They were as cheerful a body of men as I ever saw; and to hear them, you would think they were going to a party of pleasure instead of retreating from a hard fought battle.[30]

Perhaps one reason Chaplain Sheeran's troops were in high spirits was that they, unlike the wagon train drivers, were not immediately attacked or hotly pursued during the first few days of the retreat. In fact, Lee was able to wait ten days, until July 14, to get the Army of Northern Virginia across the

---

[28] Chaplain Peter Tinsley overheard a conversation between two soldiers who said that a Yankee Brigadier General in the cavalry had shot himself with his pistol to keep from being captured. No name for the supposed suicide was given. Tinsley, "Private Diary," entry of August 4, 1863, page 57.

[29] Chaplain Boudrye was the author of the *Historical Records of the Fifth New York Cavalry* (1865). The details of his capture are on page 202. The Louis Napoleon Boudrye Papers are in the Wheaton College (IL) Archives and Special Collections, Series 1, Box 1, Item 10 See http://library.wheaton.edu, accessed November 2014.

[30] Joseph T. Durkin, SJ, ed., *Confederate Chaplain: A War Journal of Rev. James B. Sheeran, c.ss.r., 14th Louisiana, CSA* (Milwaukee, WI: Bruce Publishing Co., 1960) 49–50.

Potomac. His rate of march was about 1 mile per hour. That Meade had not destroyed Lee's army immediately left President Lincoln and his chief military advisor, Maj. Gen. Henry Halleck, dissatisfied to say the least. Meade reported to them that he had his men busy "succoring the wounded and burying the dead."[31] Two letters that General Meade wrote to his wife, Margaretta, reveal some more of his concerns about resupplying the Union army with food and ammunition, and trying to get adequate intelligence as to Lee's position and intent:

> 5 July 1863 ...It was a grand battle, and it is my judgment a most decided victory, though I did not annihilate or bag the Confederate Army. This morning they retired in great haste into the mountains, leaving their dead unburied and their wounded on the field. [Our] men behaved splendidly; I really think they are becoming soldiers. They endured long marches, short rations, and stood one of the most terrific connonings I ever witnessed.... The army are in the highest spirits, and of course I am a great man. The most difficult part of my work is acting without correct information on which to predicate action.[32]

> 8 July 1863 ...From the time I took command till today, now over ten days, I have not changed my clothes, have not had a regular night's rest, and many nights not a wink of sleep, and for several days did not even wash my face and hands, no regular food, and all the time in a great state of mental anxiety. Indeed, I think I have lived as much in this time as in the last thirty years.... I never claimed a victory, though I stated that Lee was defeated in his efforts to destroy my army. I am going to move as soon as I can get the army supplied with subsistence and ammunition.[33]

It was not until July 12 that General Meade had caught up with Lee's army, and even then five of the Union corps commanders voted against attacking Lee's veterans, who were entrenched on the Maryland bank of the Potomac River. Meade informed Washington on July 13 that his attack was delayed. On the morning of July 14, the Army of Northern Virginia escaped

---

[31] War Department, *Official Records*, part 1: 135.

[32] As cited in Jay Luvaas and Harold Nelson, eds., *Guide to the Battle of Gettysburg* (Lawrence: University Press of Kansas, 1994) 195.

[33] Ibid., 196–97.

across the Potomac—with the result that the war would continue another twenty-one months.[34]

With the Confederate troops withdrawn from the town of Gettysburg, some of the citizens who had fled the rebel army began to return to their homes. Among these were about 200 African American townspeople who had worked as farmers, domestics, and hired hands. They rented homes and owned lands and businesses—many attended the African Methodist Episcopal Church in Gettysburg that was a stop on the Underground Railroad.[35] Most fled because they had heard rumors that the Confederate soldiers were capturing black people and sending them back South as escaped slaves. With the Southerners gone, it was safe to return home.

Upon arrival, many members of the African American community volunteered to help care for the wounded and bury the dead. Among them was Mrs. Lydia Hamilton Smith, the longtime housekeeper of Congressman Thaddeus Stevens. Even though Mrs. Smith was just one-quarter black, she identified with the African American community and worked with them to bring food and clothing to the wounded. Other ladies of color cooked in the hospital kitchens, washed blood-soaked scraps of uniforms, and sewed new ones. The men in the black community hired themselves out to transport the dead and bury them at the new cemetery.

After the Confederate army marched away, a little African American boy was interviewed by a Union cavalryman in the town of Gettysburg. Assuming the boy had been in or near the town during its occupation by the Confederates, the soldier asked him,

"Well, boy, which did you prefer, the men in gray or the men in blue?"

Looking at the many men in blue uniforms standing around, the boy answered predictably, "The men in blue."

"And why was that?" he was asked.

"Because I know," he said hopefully, "the men in blue won't sell me."[36]

---

[34] Knauer, *Gettysburg: A Day-by-Day Account*, 114–15.

[35] Henry Louis Gates, Jr., "Did black men fight at Gettysburg?" *Nation*, July 1, 2013, accessed January 2016, as cited in http://www.theroot.com/articles/history/2013/07/did_black_men_fight_at_gettysburg.html, 4.

[36] Oral tradition from a guide at Gettysburg Presbyterian Church, Gettysburg, PA, October 16, 2013.

A Band of Angels Coming After Me...[37]

When the two armies moved south from Gettysburg, most of the surgeons and chaplains went with them. The 5,747 dead and 21,331 wounded soldiers were left behind. Dr. Jonathan Letterman, who had the responsibility for providing medical care to legions of wounded scattered for miles, had but a few days to try to save as many lives as possible.[38] Excerpts from his official report, written three months after the battle, reveal some of the major issues he had to resolve:

> The chief want was tents and other appliances for better care of the wounded. I had an interview with the commanding general on the evening of July 3, after the battle was over, to obtain permission to order up the wagons containing the tents. This request he did not think expedient to grant but in part, allowing one-half the wagons to come to the front; the remainder were brought up as soon as it was considered by him proper to permit it.[39]
>
> Surgeon [John] McNulty, medical director [of the Twelfth Corps], reports that "it is with extreme satisfaction that I can assure you that it enabled me to remove the wounded from the field, shelter, feed them, and dress their wounds within six hours after the battle ended, and to have every capital operation performed within twenty-four hours after the injury was received." I can, I think, safely say that such would have been the result in other corps had the same facilities been allowed—a result not to have been surpassed, if equaled, in any battle of magnitude that has ever taken place.
>
> By the exertions of Colonel [Henry F.] Clark, chief commissary, 30,000 rations were brought up on July 4 and distributed to the hospitals.... Arrangements were made by him to have supplies in abundance brought to Gettysburg for the wounded; he ordered them, and if the railroad could have transported them they would have been on hand.[40]

Dr. Letterman went on to report that the 650 medical officers present for duty at the Battle of Gettysburg worked day and night with little rest until July 7, attending to the wounded:

---

[37] The spiritual "Swing Low, Sweet Chariot," 1862.
[38] If all of the wounded from both sides had been placed shoulder-to-shoulder on the ground in a straight line, the wounded would have stretched for 6 miles.
[39] War Department, *Official Records*, part 2: report no. 16, 196.
[40] Ibid., 197.

The labor performed by these officers was immense. Some fainted from exhaustion, induced by overexertion, and others became ill from the same cause. The skill and devotion shown by the medical officers of this army were worthy of all commendation; they could not be surpassed.... Thirteen of them were wounded...one of whom died on July 6 from the effects of his wounds received on the 3d. The greater portion of the surgical labor was performed before the army left [on July 7 and 8]. The time for primary operations had passed, and what remained to be done was to attend to making the men comfortable, dress their wounds, and perform such secondary operations as from time to time might be necessary. One hundred and six medical officers were left behind when the army left; no more could be left, as it was expected that another battle would within three or four days take place.[41]

While Dr. Letterman praised the efforts of the Army doctors, his opinion of civilian physicians was surprisingly low: "No reliance can be placed on surgeons from civil life during or after a battle. They cannot or will not submit to the privations and discomforts which are necessary, and the great majority think more of their personal comfort than they do of the wounded. I regret to make such a statement, but it is a fact and often a practical one."[42]

The main collection point for the wounded was at Camp Letterman on the York Pike. Camp Letterman, which was an evacuation hospital near the railroad, had large tents marked with the insignia of the various Union corps so that troops could be identified by unit. Triage was practiced by dividing the wounded into the seriously wounded and the lightly wounded, the latter sometimes waiting for hours if not days for a surgeon's attention and report.

In addition to Camp Letterman there were 160 aid stations in and around Gettysburg, forty-five of them in private homes, where wounded soldiers waited for transportation to Camp Letterman, to the Lutheran seminary hospital, or to the train station. Seventeen Gettysburg farmhouses or barns, or both, served Union wounded, while eighteen other farmhouses, schools, churches, taverns, and mills provided shelter for Confederate casual-

---

[41] Ibid. Note: by medical officers, Dr. Letterman meant surgeons and assistant surgeons. He did not include nurses or chaplains.

[42] War Department, *Official Records*, part 2: report no. 16, 197. Dr. Letterman's assessment could not have included physicians, such as Dr. Zachariah Stewart of Canonsburg, PA, who, according to oral tradition, died of overexertion on the Gettysburg battlefield. Quoted from Gettysburg tour guide, October 17, 2013.

ties.[43] In the town of Gettysburg, the train station, the Adams County Courthouse, the Cemetery Gatehouse, several churches, and parts of Pennsylvania (Gettysburg) College and the Lutheran seminary, among other buildings, were designated as temporary hospitals, and many treated soldiers from both armies.

A multitude of civilian and religious organizations and private physicians and nurses arrived in Gettysburg, even before the last shots were fired, to assist the army surgeons. For example, at the seminary hospital, twenty-eight doctors and 144 nurses, most volunteers, worked in shifts until September 16 to care for both the Union and Confederate wounded. The United States Christian Commission, formed as a ministry of the Young Men's Christian Association, sent over 300 delegates to help locate and transport wounded soldiers, bringing with them $80,000 worth of food, clothing, and blankets.[44] A Roman Catholic priest, Father Francis Burlando, and sixteen nuns from the Daughters of Charity mission in Emmitsburg, Maryland, arrived on July 5, bringing baskets of bandages, cooked hams, coffee, tea, and bedding for the soldiers.[45] The Patriot Daughters of Lancaster (Pennsylvania) raised money and brought volunteers and supplies to Christ Lutheran Church hospital on July 10.[46] The United States Sanitary Commission, a private relief organization created by Federal legislation in 1861, sponsored nurses and provided medical supplies and money to buy any other necessities for soldiers.

Some soldiers were apparently left on the field for dead until an angel of mercy picked them up. Private Enoch K. Miller, 108th New York Infantry, Hays' Division, US Second Corps, who lay on the field for twelve days, and was visited by his regimental chaplain, the Reverend Thomas Grassie,[47] his regimental surgeon, and cared for by his friend, Sgt. John O'Connell, left this account of his ordeal:

---

[43] Historic Gettysburg-Adams County, *Gettysburg Civil War Field Hospital Tour* (Harrisburg, PA: The Hospital & Healthsystem Association of Pennsylvania, 2001) 3–4.

[44] Edward Smith, *Incidents among Shots and Shell* (Memphis, TN: General Books, 2012) 50–51.

[45] Betty Ann McNeil, ed., *Dear Masters: Extracts from Accounts by Sister Nurses* (Emmitsburg, MD: Daughters of Charity of Saint Vincent de Paul, 2011) 85.

[46] G. Craig Caba, ed., *Hospital Scenes after the Battle of Gettysburg* (Craig Caba: Gettysburg, PA, 1993) 48.

[47] Chaplain Thomas Gordon Grassie (1831–1898) was a Dutch Reformed pastor and regimental chaplain for the 108th New York Infantry.

A minie ball had pierced my breast, passing through my left lung and coming out a little under my shoulder blade. The Surgeon of our regiment made an examination of my wound, but as I supposed that at that time the ball was in me, he only looked at my breast. He gave me a sleeping powder, and throwing a rubber blanket over me, left me as he supposed, to die. During the next three or four days, without a pillow or sufficient covering, my clothes saturated with my own blood, with no proper food, attended by a faithful comrade, Sergeant John O'Connell, I lay scarcely daring to hope for life.

About noon one day I saw the silver badge of the Christian Commission, and sending my comrade, I soon had its Delegate by my side. In that Delegate I recognized Brother Stillson. He was an old friend, and we had been co-laborers in the Sunday School work before the war commenced. He knew me in an instant, supplied me with a feather pillow—the first I had had in a year—a quilt, a draught of wine, some nice soft crackers and a cup of warm tea. After offering up an earnest prayer by my side, he hastened away to secure some clean clothes. He then removed my filthy garments, and in doing that it was found that the ball had passed through me.

After all this had been done, I felt as though I was at home; for...the Delegate of the Commission acts the part of a tender, loving mother, a willing father, an affectionate sister, a sympathizing brother and a beloved pastor.[48]

Thirty-year-old Georgeanna Woolsey, a volunteer nurse from New York serving with the US Sanitary Commission, had to overcome opposition to female nurses before she could do her work. While she was training in Washington, DC, she found the attitudes of some army doctors hard to bear:

No one knows who did not watch the thing from the beginning, how much opposition, how much ill will, how much unfeeling want of thought, these women nurses endured. Hardly a surgeon whom I can think of received or treated them with even common courtesy. Government had decided that women should be employed, and the Army surgeons—unable therefore to close the hospitals against them—determined

---

[48] Smith, *Incidents among Shots and Shell*, 50–51. Delegate J. B. Stillson, US Christian Commission.

to make their lives so unbearable that they should be forced in self-defense to leave.[49]

Georgeanna, however, stuck to her guns under the kind but strict supervision of Dorothea Dix, superintendent of Army Nurses, and was able to join the Army of the Potomac at Gettysburg. At Camp Letterman, where she worked for three weeks, she related how the wounded soldiers were evacuated:

> This is the way the thing was managed at first: The surgeons, left in care of the wounded 3 or 4 miles out from the town, went up and down among the men in the morning and said, "Any of you boys who can make your way to the cars, can go to Baltimore." So off start all who think they feel well enough, anything better than the "hospitals," so called, for the first few days after a battle....
>
> Twice a day the trains left for Baltimore or Harrisburg, and twice a day we fed all the wounded who arrived for them. Things were systematized now, and the men came down in long ambulance trains to the cars: baggage cars they were, fitted with straw for the wounded to lie on, and broken open at either end to let in the air. A government surgeon was always present to attend to the careful lifting of the soldiers from ambulance to car.
>
> When the surgeons had the wounded all placed, with as much comfort as seemed possible under the circumstances, on board the train, our detail of men would go from car to car, with soup made of beef stock or fresh meat, full of potatoes, turnips, cabbage, and rice, with fresh bread and coffee, and when stimulants were needed, with ale, milk punch, or brandy. Water pails were in great demand for use in the cars on the journey, and empty bottles, to take the place of canteens. All our whiskey and brandy bottles were washed and filled up at the spring, and the boys went off, carefully hugging their extemporized canteens, from which they would wet their wounds, or refresh themselves, till the journey ended.[50]

Although in some cases the Confederate casualties were treated last, it was Superintendent Dix's policy that rebels would be afforded the same nursing care as Union soldiers. Georgeanna noted that they did get equal care once they got to the hospital: "The surgeon in charge of our

---

[49] "Civil War Nurses: Georgeanna Woolsey," accessed November 2014, http://civilwarwomenblog.com/georgeanna-woolsey/, 8.

[50] As cited in Henry Woodhead, ed., *Voices of the Civil War: Gettysburg* (Richmond, VA: Time-Life Books, 1995) 152.

camp...looked after all their wounds, which were often in a most shocking state, particularly among the rebels. Every evening and morning they were dressed."[51] Another Dix nurse, Julia Susan Wheelock, said, "Many of these were Rebels. I could not pass them by neglected. Though enemies, they were nevertheless helpless, suffering human beings."[52]

The Chaplains Who Stayed Behind

When the Army of the Potomac left the battlefield, six surgeons and one chaplain per division were left behind to tend the wounded.[53] This order would have left 106 surgeons and twenty-two Union army chaplains behind. It is not known if the number of Union chaplains was actually met, but Chaplain Joseph Twichell's letters to his family indicated that he remained behind for at least sixteen days. In a letter to his brother dated July 15, Chaplain Twichell summed up his labors to relieve suffering:

> I would have written oftener but for the absolute want of time. Owing to the scarcity of Surgeons—as few as possible having been left behind—much more than usual has devolved on Chaplains.... Within three days the condition of our hospital has much improved. Nearly all of the slightly wounded have been sent away, making more room for the bad cases, and assistance has reached us in the shape of stores, nurses and surgeons sent by the authorities and benevolent persons of various cities. I shall never forget this hospital. It has been the scene of great sufferings, also a place in which the love of God and the preciousness of Redemption have been strikingly manifested. All the country round about is a graveyard—not an acre for miles but has some mark of death upon it, yet if it only brings the blessing, we will rejoice.
>
> I have been considerably among the Confederate wounded. Thousands of them were left in our hands and they fared miserably. Many were not taken from the field until the fourth day. The Confed. Surgeons left with them were too few to care for a twentieth of the number—we had more of our own than we could attend to, and the poor creatures had to suffer and die for want of care. Nearby us is a barn, within and around

---

[51] As cited at http://en.wikipedia.org/wiki/ Dorothea_Dix, 8.

[52] Cornelia Hancock, *South after Gettysburg: Letters of Cornelia Hancock from the Army of the Potomac, 1863–1865* (University of Pennsylvania Press, original from the University of Michigan, Digitized October 27, 2006) as cited at http://en. wikipedia.org/wiki/ Dorothea_Dix, 8, accessed November 2014.

[53] Memoir of Chaplain John H. W. Stuckenberg, 145th Pennsylvania Infantry, as cited in Hedrick and Davis, *Diary of John H. W. Stuckenberg*, 86.

which were 150 of the wretches, mangled in every way, left for days without hardly a look. Some of us would snatch an hour to go over, and fetch them water—bind up simple wounds, etc. But their misery was almost unmitigated. Their appeals for help would have moved a heart of stone. Food they had, and a few men were sent to keep them from dying of hunger, thirst or cold, but, as wounded men, they were in great tribulation. Now, those that are left are well nursed, but many a one did not live to be helped.... Many of the Confederates are gentlemen, evidently of good birth and education, and there are not a few pious men among them. There was one, a sweet handsome boy with beautiful deep eyes, with whom I fell in love. He was mortally wounded and for days bore his sufferings with most admirable fortitude. I procured a bed and a pillow for him and went to see him as often as possible. He possessed a most cheerful Christian spirit.... I buried him yesterday before I came away, and mourned for him sincerely.[54]

The Gettysburg Sixteen

Of the 110 Confederate chaplains who served with their units at Gettysburg, sixteen are known to have voluntarily stayed behind with their wounded. This was an average of almost two chaplains per division, but a ratio of just one chaplain per 425 wounded soldiers left on the field. Since Confederate chaplains were commissioned officers but most also noncombatants, the Federal Provost Marshal put them under arrest but with the freedom to minister to their patients in the hospitals. These "Gettysburg Sixteen" were kept together at Gettysburg until their work was done, then split up and sent to prisons at Fort Delaware, Delaware; Norfolk, Virginia; and Fort McHenry, Maryland.

The Confederate chaplains who volunteered to remain with the surgeons and the wounded were identified in almost equal numbers from each infantry corps. Longstreet's First Corps left Chaplains George E. Butler (3rd Arkansas); William B. Owen (17th Mississippi); William G. Perry (44th Alabama); and Peter Tinsley (28th Virginia). Ewell's Second Corps contributed Chaplains Henry E. Brooks (2nd North Carolina Battalion); James H. Colton (53rd North Carolina); James H. Gilmore (21st Virginia); Paul C. Morton (23rd Virginia); Joseph W. Murphy (32nd North Carolina); and John L. Pettigrew (31st Georgia). Hill's Third Corps allowed Chaplains James N. Bouchelle (13th South Carolina); James O. A. Cook (2nd Georgia Battalion); Augustus G. Raines (14th Alabama); James M. Stokes (3rd

---

[54] Messent and Courtney, *Civil War Letters*, 254–55.

Georgia); Moses L. Whitten (9th Alabama); and Thomas D. Witherspoon (42nd Mississippi) to stay behind even though they all knew they would be going to a military prison eventually.

By denomination the sixteen chaplains included seven Methodists, four Presbyterians, three Baptists, and two Episcopalians in their number. One additional chaplain, Madison W. Frierson (2nd Mississippi), a Presbyterian, was captured at Greencastle, Pennsylvania, on July 5, making seventeen the total number of Confederate chaplain detainees from Gettysburg.

Chaplain Peter Tinsley, one of the Gettysburg Sixteen, kept a daily diary during the year 1863 to include his period of detention at Gettysburg and at Fort McHenry. In general, Tinsley recorded very courteous treatment of the Confederate chaplains by the Union officers. Since his diary consists of 149 pages, a summary is necessary to maintain brevity and the focus of his story.[55]

According to Tinsley's diary, during the two days after the battle, July 4 and 5, most of the buildings around Currens Farm, Bream's Mill, and the Black Horse Tavern, southwest of Gettysburg, were utilized as Pickett's Division hospital. Chaplain Tinsley ministered to about 250 wounded soldiers and to Gen. James Kemper, whose coffin had already been constructed when he surprisingly recovered from his wound.

On Sunday afternoon, July 5, the first Union troops arrived at Tinsley's hospital:

> About 2 oClock Gen'l Sedwick [Sedgwick] 6th Corps advances and takes possession of our Hosp[ital]. They are Jerseymen & both officers and soldiers are very polite & kind. They are the best specimen of Yankee soldiers I have ever seen. Gen'l Sedwick visits Gen'l Kemper. I also see Gen'l Warren, Chief of engineers. They promise to send medical & other supplies immediately. They are evidently elated but are not insulting. In a short time they pass on pretending to be "inclined to press" our army & we are left entirely to ourselves. They are halted in front of our Hosp[ital] & from the free and friendly conversations between them & our wounded, you would suppose they were friends & acquaintances.[56]

It must be admitted that not all of the chaplains felt so appreciative, although gifts of food and medicine went a long way toward creating friendly relations. Chaplain Thomas Witherspoon, the fighting chaplain of the

---

[55] Tinsley, "Private Diary," box 1, folder 51.
[56] Ibid., 31–32.

42nd Mississippi Infantry, was arrested in a hospital tent with the rest of his wounded rebels. Chaplain Witherspoon was evidently placed under closer guard than was Chaplain Tinsley.

The Confederate surgeons and chaplains were kept at Gettysburg for thirty-two days, until August 7. During that time most were allowed to look after their own wounded, many of whom still remained under tentage around the battlefield.

On July 6, Chaplain Tinsley and Dr. Alexander Grigsby, surgeon of the 1st Virginia Infantry, went into Gettysburg, apparently unsupervised, to buy more supplies. Tinsley noted that they were "politely and kindly" treated.[57] While in the town they met Dr. Henry Janes, who had replaced Dr. Letterman as the superintendent of the Union hospitals. Dr. Janes had a wagon loaded with supplies, including medicine, bandages, a ham, sugar, lemons, and liquor, all from the Union commissary and medical departments. In comparison with the normal Confederate diet of parched corn and bacon, the Union rations were a godsend.

The Confederate surgeons and chaplains remained at their work until August 7 when it was determined that enough wounded had been evacuated or imprisoned to make their presence in Gettysburg no longer necessary. The hospitals were broken up and the surgeons and chaplains marched out under guard. They were told that they were not prisoners of war and would not be treated as such in Baltimore, which was their destination. They were packed into boxcars for the four-and-a-half-hour journey by train, which Tinsley said was a "tolerably pleasant journey."[58]

When the passengers arrived in Baltimore, they were marched to the Gilmore House, which was used as a military prison.[59] The surgeons and chaplains were separated from the other political and military inmates and put in two rooms, 12 by 20 feet each. Meals consisted of hardtack and meat for breakfast and supper, hardtack and meat and soup for the noon meal. Tinsley thought the meat was chewable, but the soup was thin.[60]

Two days later, on August 9, the noncombatant detainees were moved to Fort Monroe, Virginia, and then to Fort Norfolk, where Tinsley found

---

[57] Ibid.

[58] Ibid., 60–62.

[59] Gilmore House was subsequently renamed as the St. Clair Hotel, located on the west side of Calvert Street in Baltimore.

[60] Ibid.

seven of the other chaplains who surrendered at Gettysburg.[61] The temperature was a stifling 100 degrees, so the men remained in as much shade as they could find when they were allowed outside. While he waited for transfer to "Dixie," Tinsley read his Greek New Testament, attended worship services, and participated in debates on such questions as "Is practical utility or social ethics the principal strength of civilized society?" and "Should Confederate prayers be offered in mixed audiences of Yankees and Confederates?"[62]

The next stop was Fort McHenry on August 10, where the group was assigned to rooms that featured bunk beds, two men to a bed.[63] Most of the chaplains and surgeons remained at Fort McHenry for two months while they waited for exchange. However, during that time three of their number escaped without their absence being noted. On Monday, October 5, the announcement was made that they would all attend a roll call that evening and then be loaded on a boat bound for Fort Monroe, Portsmouth (Virginia) and City Point (Virginia), where they would be returned to the Confederate lines.[64]

The chaplains and surgeons were in a dilemma. If their three comrades, surgeons Martin, Carson, and Chaplain Brooks, were discovered missing, it might derail the hope of the prisoners to go home. Since their guard was a new and young Union lieutenant, they decided to bunch up and answer the roll call for the missing men. Three chaplains were carefully selected to change their voices and impersonate the absent brothers. While risky, this strategy worked because it was already dark before the roll call was held. As far as the commissioners at City Point could tell, three men had been lost in the voyage from Fort McHenry to City Point. Gen. John H. Winder, to whom Chaplain Tinsley reported in Richmond, thought the chaplains and surgeons had played a good joke on their captors.[65]

On October 10, 1863, thirteen weeks after he had been captured, Chaplain Peter Tinsley rejoined the 28th Virginia Infantry, his old regiment, and remained with them until the end of the war.[66]

---

[61] Ibid. Chaplains Whitten, Pettigrew, Owen, Murphy, Witherspoon, Stokes, and Brooks.

[62] Ibid., 80, 96.

[63] Tinsley, "Private Diary," 66–68.

[64] Tinsley, "Private Diary," 100–103.

[65] Ibid., 105–106.

[66] Ibid., 107. Chaplain Peter Tinsley remained with his regiment until April 9, 1865, when he and forty-nine other Confederate chaplains surrendered at Appomattox with their units.

The extraordinary treatment the Gettysburg chaplains recorded must be regarded as an exception to the experiences the enlisted prisoners, North and South, endured in prison camps. An estimated 56,000 men perished in Civil War prisons—more casualties than in any battle of the war.[67] Shortages of food, shelter, clothing, and medical care, coupled with the weakened condition of many prisoners unable to withstand dysentery, typhoid fever, or smallpox, contributed to the horrific death toll.

Among the more notorious prison camps were Andersonville, Georgia, which contained a total of 45,000 Union captives during its existence in 1864, and Elmira Prison in New York, which had a total population of 12,100 Confederate prisoners from July 1864 to fall 1865. Andersonville's mortality rate was 29 percent, while Elmira's was nearly 25 percent.[68] At the end of the war, the surviving Confederate prisoners were required to take a loyalty oath to the United States and then given a train ticket home. Most of the dead from these prisons, Union and Confederate, were buried outside their respective camps.

The Last Full Measure of Devotion: Honoring the Dead

The last service to be performed for the soldiers who fought at Gettysburg was the honorable burial of the dead. It is difficult, in retrospect, to know how many soldiers, Union and Confederate, were killed in the three-day battle. A comparison of the official Union army returns for June 30 and July 10, 1863, shows a difference of 20,366.[69] Of these, 14,529 were wounded and 5,365 captured or missing. Subtracting the wounded and missing from the July 10 report of 20,366 would mean that the Union dead from the battle numbered just 472. Obviously this is incorrect since more than 3,500 Union soldiers were eventually buried in the Gettysburg National Cemetery. A later official report raised the death total for the Union to 3,155 which is probably closer to the elusive truth, with the difference in casualty reports

---

[67] Yancey Hall, "U.S. Civil War Prison Camps Claimed Thousands," *National Geographic News*, July 1, 2003, 1 at http://news.nationalgeographic.com/news/2003/07/0701_030701_civilwarprisons.html, accessed November 2014.

[68] "Elmira Prison," accessed November 2014, http://en.Wikipedia.org/wiki/Elmira_Prison, 1, and Admiral Jim Stockdale, "Andersonville Memorial Day Speech," in Jim Stockdale, *Thoughts of a Philosophical Fighter Pilot* (Stanford, CA: Hoover Institution Press, 1995) 122.

[69] War Department, *Official Records*, part 1: 151–52.

and actual burials explained by the wounded who died in aid stations and hospitals after the battle.[70]

Counting the Confederate dead was even more challenging, for most of the remains were placed in shallow graves on the battlefield, some in mass graves. Over 3,000 burials remained on or around the battlefield for at least seven years, until the bones were exhumed and reinterred in the South.[71] The Army of Northern Virginia reported 2,592 soldiers killed during the battle,[72] but General Meade telegraphed General Halleck in Washington on October 3, 1863, that Union soldiers had buried 126 Confederate officers and 2,764 enlisted men at Gettysburg, not including those buried by details from the US Twelfth Corps.[73] An even greater number was reported when a total of 3,320 Confederate remains were relocated to Southern cemeteries by 1873. One possible explanation for the difference, again, is that hundreds, if not thousands, of Confederate wounded died after the battle.

One of the things soldiers dreaded was to be killed and then have their bodies placed in a grave marked "unknown." This concern was amplified by the observation of graves marked with just a wooden marker, perhaps a board from a cracker box with the name and unit of the deceased scratched on the front. It was obvious that these wooden headboards would not last very long. Regimental chaplains tried to provide some assurances to the soldiers that they would not be forgotten. Chaplains on both sides accepted letters, money, watches, and keepsakes to be sent home with a letter of condolence in case of a soldier's death. Many soldiers, however, carried identification with them into battle, including round identification disks, pictures of their loved ones, New Testaments with their names inscribed, personal diaries, and letters from family members.[74] These helped gravediggers later with the identification process.

---

[70] Ibid., part 2: 283 ff.

[71] Drew Gilpin Faust, *This Republic of Suffering: Death and the American Civil War* (New York: Vintage Books, 2008) 125–26. In 1873 a number of ladies associations from the South paid to move these remains to Richmond, Virginia; Charleston, South Carolina; Raleigh, North Carolina; and Savannah, Georgia. By 1873 some 3,320 Confederate soldiers had been relocated from Pennsylvania to alternate cemeteries. The last Confederate to be discovered at Gettysburg to date was found in the railroad cut in 1996. Those remains were buried in the Gettysburg National Cemetery with full military honors.

[72] War Department, *Official Records*, part 2: 346.

[73] Ibid., ch. 39, 119.

[74] Gabor Boritt, *The Gettysburg Gospel* (New York: Simon and Schuster Paperbacks, 2006) 48.

Chaplain Stuckenberg, 145th Pennsylvania Infantry, left Gettysburg with the army on July 7. As he rode through the Confederate lines he noted that "they had buried some of their dead, others had been carried together ready for burial. The stench was fearful, almost intolerable."[75]

Because the Confederates had rebelled against the Federal Government, it was decided that only Union soldiers would be exhumed and buried in what would become the Gettysburg National Cemetery. The task of deciding which set of remains was Union and which Confederate was often a difficult one. Before he departed, Chaplain Corby of the Irish Brigade recommended that the burial details find as many bottles as possible, then put the name of the deceased and his unit on a piece of paper, place the paper in the bottle, and bury the bottle with the body. That way soldiers could be identified later if the bodies were moved.

The Union chaplains left behind attempted to have at least a prayer for the deceased. Chaplain Joseph Walker from Wisconsin explained how he worked to be respectful and yet efficient in his treatment of the dead. "It was our habit to have one service for several bodies that were uncovered in adjacent graves varying the service to suit the numbers, or to have a general service over the coffins while still above ground."[76]

Many of the Confederate dead were simply put in mass graves without any effort to identify them. Some were left unburied for weeks. However, Dr. John O'Neal, a Gettysburg physician, kept a record of the names and locations of Confederate graves he encountered as he traveled around the county visiting patients. These men had their graves marked by their fellow Confederate soldiers. O'Neal documented their often hasty interments in hope of someday transmitting the information to family or friends. Into his journal Dr. O'Neal entered the lists of dead Confederates, their companies, regiments, and gravesites.[77] Ultimately it was discovered that seven Confederate soldiers had been buried with the Union troops through a case of mistaken identity.[78]

The Union dead did not fare much better. Although 3,564 Union soldiers were buried in what became the Gettysburg National Cemetery, some 1,664 of them were placed in the unknown section. Some Union soldiers,

---

[75] As cited in Hedrick and Davis, *Diary of John H. W. Stuckenberg*, 86.

[76] Faust, *This Republic of Suffering*, 82.

[77] Ibid., 125–26.

[78] Supervisory Park Ranger Clyde Bell, "What Happened to Gettysburg's Confederate Dead?" From the Fields of Gettysburg, The Blog of Gettysburg National Military Park, 1, accessed November 2014, http://npsgnmp.word-press.com, 2012.

identified by name but not by state, were buried in the unknown section because the cemetery was organized by state and not by last name.

The exhumation and reburial of the Union dead was under the supervision of Mr. Bail Biggs, an African American farmer and veterinarian who owned his own farm on Cemetery Ridge, including the copse of trees toward which Pickett and Pettigrew had led their men.[79] Black men, mostly from Gettysburg, worked in teams of eight to ten men from dawn to dusk trying to dig up, identify, and transport remains to the cemetery. The pay was minimal, $1.59 per body for the Union dead. Since there was no pay for Confederate bodies, if discovered they were covered back up and left where they lay.[80] The 1,500 horses and mules killed in the battle were left for farmers to bury or cremate.[81] As the Duke of Wellington noted fifty years before, "Nothing except a battle lost can be half so melancholy as a battle won."[82]

When President Lincoln arrived in Gettysburg on November 18 to dedicate the cemetery, the reinterment of the Union dead was not yet complete. Lincoln spent the night at the Wills House in Gettysburg, where his host, attorney David Wills, was sure the president put the finishing touches on his speech. It must have been a disconcerting task, for some thirty-seven other people crowded into Wills's home to spend the night.[83] Governor Andrew Curtin of Pennsylvania arrived late and had to seek accommodations elsewhere. William Saunders, the designer of the National Cemetery, slept in a chair in the parlor.[84]

The crowds that gathered to welcome the president were huge—approaching 20,000 or ten times the peacetime population of the town. A military band played late into the night and serenaders, some a bit tipsy if not drunk, twice gathered outside the Wills House. A newspaper reporter wondered whether it was "the want of sleeping quarters" or an "irrepressible enthusiasm" that kept people celebrating. But he noted that "bands of people walked the street through the night." The morning hours still found the

---

[79] Boritt, *The Gettysburg Gospel*, 6.

[80] Ibid., 44.

[81] Deborah Grace, "The Horse in the Civil War," accessed November 2014, http://www.reillysbattery.org/Newsletter/Jul00/deborah_grace.htm, 1 (July 2000).

[82] Christopher Morley, ed., *The Shorter Bartlett's Familiar Quotations* (New York: Permabooks, 1957) 420.

[83] Boritt, *The Gettysburg Gospel*, 84–85.

[84] Garry Wills, *Lincoln at Gettysburg: The Words That Remade America* (New York: Simon and Schuster, 1992) 30.

"Bonnie Blue Flag" and "The Star-Spangled Banner" echoing "up and down the would be silent streets and lanes."[85]

After a short night and a telegram from his wife, Mary, telling Lincoln that his son Tad was "slightly better" in a battle with fever, the president and Secretary of State William Seward toured the battlefield by carriage on the morning of November 19. Because the dedication would take place on Cemetery Hill, Lincoln and Seward headed for Seminary Ridge and the former Confederate lines. Although no one recorded their conversation in writing, Lincoln was reported to have remarked when opposite the copse of trees, "I am proud to be a countryman of the men who made that charge."[86] If he did say those words, they were not repeated again, for Lincoln was to dedicate the cemetery later in the day to the men in blue who had paid with their lives to defend the wall of freedom across the wide fields of Gettysburg.

---

[85] As cited in Boritt, *The Gettysburg Gospel*, 85.

[86] Quoted from a Gettysburg tour guide, October 17, 2013; see also Boritt, *The Gettysburg Gospel*, 92.

Chapter 7

Reflections: The Commanders, the Soldiers, the Chaplains

"No man can begin to tell the whole story of such a conflict, for more than earthly powers were engaged in it."[1]
—Capt. S. C. Armstrong, 125th New York Infantry

After such an awe-inspiring sequence of battles as Gettysburg turned out to be, it was inevitable that the participants would reflect on all they had done and seen. Some men, both officers and enlisted soldiers, began to find some pity and even compassion for their wounded opponents. Captain S.G. Armstrong, 125th New York Infantry, wrote about the night of July 3rd:

> Those days were full of horrible sights: the night after the great charge was unearthly from the cries of the wounded who could not be cared for: the air was full of groans and prayers; we had supper with the dead all about us; yet in all of these sickening scenes there was, I think, no hatred; the malice and rascality engendered by the war is at the rear. There is a certain mutual respect among those who accept the wager of battle.... In the presence of such tremendous issues men thought in a way that affected their whole future.[2]

Before the guns grew silent, Brigadier General Armistead, twice wounded leading his brigade forward, was already thinking about his old friend, Maj. Gen. Winfield Scott Hancock. As Capt. Henry Bingham, a fellow Mason and a member of Hancock's staff, knelt next to the wounded officer, Armistead asked him to deliver a message: "Tell General Hancock for me that I have done him and you all an injury which I shall regret the longest day I live." Bingham then took Armistead's spurs, pocketbook, watch, chain, and seal, which he later gave to General Hancock, who himself had been wounded, ironically, at about the same time as Armistead.[3]

Evidently Armistead thought again about his words two days later as he lay dying at the US Eleventh Corps Hospital at the George Spangler

---

[1] As cited in Richard Rollins, ed., *Pickett's Charge: Eyewitness Accounts* (Torrance, CA: Rank and File Publications, 1994), v.

[2] Ibid.

[3] Wayne E. Motts, *"Trust in God and Fear Nothing": Gen. Lewis A. Armistead, CSA* (Gettysburg, PA: Farnsworth House Military Impressions, 1994) 46.

farmhouse. As his end came near, Lewis Armistead mustered what little strength he had and made one final defiant comment to his Union captors. As Union doctors dressed his arm wound, the general reached into his trouser pocket and pulled from his soiled pants some raw corn. Holding the kernels in his hand, he looked the surgeon directly in the eye and said, "Men who can subsist on raw corn can never be whipped." Armistead died at the Spangler Farm at 9 A.M. on July 5, 1863.[4]

Of course General Armistead was not alone in his reflections. Generals A. P. Hill, Richard Ewell, J. E. B. Stuart, Winfield Scott Hancock, Oliver O. Howard, James Longstreet, and many others drafted official reports or wrote memoirs about the role of their units in the great battle. Dozens of surgeons, chaplains, and enlisted soldiers also wrote letters or reminiscences, reflecting what they had seen and felt. But perhaps the most dramatic reactions came from the two commanding generals, George G. Meade and Robert E. Lee, both of whom offered to be relieved of their commands following the battle.

On July 14, the day Lee made his successful escape across the Potomac, General Meade, smarting under criticism from President Lincoln for allowing Lee's army to reach Virginia, sent the following telegram at 2:30 P.M. to Maj. Gen. Henry Halleck, Lincoln's general-in-chief: "Having performed my duty conscientiously and to the best of my ability, the censure of the President conveyed in your dispatch of 1 P.M. this day, is, in my judgment, so undeserved that I feel compelled most respectfully to ask to be immediately relieved from the command of this army."[5]

General Halleck replied two hours later saying he did not mean to censure Meade, but to stimulate him to an active pursuit. Meade's application for relief was denied. Although he remained in command of the Army of the Potomac through the end of the war, the commander of all Union armies, Lt. Gen. U. S. Grant, overshadowed him.

General Lee's request to be relieved from command of the Army of Northern Virginia came on August 8 from his headquarters at Orange, Virginia. He wrote to President Jefferson Davis that "the general remedy for the want of success in a military commander is his removal," and that his reflections had prompted him "to propose to your Excellency the propriety of selecting another commander for this army." Moreover, Lee wrote, "I urge the

---

[4] Ibid., 48.
[5] War Department, *Official Records*, part 3: ch. 39, 93.

matter upon your Excellency from my belief that a younger and abler man than myself can readily be obtained."[6]

President Davis disagreed with Lee that an abler general could be found and declined to accept his resignation. Nevertheless it was one of the few times in military history that commanding generals from opposing forces had both offered to be replaced after the same battle.

Explanations

The point of many of the reports and memoirs, of course, was who or what was responsible for Meade's victory and Lee's defeat. On the Union side, General Meade credited the Army of the Potomac, and especially the men who were "becoming soldiers."[7] On July 5, Meade wrote General Orders No. 68, in which he stated, "The privations and fatigue the Army has endured, and the heroic courage and gallantry it has displayed will be matters of history to be remembered."[8] In a broad sense General Meade was right. The Army of the Potomac had endured five major confrontations with the Army of Northern Virginia in two years, four times losing key battles to Lee. Yet of the 272 Union regiments that fought at Gettysburg, 116 of them were veterans of Antietam, Fredericksburg, and Chancellorsville, as was Meade himself and most of his senior commanders. In the crucible of war, the Army of the Potomac had learned to fight as a unit even though Meade had been in command less than a week when the Battle of Gettysburg began.

General Hancock attributed the victory in his part of the field to the combined efforts of the artillery and infantry fighting in the defense. These efforts were possible because division and brigade commanders, such as Brig. Gen. Alexander Webb and Col. Norman Hall, led their men with conspicuous personal bravery. Moreover, Hancock pointed out, the men had taken cover behind the stone wall and hastily constructed breastworks, which gave them an advantage over the attackers.[9]

Brig. Gen. Henry Hunt, Meade's chief of artillery, placed the blame for Lee's loss on a lack of coordination between the Confederate commanders:

---

[6] Fitzhugh Lee, *General Lee* (Greenwich, CT: Faucett Publications, 1964) 297–98.

[7] As cited in Jay Luvaas and Harold Nelson, eds., *Guide to the Battle of Gettysburg* (Lawrence: University Press of Kansas, 1994) 195.

[8] Ibid.

[9] Ibid., 179.

The attacks on the part of the enemy were not well managed. Their artillery fire was too much dispersed, and failed to produce the intended effect.... The two assaults, had they been simultaneous, would have divided our artillery fire. As it was, each attack was met by a heavy front and flank fire of our artillery.... The expenditure of ammunition in the three days amounted to 32,781 rounds, averaging over 100 rounds per gun.[10]

The junior officers and the men in the ranks, seeing just a part of the battlefield, thought their units, artillery, or infantry had performed the best. Lt. Tully McCrea, 1st United States Artillery, supporting Brigadier General Hays's Division, wrote later to a friend,

When I saw this mass of men, in three long lines, approaching our position, and knowing that we had but one thin line of infantry to oppose them, I thought that our chances for Kingdom Come or Libby Prison were very good. Now this is where our Artillery came in, saved the day, and won the battle. I have always been of the opinion that the Artillery has never received the credit which was its due for this battle.[11]

On the other end of the field, the men of Col. Joshua Chamberlain's 20th Maine Regiment could have made the same argument for the infantry. Out of ammunition and without artillery support on July 2, they had held their ground at Little Round Top with a lengthening of their line and a final bayonet attack.

Some historians have observed that with 20,000 more infantry, 7,500 more cavalrymen, and 100 more artillery pieces at the beginning of the campaign, by holding the high ground with shorter interior lines and some entrenchments, and with a secure route of supply, it would have been hard for General Meade to lose the battle.[12] But four times on July 2 and 3, the Confederate infantry found weak points in the Union line. The penetrations failed only because of a lack of support and the arrival of valiant Union soldiers in the nick of time.[13] General Meade knew this, which is why he went without adequate sleep and food for three days.

---

[10] Ibid., 177.

[11] Tully McCrea to John Backhelder, 30 March 1904, as cited in Rollins, *Pickett's Charge*, 290.

[12] Statistics from Kelly Knauer, ed., *Gettysburg: A Day-by-Day Account of the Greatest Battle of the Civil War* (New York: Time Books, 2013) 14, and War Department, *Official Records*, part 1: 151.

[13] Even on July 3rd, Confederate soldiers said they broke the Union line at the stone wall and waited for 20 minutes for reinforcement which never arrived. Private J. R. Morrison, 28th Virginia Infantry, wrote that he saw reinforcing units at the

General Lee's explanation to President Davis was a bit more detailed. Lee actually wrote two reports, one on July 31, 1863, and the second in January 1864. In his second report, addressed to Davis's adjutant general Samuel Cooper in Richmond, Lee noted that he had not planned to fight at Gettysburg:

> It had not been intended to deliver a general battle so far from our base unless attacked, but coming unexpectedly upon the whole Federal army, to withdraw through the mountains with our extensive trains would have been difficult and dangerous. At the same time we were unable to wait an attack, as the country was unfavorable for collecting supplies in the presence of the enemy, who could restrain our foraging parties by holding the mountain passes with local and other troops. A battle therefore had become, in a measure, unavoidable, and the success already gained gave hope of a favorable issue.[14]

It is hard to know what General Lee meant by not intending to deliver a general battle so far from his base of supply since he brought almost his whole army with him, but it is clear that he was surprised to find the Union Army so close at hand on July 1. Certainly, General Lee felt that he was without adequate intelligence as to Union movements and Union strength, which meant that his maneuver options were reduced.

With regard to ordering the Pettigrew-Pickett charge on July 3, Lee reported simply that the "partial successes" of the Confederate attacks on July 2 had persuaded him to attempt another attack the next day.[15] General Longstreet was to direct the final attack with all three of his divisions from the First Corps toward the center of the Union line while Ewell assaulted Cemetery Hill with seven brigades from the Second Corps. Thus, the equivalent of five divisions, with "increased support" from the artillery, would assail the Union lines.[16]

Lee went on to say that this plan was almost immediately modified because General Longstreet wanted to keep two of his divisions ready to de-

---

edge of the Confederate woods on Seminary Ridge in total confusion. Charles T. Loehr, "The 'Old First' Virginia at Gettysburg," *Southern Historical Society Papers* vol. XXXII (January–December 1904): 190–94.

[14] J. William Jones, ed., "General Lee's Report of the Gettysburg Campaign," *Southern Historical Society Papers*, vol. II (July to December, 1876) 41.

[15] As cited in Luvaas and Nelson, *Battle of Gettysburg*, 169, and J. William Jones, ed., "General Lee's Report of the Gettysburg Campaign," *Southern Historical Society Papers*, vol. II (July to December 1876) 43.

[16] Jones, "General Lee's Report," *Southern Historical Society Papers*, 43.

fend his right flank in front of Big and Little Round Top, so Pickett's Division was joined by Heth's Division and two additional brigades from General Hill's Third Corps, a total of nine brigades. This plan was modified yet again with the addition of two more brigades from Anderson's Division of Hill's Corps. Lee made it clear that the combined artillery from all three of his corps were to provide covering fire for the infantry and "*to be pushed forward as the infantry progressed, protect their flanks, and support their attacks closely.*"[17]

While Lee did not fault Longstreet for failing to attack on time in the morning, he did mention that "General Longstreet's *dispositions were not completed as early as was expected*, but before notice could be sent to General Ewell, General Johnson had already become engaged, and *it was too late* to recall him."[18] The coordinated attack by Longstreet and Ewell was therefore disrupted by a Federal counterattack at Culp's Hill. According to Lee, by 1 P.M. Ewell's attack was over. Thereafter, Union troops and artillery from Cemetery Hill could direct their attention toward the attack on their center.

General Lee mentioned one additional factor that determined the outcome of Pickett's Charge, and thus of the battle, in his view:

> The troops moved steadily on under a heavy fire of musketry and artillery, the main attack being directed against the enemy's left-centre. His batteries reopened as soon as they appeared. Our own having nearly exhausted their ammunition in the protracted cannonade that preceded the advance of the infantry, were unable to reply, or render the necessary support to the attacking party. Owing to this fact, *which was unknown to me when the assault took place*, the enemy was enabled to throw a strong force of infantry against our left, already wavering under a concentrated fire of artillery from the ridge in front, and from Cemetery Hill on the left.[19]

Thereafter, Lee's report dealt with the double envelopment of Pickett's attacking force by the Union infantry, and by the large number of "brave officers and men [who] fell or were captured on this occasion."[20] He named five of them: Armistead, Garnett, Kemper, Trimble, and Pettigrew. Then Lee spent seven paragraphs indicating how the absence of Maj. Gen. J. E. B. Stuart's cavalry "much embarrassed" the movements of the army, but he added "the day after its arrival at Gettysburg it [Stuart's Division] engaged

---

[17] Ibid., 43–44 (emphasis added).
[18] Ibid., 43 (emphasis added).
[19] Ibid., 44 (emphasis added).
[20] Ibid., 44.

the enemy's cavalry with unabated spirit, and effectively protected our left. In this action Brigadier General Hampton was seriously wounded while acting with his accustomed gallantry."[21]

Some years later, when asked why the Battle of Gettysburg was lost, General Lee replied simply, "I will only say that the failure of the Confederate army at Gettysburg was owing to a combination of circumstances, but for which success might have been reasonably expected."[22] General Pickett was even more succinct when asked why he thought his valiant charge had failed: "I always thought the Yankees had something to do with it."[23]

Meditations

Since the Civil War generation did not hesitate to attribute victory to the providence of God, it is not surprising that many of the senior leaders made public proclamations of gratitude to the Almighty. President Lincoln was quick to declare a Day of Thanksgiving for the victories at Gettysburg and Vicksburg to be observed on Thursday, August 6, 1863. Chaplain Peter Tinsley, still in Gettysburg, wrote in his diary, "I got to town—most of the stores closed, it being Old Abe's Thanksgiving."[24] There is little evidence that August 6 was set aside for any observances in the Army of the Potomac, for those men were back on campaign in Virginia, but Lincoln renewed his proclamation on October 3, which established a National Day of Thanksgiving on the fourth Thursday in November:

> In the midst of a civil war of unequaled magnitude and severity, which has sometimes seemed to foreign States to invite and to provoke their aggression, peace has been preserved with all nations, order has been maintained, the laws have been respected and obeyed, and harmony has prevailed everywhere except in the theatre of military conflict; while that theatre has been greatly contracted by the advancing armies and navies of the Union.... No human counsel hath devised nor any mortal hand

---

[21] Ibid., 45. General Lee did not mention that four brigades of Stuart's Cavalry Division were defeated in their attempt to break through to the rear of the Union army, nor that some of Stuart's troopers had run low on ammunition in their fight with General Gregg's and General Custer's Union cavalrymen on the afternoon of July 3rd.

[22] Rev. J. William Jones, *Personal Reminiscences, Anecdotes, and Letters of General Robert E. Lee* (New York: D. Appleton and Co., 1875) 238.

[23] Knauer, *Gettysburg: A Day-by-Day Account*, 104.

[24] Peter Archer Tinsley (1833–1908), "Private Diary," in John and Joyce Schmale Civil War Collection, Wheaton (IL) College Archives, box 1, folder 51: 58.

worked out these great things. They are the gracious gifts of the Most High God, who, while dealing with us in anger for our sins, hath nevertheless remembered mercy.... I do therefore invite my fellow citizens in every part of the United States, and also those who are at sea and those who are sojourning in foreign lands, to set apart and observe the last Thursday of November next, as a day of Thanksgiving and Praise to our beneficent Father who dwelleth in the Heavens.[25]

On the Southern side, the mood after Gettysburg was more somber but no less fervent in seeking God's favor. In a letter to his wife, Mary, dated July 12 and written while he was still waiting to cross the Potomac, General Lee discussed a prayer he had:

The waters have subsided to about four feet, and if they continue, by tomorrow I hope our communications will be open. I trust that a merciful God, our only hope and refuge, will not desert us in this hour of need, and will deliver us by his almighty hand, that the whole world may recognize his power, and all hearts be lifted up in adoration and praise of his unbounded loving-kindness. We must, however, submit to his almighty will whatever that may be. May God guide and protect us is my constant prayer.[26]

President Jefferson Davis, like President Lincoln, had been thinking about the results of the battles at Vicksburg and Gettysburg. Accordingly, he designated Friday, August 21, 1863, a day of fasting, humiliation, and prayer. When he was apprised of this proclamation, General Lee issued General Order No. 83, which required strict observance of August 21 by all under his command:

The President of the Confederate states has, in the name of the people, appointed August 21 as a day of fasting, humiliation and prayer. A strict observance of the day is enjoined upon the officers and soldiers of this army. All military duties, except such as are absolutely necessary, will be suspended. The commanding officers of brigades and regiments are

---

[25] As cited in Margaret E. Wagner, Gary W. Gallagher, and Paul Finkelman, eds., *The Library of Congress Civil War Desk Reference* (New York: Simon and Schuster, 2002) 689. While President Lincoln did not know it at the time, the first Thanksgiving under his proclamation would also celebrate General Grant's victories at Chattanooga and Missionary Ridge, November 25, 1863.

[26] Fitzhugh Lee, *General Lee* (Greenwich, CT: Fawcett Publications Inc., 1964) 294.

requested to cause divine services, suitable to the occasion, to be performed in their respective commands.

Soldiers! We have sinned against Almighty God. We have forgotten his signal mercies, and have cultivated a revengeful, haughty, and boastful spirit. We have not remembered that the defenders of a just cause should be pure in his eyes.... God is our only refuge and our strength. Let us humble ourselves before Him. Let us confess our many sins, and beseech Him to give us a higher courage, a purer patriotism, and more determined will; that He will convert the hearts of our enemies; that He will hasten the time when war, with its sorrows and sufferings, shall cease, and that He will give us a name and place among the nations of the earth.

R. E. Lee, *General*[27]

Among the more junior officers, there were also expressions of thanksgiving—mostly just gratitude for being alive. Of the 160,000 men who took various parts in the Battle of Gettysburg, there were as many stories and reflections. However, Captain S. C. Armstrong of the 125th New York Volunteer Infantry probably summarized very succinctly the feelings of many. "No man can begin to tell the whole story of such a conflict," he wrote, "for more than earthly powers were engaged in it."[28]

The Soldiers

Sometime after the Civil War, a former Confederate soldier wrote a poem entitled "And What Do the Privates Do?"[29] In essence, it was a reminder that wars are not fought by officers alone, but for the most part by the men in ranks. Privates in both armies, of course, did what they were told to do or risk punishments that were not only corporal but also psychological. If they were convicted of stealing, they could be confined in a tiny guardhouse, made to stand all day on a barrel with a sign around their necks, or tied to a tree. In more severe cases, they could be forced to ride a rail out of camp, or, if convicted of desertion, shot by firing squad.

Yet the majority of enlisted men did not face these penalties. Like the officers, most wanted to do their duty, win their battles and the war as a whole, and go home. Meanwhile they could look forward to short rations, long marches, and pitiful pay. By US Army Regulations, a colonel of Infan-

---

[27] Jones, *Personal Reminiscences*, 412–22 (emphasis in the original).

[28] As cited in Rollins, *Pickett's Charge*, v.

[29] By James B. Evans, Company B, 8th North Carolina Infantry, as cited in *Confederate Veteran* 71/2 (March/April 2013): 23.

try was paid $95 a month plus forage for four horses and a maximum of two servants. A private received $13 a month without any other allowances.[30] However, a private could receive an additional $2 a month if he reenlisted and $1 a month for each subsequent period of five years' service, but $2 a month was subtracted from each private soldier's pay until the expiration of his term of enlistment. Presumably this gave him a bonus when he was discharged. If he served for three years, he would be entitled to $72 and transportation home.

In the Confederate armies, most privates were paid approximately $11 a month. Pay was often not available on schedule, so if a soldier received his $33 every three months, he was fortunate. Likewise rations, blankets, shoes, uniforms, and ammunition depended on commissary and ordnance channels, which, in turn, depended on how fast horses could pull wagons.

Why, then, were thousands of men willing to risk their lives on battlefields such as Gettysburg? What motivated them to march at a steady pace into a hailstorm of lead and iron without firing a shot until they were within range of their one-shot muskets? What made them stand firm in a storm of artillery shells facing the possibility of being overrun, killed, wounded, or captured?

Many eminent historians, Brig. Gen. S. L. A. Marshall, Sir John Keegan, Stephen Ambrose, William Manchester, and Professor James M. McPherson, have written about the reasons brave men behave the way they do in battle. Most agree that men fight for a cause, for their country, and for their comrades in varying degrees. Yet these are not simple concepts because even on the same side there are shades of difference.

What does fighting for cause and country mean? Many Northern soldiers understood that they were fighting for the Union, to preserve a democratic government established by their grandfathers, a government that respected the law. They also understood that an independent South as a whole might not only perpetuate slavery, but also weaken the Union for future generations. Southern soldiers were convinced that they were fighting for their independence, to preserve their way of life from tyranny. Both sides were fighting for freedom by July 1863, the South for freedom for some, the North for freedom for all.

But the memoirs of soldiers at Gettysburg, or about the soldiers at Gettysburg, reveal some other motivations. With almost two-thirds veteran soldiers in both armies, ideas of adventure and glory had virtually disappeared.

---

[30] War Department, *Revised United States Army Regulations of 1861* (Washington, DC: Government Printing Office, 1863) 361–62.

JOHN W. BRINSFIELD, JR.

Chaplain Peter Tinsley in Pickett's Division noted on the morning of July 3 that the men expected the worst, not the best, from the battle. But both Tinsley and Father Sheeran recorded that some soldiers were fighting for revenge. General Lee referred to the same motive in his General Order No. 83. A revengeful spirit was not what General Lee wanted, but it was surely present. Soldiers were fighting to drive Union forces out of their home states to stop the pillage, arson, and other depredations that characterized some of the Union soldiers' behavior. The killing of livestock, burning of houses, and turning women and children into the woods without food or shelter brought more Southern soldiers to Gettysburg than any Conscription Acts or appeals to patriotism. When General Pickett sent his men forward with the challenge, "Charge the enemy and remember old Virginia!" it was probably not an appeal simply to uphold the reputation of the state.

One South Carolina soldier, whose name was withheld by his hometown newspaper, described his feelings in the midst of an attack early in the war:

With the first shot you become a new man. Personal safety is your least concern. Fear has no existence in your bosom. Hesitation gives way to an uncontrollable desire to rush into the thickest of the fight. The dead and dying around you, if they receive a passing thought, only stimulate you to revenge. You become cool and deliberate, and watch the effect of bullets, the showers of bursting shells, the passage of cannon balls as they rake their murderous channels through your ranks...with a feeling so callous...that your soul seems dead to every sympathizing and selfish thought.[31]

Union soldiers also fought for revenge, but for their comrades killed at Fredericksburg or Chancellorsville. They blamed the South for starting an unholy and unjust war, but mostly for wantonly killing so many of their fellow soldiers and causing so many families to grieve. At the height of Pickett's Charge some Union soldiers began chanting "Fredericksburg, Fredericksburg," their equivalent of "Remember the Alamo," for they remembered a similar disastrous charge they had to make at Fredericksburg the previous year and the casualties they suffered at the hands of some of the same men they now faced at Gettysburg. Southern soldiers were treasonous

---

[31] Bell I. Wiley, *The Life of Johnny Reb* (New York: Book-of-the-Month Club, 1994) 29.

rebels and as such posed dangers not just to the loyal men in the field, but also to the entire Federal government.

Comrades

It is not surprising that men would fight for cause and country, even if they did not completely agree on why they were all there. But beyond these factors, it is also true that soldiers fought for their regiments. When a soldier joined a regiment, over time they formed a "band of brothers," bonded for survival.[32] Within a full-strength regiment of 1,000 soldiers there were normally ten companies of 100 men each. Companies were further divided into two platoons of fifty men each. The tallest and largest men were in the first platoon, the shorter or smaller men in the second platoon.[33] The platoons were further subdivided into even smaller units called squads or messes. A mess was a group of eight to twelve men who often pooled their rations to make a common meal in camp. Each member of the mess carried either a pot, a skillet, a fork, knife and spoon, or other cooking implements on the march so that at night and in the morning they could collectively cook their rations. In later years army cooks would prepare food for the officers' mess or for the enlisted mess, a tradition that grew from the earliest field armies.

Not only did the regiment bond men around the necessity of eating, but the regiment also provided leadership, supplies, a surgeon, sometimes an ambulance, a small band, and a chaplain. The regiment also forwarded mail and provided identity for soldiers to be paid and receive furloughs. In modern psychological terms, the regiment became the soldier's primary group "whose members shared close, personal, and often enduring relationships."[34] In many cases, the regiment was a soldier's surrogate family.

The primary symbol of the regiment was the flag, often made by ladies at home and presented with ceremony to the men as they marched off to war. Regimental battle flags were symbols of unity of purpose, unity of spirit, and common identity. They might be state flags or a Confederate battle flag,

---

[32] "We few, we band of brothers," William Shakespeare, *Henry V*, Act IV, Scene 3, line 60.

[33] John Curry, *Volunteers' Camp and Field Book* (1862), eds. William B. Sargeant and John W. Brinsfield (Macon, GA: Mercer University Press, 2009) 102.

[34] The concept of primary group identification was introduced by Professor Charles Cooley, a sociologist from the Chicago School of Sociology, in his book *Social Organization: A Study of the Larger Mind*. See "Primary and Secondary Groups," accessed November 2014, http://en.wikipedia.org/wiki/Primary_and_ secondary_groups, 1.

but usually, as the regiment passed through one campaign after another, the flags were embossed with the names of the battles in which the regiment had participated.

Moreover, the flags had a practical purpose. In the midst of the noise and smoke of battle, the men could not always hear the bugle or the drum telling them whether to charge, march in one direction or another, or retire. But if a soldier could see his regimental flag, he could guess that his commander was near and that he was moving in the right direction or maintaining the right position.

Regimental flags were so important that whole squads of men would give their lives to protect them. During the battles at Gettysburg it was not unusual for eight to ten men, serving as color-bearers, to be wounded or killed protecting the colors. The number of captured enemy regimental flags was also mentioned in after-action reports and served at times to justify the award of the Medal of Honor for a soldier who could bring one back.

While fighting for one's fellow soldiers may seem different than fighting for a flag, both motivations were commonly united, for flags also represented organizational survival, which was important for group and personal security on the battlefield. At the conclusion of Pickett's Charge, Maj. Gen. Winfield Scott Hancock, US Second Corps, noted the battle for flags at the Angle:

> The colors of the different regiments were now advanced, waving in defiance of the long line of battle flags presented by the enemy. The men pressed firmly after them, under the energetic commands and example of their officers, and after a few moments of desperate fighting the enemy's troops were repulsed, threw down their arms, and sought safety in flight or by throwing themselves on the ground to escape our fire. The battle flags were ours and the victory was won.[35]

Major Charles S. Peyton, CSA, of the 19th Virginia Infantry, Garnett's Brigade, described the same scene:

> At this moment, General Kemper came up on the right and General Armistead in rear, when the three lines, joining in concert, rushed forward with unyielding determination and an apparent spirit of laudable rivalry to plant the Southern banner on the walls of the enemy. His strongest and last line was instantly gained: the Confederate battle-flag waved over his defenses, and the fighting over the wall became hand to hand...but our line was found too weak to rout the enemy. We hoped for

---

[35] War Department, *Official Records*, part 1: 373–74.

support on the left...but hoped in vain...and those who were not killed or wounded were captured with the exception of about 300 who came off slowly, but greatly scattered, the identity of every regiment being entirely lost, and every regimental commander killed or wounded.[36]

Another motivation for soldiers to fight was out of obedience, respect, and even affection for their commanders. A good commander was something of a father figure to the younger soldiers; a competent and caring commander was appreciated by the older men. A poor commander was often simply endured until there was a change, which could come by the commander being promoted, relieved, severely wounded, or killed. Commanders might also resign and hope their resignations would be accepted.

During the three days' fighting at Gettysburg, it was not hard to see which commanders were most appreciated. Immediately after his death on July 1, Maj. Gen. John Reynolds's body was carefully transported back to Taneytown for embalming and returned to his family. Maj. Gen. Dan Sickles, hit in the leg on July 2, was evacuated not only by his staff but also attended by both Chaplains Twichell and O'Hagan. Maj. Gen. John B. Hood, wounded the same day, was carefully removed from the field by his men. Maj. Gen. James Kemper, twice wounded during Pickett's Charge and captured, was rescued by Sgt. Leigh Blanton of the 1st Virginia Infantry and taken back to the Seminary Ridge line. These were but a few of the officers and noncommissioned officers attended by their fellow soldiers on the battlefield. At a higher echelon it was said that by 1863 some men fought as much for Gen. Robert E. Lee as they did for the Confederacy, for they trusted him as their model commander and their main hope for victory.

The problem with these complex motivations is that they were all contingent and temporary. If a regiment lost its commander, its regimental colors, and up to 50 percent of its fighting strength, it was usually done as an effective unit. Without direction from a commander and a reasonable hope of success, retreat or capture seemed the only options. That's what happened to Pickett's Division on July 3 when Maj. Charles Peyton noted that at the end of the day the men were scattered and the identity of every regiment was entirely lost. There were some exceptions during the three-day battle, such as the 26th North Carolina Infantry and the 1st Minnesota Infantry regiments, both of which lost 80 percent of their officers and soldiers and yet maintained a remnant of their presence on the field. For those who have counted the citations for valor, it has been verified that at least sixty-one soldiers in the Army of the Potomac were awarded the Medal of Honor for

---

[36] Ibid., part 2: 385–87.

valor beyond the call of duty at Gettysburg, including three general officers.[37] The number of heroes was much higher on both sides. Nevertheless, as expected, many of the bravest and the best soldiers in both armies became the first casualties. When the senior officers summoned only the brave, they knew there would be a high price to pay.[38]

The Chaplains' Contributions

Though sometimes overlooked and underappreciated, the contributions chaplains made to their respective armies were not insignificant in supporting the morale and fighting strength of the soldiers. In addition to doing the work of normal clergy, preaching, counseling, praying, visiting hospitals, and burying the dead, many chaplains were also involved with the practical aspects of the campaign. Some fought side by side with their soldiers, Chaplains Thomas Witherspoon, 42nd Mississippi Infantry, and Lorenzo Barber, 2nd US Sharpshooters, in particular. Others performed duties associated with assistant surgeons, such as driving ambulances, providing water and bandages, administering chloroform, and assisting with amputations. Still others held precious letters and personal effects for soldiers going into battle and wrote letters home to families who wondered what had happened to their son, husband, or brother. A few advised and assisted commanders with their personal responsibilities for looking after the welfare of their soldiers, as did Father Sheeran in organizing care for the wounded at Winchester for

---

[37] On November 6, 2014, President Barack Obama awarded the Medal of Honor posthumously to Lt. Alonzo Cushing, Battery A, Fourth US Artillery, who died at his gun during Pickett's Charge. The three general officers awarded the Medal of Honor were major generals Daniel Sickles and Joshua Chamberlain and Brig. Gen. Alexander Webb. Maj. Gen. O. O. Howard also received the Medal of Honor, but for heroism in a previous engagement.

[38] There has not been a detailed study of the after effects of combat on Civil War veterans. There were accounts of suicide, murder, addiction, and desertion during the war, and records of soldiers and officers suffering from what seems to be post-traumatic stress disorder (PTSD) for years thereafter. In his article "Whose Graves Are These: The Quiet Crisis of Mentally Ill Civil War Veterans," Allen Cornwell estimated that "approximately 100,000 soldiers suffered from what is now referred to as post-traumatic stress disorder," many of whom lived out their lives in mental hospitals and Soldiers' Homes. For example, the Dixmont Asylum in western Pennsylvania houses more than 1,300 graves belonging to Civil War veterans, and the Milledgeville Mental Asylum cemetery in Georgia has well over 30,000 graves, "quietly hidden behind massive sprawling structures." See Allen Cromwell's article in *Civil War Historian*, 2/ 2 (May/June 2006): 60–65.

General Ewell early in the campaign. Still more chaplains tried to reinforce moral and ethical standards among the soldiers, a task that met with mixed results at best.

Commanders and soldiers were not without appreciation for their chaplains. They realized that chaplains were volunteers, that most were non-combatants, that they could resign at almost any time, and that they were there to answer a calling and not a conscription.[39] In other words, the chaplains, unlike the soldiers, did not have to be there.

General Meade referred to the work of chaplains as a sacred office in comforting the wounded and dying. Impressed by his devotion and fidelity, General Lee described Chaplain Alexander Betts of the 30th North Carolina Infantry as "that model chaplain."[40] Maj. Gen. Oliver O. Howard wrote in retrospect of Chaplain William Eastman, 72nd New York Infantry, who ministered to the wounded even after he was disabled, "It has struck me that there was no display of self-abnegation and generous heroic conduct superior to that of Chaplain William R. Eastman."[41] Maj. Gen. Daniel Sickles believed his life had been saved at least in part by the ministrations of two of his chaplains. When 93-year-old General Sickles attended the 50th anniversary of the battle at Gettysburg in 1913, he took his former chaplain, Rev. Joseph H. Twichell, with him.[42] The Right Reverend Boyd Vincent, Episcopal Bishop of Ohio, wrote in Chaplain Peter Tinsley's obituary, "He was possessed of a most genial, gentle nature, always courteous and considerate of others, and won friends wherever he went, who became deeply attached to him for his many noble traits and fidelity to duty."[43]

---

[39] Chaplain Moses Smith, Eighth Connecticut Infantry, was drafted as a private in August 1863 but was commissioned a chaplain the next month. Benedict R. Maryniak and John Wesley Brinsfield, Jr., *The Spirit Divided: Memoirs of Civil War Chaplains—The Union* (Macon, GA: Mercer University Press, 2007) 13.

[40] Dr. T. B. Kingsbury (Wilmington, NC), as cited in Alexander Davis Betts, DD, *Experience of a Confederate Chaplain 1861–1864*, ed. W. A. Betts. (Greenville, SC: Privately printed, 1904). See digital copy at http://docsouth.unc.edu/fpn/betts/betts.html, 22, accessed November 2014.

[41] General O. O. Howard, "Minor Incidents and Great Events," 339, as cited in The O. O. Howard Papers, Special Collections, Bowdoin (College) Library, catalog number M 91.8, item 43, number 19.

[42] Peter Messent and Steve Courtney, eds., *The Civil War Letters of Joseph Hopkins Twichell* (Athens: University of Georgia Press, 2006) 313.

[43] Rt. Rev. Boyd Vincent, "Death of the Rev. Dr. Tinsley," *Southern Churchman* 73/1 (January 25, 1908): 7.

Soldiers, too, left evidence of their regard for their chaplains. On the Gettysburg battlefield, veterans of the Irish Brigade helped fund a statue of Father William Corby in gratitude for his ministry to them. In the town of Gettysburg, the veterans of the 90th Pennsylvania Infantry left a bronze open Bible in memory of their chaplain, Horatio Howell, killed in front of Christ Lutheran Church. These were the first, and so far the only, battlefield monuments dedicated to chaplains.

But the soldiers showed their regard for the ministry of chaplains more by actions than by monuments. Chaplain J. William Jones and Chaplain L. C. Vass, both Confederate chaplains who served at Gettysburg, estimated that at least 15,000 soldiers in the Army of Northern Virginia made professions of faith during the war. The Reverend W. W. Bennett, post chaplain at Richmond and future president of Randolph-Macon College, believed that 150,000 soldiers from all of the Confederate armies had been converted and become members of some branch of the Christian faith after the war. Most Confederate chaplains who left records agreed that it was the most amazing display of spiritual power ever witnessed among fighting men on the American continent.[44]

In the Union armies the work of chaplains and the US Christian Commission had some measure of success as well. As Gardiner H. Shattuck, Jr., discovered in his research covering the period just after Gettysburg:

> In the Army of the Potomac, a great religious excitement appeared during winter 1863 to 1864 as many brigades built churches and chapel tents for prayer meetings. In February 1864, a Christian Commission agent recorded in his diary that a period of unusual spiritual interest had begun in the army, and brigade chapels were so full that some men were not able to come inside to join in prayer. General [Robert] McAllister wrote to his wife that he had never seen "a better state of feeling in religious matters" in the Army of the Potomac.[45]

In short, as Professor Robert L. Dabney of the Union Theological Seminary in Richmond, formerly chaplain of the 18th Virginia Infantry, wrote after the war, "The strange spectacle was now presented, of a people among whom the *active religious life seemed to be transferred from the churches at home—the customary seats of piety—to the army*; which, among other na-

---

[44] Rev. J. William Jones, *Christ in the Camp: Or Religion in the Confederate Army* (Harrisonburg, VA: Sprinkle Publications, 1986) 390.

[45] Gardiner H. Shattuck, Jr., *A Shield and a Hiding Place: The Religious Life of the Civil War Armies* (Macon, GA: Mercer University Press, 1987) 79–80.

tions, has always been dreaded as the school of vice and infidelity."[46] Given the work of the Union and Confederate chaplains and their colleagues in the US Christian Commission for at least three years, the result was not as surprising as it was confirming.

But Whose Side Was God On?

If there was a lingering question the chaplains left on the field after so many exhortations and sermons that encouraged soldiers on both sides to do their duty, it was whose side God was really on.

Such a question in more modern times may seem to have been just a matter of belief, but for the Civil War generation it was an issue of public discussion and debate.

President Abraham Lincoln had sought to understand God's will for the country and for himself for months. In a fragment of Lincoln's writings preserved by his secretary, John Hay, is a brief record of the President's thoughts:

Washington, D.C.
September, 1862
The will of God prevails. In great contests each party claims to act in accordance with the will of God. Both *may* be, and one *must* be, wrong. God cannot be *for* and *against* the same thing at the same time. In the present civil war it is quite possible that God's purpose is something different from the purpose of either party—and yet the human instrumentalities, working just as they do, are of the best adaptation to effect His purpose. I am almost ready to say that this is probably true—that God wills this contest, and wills that it shall not end yet. By his mere great power, on the minds of the now contestants, He could have either *saved* or *destroyed* the Union without a human contest. Yet the contest began. And, having begun He could give the final victory to either side any day. Yet the contest proceeds.[47]

In Montgomery, Alabama, former Chaplain Isaac Tichenor, pastor of the First Baptist Church in that city, delivered a Fast-Day sermon on Au-

[46] Robert Dabney, *Life and Campaigns of Lt. General Thomas J. Jackson* (Harrisonburg, VA: Sprinkle Publications, 1983) 657 (emphasis in the original).

[47] Abraham Lincoln, "Meditation on the Divine Will," Abraham Lincoln Online: Speeches and Writings, 1. See http://www.abrahamlincolnonline.org/ lincoln/speeches/meditat.htm, accessed November 2014. Some of these same thoughts are found in Lincoln's Second Inaugural Address, March 4, 1865.

gust 21, 1863, before the Alabama Legislature in which he agreed with Lincoln but to a different end:

> If God governs the world then His hand is in this war in which we are engaged. It matters not that the wickedness of man brought it upon us, that it was caused by the mad attempts of fanaticism to deprive us of our rights, overthrow our institutions, and impose upon us a yoke, which, as freemen, we had resolved *never to bear*.... While the storm cloud sweeps over our land, let us remember that God rides upon the wings of the tempest, and subjects it to His will.[48]

Chaplain Thomas W. Caskey of the 18th Mississippi Infantry had a closer look at what impact the idea of a holy war had upon the soldiers. He wrote from his new home in Fort Worth, Texas:

> Oh, how many of my fondly-loved spiritual children quietly slept, without coffins or shrouds, in far distant graves! How many had lost faith in God, when the cause they believed was right, and which they fondly loved, went down in a sea of blood. Our chaplains prophesied success, as among the certainties, since our cause was right, and God was on the side of right; therefore, the right was bound to triumph. I told them that they were sowing the seeds from which an abundant harvest of infidelity would be garnered in the event that our cause went under; that I did not believe that God had anything to do with the accursed thing from beginning to end on either side; that final victory would depend on courage, skill, numbers, and the heaviest guns best handled; that right and wrong would not weigh as much as a feather on the scale. What had I left to cheer my poor sad heart? Nothing but a consciousness of what to me was sacred—duty faithfully discharged. I had done the very best I could.[49]

Former Confederate Lt. Gen. Alexander P. Stewart, the postwar chancellor of the University of Mississippi, took a different theological view—based on results not on causes. A Presbyterian elder who believed in Divine Sovereignty, he remarked in 1874: "I do not know who was finally right or wrong in the last war. I do not even know whose side God was on. I do believe that in the end, God had need of a *United* States of America."[50]

---

[48] John Wesley Brinsfield, Jr., *The Spirit Divided: Memoirs of Civil War Chaplains—The Confederacy* (Macon, GA: Mercer University Press, 2005) 209, 212–13.
[49] Ibid., 250–51. Thomas Caskey published *Caskey's Book: Lectures on Great Subjects* (self-published) in St. Louis, MO, in 1884.
[50] Dumas Malone, ed., *Dictionary of American Biography*, vol. 18 (New York: Charles Scribner's Sons, 1946) 3.

Chancellor Stewart's religious beliefs may have been reasonable, but in light of the challenges to America in the next century, which included two World Wars, they were unquestionably prophetic. The legacies of courage and faith that marked those who fought at Gettysburg would not cease to inspire those around the world who would fight in defense of freedom. No matter how the commanders, soldiers, and chaplains on both sides defined their just cause or freedom or faith on the fields of Gettysburg, they unquestionably redefined courage for those who followed them. As Thucydides wrote centuries before about the heroes of Greece, "The bravest are surely those who have the clearest vision of what is before them, glory and danger alike, and yet notwithstanding, go out and meet it."[51]

---

[51] As cited in Jeff Shaara, *The Rising Tide* (New York: Ballentine Books, 2006) xxxvii.

Appendix I

Rosters of the Union and Confederate Chaplains at Gettysburg

Roster of Union Army Chaplains at Gettysburg

Army of the Potomac (Maj. Gen. George G. Meade)

First Corps (Maj. Gen. John R. Reynolds)

Barnett, Thomas (Methodist) 19th Indiana Infantry
Bullen, George (Baptist) 16th Maine Infantry
Calkins, James F. (Presbyterian) 149th Pennsylvania Infantry
Clothier, Charles W. (Unknown) 88th Pennsylvania Infantry
Cook, Philos G. (Presbyterian) 94th New York Infantry
Eaton, Samuel (Congregational) 7th Wisconsin Infantry
Ferguson, John V. (Methodist) 97th New York Infantry
Howell, Horatio (Presbyterian) 90th Pennsylvania Infantry (KIA)
Locke, William H. (Methodist) 11th Pennsylvania Infantry
McCormick, William (Unknown) 150th Pennsylvania Infantry
Moore, William P. (Presbyterian) 142nd Pennsylvania Infantry
Smart, William S. (Congregational) 14th Vermont Infantry
Ward, Ferdinand (Presbyterian) 104th New York Infantry
Way, William C. (Methodist) 24th Michigan Infantry
Webster, Alonzo (Methodist) 16th Vermont Infantry

Second Corps (Maj. Gen. Winfield S. Hancock)

Brown, John N. (Methodist) 111th New York Infantry
Collins, Gamaliel (Universalist) 72nd Pennsylvania Infantry
Condron, George (Unknown) 2nd Delaware Infantry
Conwell, Francis (Methodist) 1st Minnesota Infantry
Corby, William (Roman Catholic) 88th New York Infantry
Grassie, Thomas G. (Dutch Reformed) 108th New York Infantry
Harrison, T. Spencer (Baptist) 126th New York Infantry
Hathaway, George W. (Congregational) 19th Maine Infantry
Hibbard, Oliver (Presbyterian) 64th New York Infantry
Miller, Alexander (Unknown) 8th Ohio Infantry
Murphey, Thomas (Presbyterian) 1st Delaware Infantry

Sabin, Elias (Unknown) 14th Indiana Infantry
Simons, Ezra (Baptist) 125th New York Infantry
Steffen, Peter (Lutheran) 52nd New York Infantry
Stevens, William (Methodist) 148th Pennsylvania Infantry
Strong, Daniel (Methodist) 4th Ohio Infantry
Stuckenberg, John (Lutheran) 145th Pennsylvania Infantry
Vogel, Henry (Baptist) 61st New York Infantry
Wilson, Stacy (Methodist) 81st Pennsylvania Infantry

Third Corps (Maj. Gen. Daniel E. Sickles)

Ambrose, Thomas L. (Church of Christ) 12th New Hampshire Infantry
Barber, Lorenzo (Methodist) 2nd US Sharpshooters
Beck, Charles A. (Church of Christ) 26th Pennsylvania Infantry
Bradner, Thomas S. (Presbyterian) 124th New York Infantry
Chase, Benjamin A. (Methodist) 4th Maine Infantry
Chase, Stephen F. (Methodist) 3rd Maine Infantry
Cudworth, Warren (Unitarian) 1st Massachusetts Infantry
Eastman, William R. (Congregational) 72nd New York Infantry (Injured)
Gilder, William H. (Methodist) 40th New York Infantry
Hartwell, Foster (Baptist) 120th New York Infantry
Hayden, Jeremiah (Baptist) 17th Maine Infantry
McAdam, William T. (Presbyterian) 57th Pennsylvania Infantry
Moore, Samuel T. (Methodist) 6th New Jersey Infantry/8th New Jersey Infantry
O'Hagan, Joseph (Roman Catholic) 73rd New York Infantry
Porter, William C. (Presbyterian) 20th Indiana Infantry
Pritchard, Benjamin F. (Methodist) 5th Michigan Infantry
Rose, Julius (Episcopal) 7th New Jersey Infantry
Sittler, Robert (Protestant) 74th New York Infantry
Sovereign, Thomas (Methodist) 5th New Jersey Infantry
Twichell, Joseph H. (Congregational) 71st New York Infantry
Watson, Elisha (Episcopal) 11th Massachusetts Infantry
Watts, Jonathan (Methodist) 86th New York Infantry

Fifth Corps (Maj. Gen. George Sykes)

Clark, Orson (Universalist) 83rd Pennsylvania Infantry
Crain, Cyrus (Baptist) 44th New York
Erdman, Albert (Presbyterian) 146th New York Infantry
French, Luther (Methodist) 20th Maine Infantry

MacLauren, John F. (Presbyterian) 10th Pennsylvania Reserves/39th Pennsylvania Infantry

McFarland, James (Presbyterian) 9th Pennsylvania Reserves/38th Pennsylvania Infantry

O'Neill, William (Methodist) 118th Pennsylvania Infantry

Seage, Johnne B. (Baptist) 4th Michigan Infantry

Torrence, Adam (Unknown) 11th Pennsylvania Reserves/40th Pennsylvania Infantry

Tyler, Charles (Congregational) 22nd Massachusetts Infantry

Sixth Corps (Maj. Gen. John Sedgwick)

Adams, John R. (Congregational) 5th Maine Infantry

Benson, Henry (Presbyterian) 49th New York Infantry

Burghardt, Peter H. (Presbyterian) 65th New York Infantry

Fox, Norman Jr. (Baptist) 77th New York Infantry

Haines, Alanson (Presbyterian) 15th New Jersey Infantry

Harvey, John (Unknown) 62nd New York Infantry

James, Joseph H. (Methodist) 3rd New Jersey Infantry

Kelley, Moses (Baptist) 6th Maine Infantry

Lane, Joseph S. (Methodist) 93rd Pennsylvania Infantry

Mack, Daniel (Methodist) 3rd Vermont Infantry

McPherson, Robert (Presbyterian) 139th Pennsylvania Infantry

Miller, Benjamin R. (Methodist) 119th Pennsylvania Infantry

Morse, Frank (Methodist) 37th Massachusetts Infantry

Osborne, Corra (Unknown) 43rd New York Infantry

Proudfit, Robert R. (Presbyterian) 2nd New Jersey Infantry

Purington, Collamore (Baptist) 7th Maine Infantry

Shinn, James G. (Unknown) 23rd Pennsylvania Infantry

Stephenson, Thomas (Unknown) 49th Pennsylvania Infantry

Stone, Edward (Congregational) 6th Vermont Infantry

Yard, Robert B. (Methodist) 1st New Jersey Infantry

Eleventh Corps (Maj. Gen. Oliver O. Howard)

Bogen, Frederick (Unknown) 41st New York Infantry

Burke, John (Unknown) 82nd Ohio Infantry

Fletcher, Frank (Baptist) 134th New York Infantry

Foster, Daniel (Unitarian) 33rd Massachusetts Infantry

Hall, William K. (Congregational) 17th Connecticut Infantry

Kabus, Robert (Unknown) 107th Ohio Infantry
Lowring, Henry D. (Congregational) 154th New York Infantry
Mussehl, William (Unknown) 68th New York Infantry
Reichhelm, Emanuel (Disciples of Christ) 82nd Illinois Infantry
Sarner, Ferdinand (Jewish), 54th New York Infantry (WIA)
Seymour, O. Hoyt (Presbyterian) 157th New York Infantry
Sprague, Ezra (Universalist) 119th New York Infantry
Vette, William (Unknown) 26th Wisconsin Infantry
Wheeler, Alfred (Methodist) 55th Ohio Infantry

Twelfth Corps (Maj. Gen. Henry Slocum)

Ames, Lyman (Christian) 29th Ohio Infantry
Beck, Theodore (Dutch Reformed) 13th New Jersey Infantry
Bowdish, Arvine (Methodist) 149th New York Infantry
Crane, Ezra (Baptist) 107th New York Infantry
Dean, Martin (Unknown) 145th New York Infantry
Drumm, Thomas (Episcopal) 102nd New York Infantry
Parsons, Wilson (Unknown) 66th Ohio Infantry
Poulson, Thomas (Methodist) 1st Maryland Infantry (Eastern Shore)
Quint, Alonzo (Congregational) 2nd Massachusetts Infantry
Roberts, Eli (Methodist) 137th New York Infantry
Sewell, Benjamin (Unknown) 29th Pennsylvania Infantry
Vassar, Thomas (Baptist) 150th New York Infantry
Welch, Moses (Congregational) 5th Connecticut Infantry

Cavalry Corps (Maj. Gen. Alfred Pleasonton)

Beale, James H. (Presbyterian) 1st Pennsylvania Cavalry
Boudrye, Louis N. (Methodist) 5th New York Cavalry (POW)
Brickman, Arthur (Unknown) 1st Maryland Cavalry
Crocker, George (Baptist) 6th New York Cavalry
Crowell, Ezra (Baptist) 10th New York Cavalry
Gracey, Samuel (Methodist) 6th Pennsylvania Cavalry
Greeley, Stephen (Congregational) 6th Michigan Cavalry
Hudson, Jonathan (Unknown) 1st Michigan Cavalry
Hunter, Moses H. (Episcopal) 3rd Pennsylvania Cavalry
Keyes, Charles (Baptist) 9th New York Cavalry
Pyne, Henry (Episcopal) 1st New Jersey Cavalry
Taylor, Oliver (Episcopal) 5th Michigan Cavalry

Truman, David (Unknown) 1st West Virginia Cavalry
Van Ingen, John (Episcopal) 8th New York Cavalry
Woodward, John (Congregational) 1st Vermont Cavalry

Other Unit:
Kirkpatrick, John A. (Presbyterian) 26th Pennsylvania Emergency Militia
(fought on June 26, 1863)

A total of 128 Union Army chaplains served at Gettysburg; 144 regiments were
without chaplains.

KIA: Killed in Action
WIA: Wounded in Action
POW: Prisoner of War

Roster of Confederate Chaplains at Gettysburg

Army of Northern Virginia (Gen. Robert E. Lee)

First Corps (Lt. Gen. James Longstreet)

Burnham, Joel C. (Unknown) 9th Georgia Infantry
Butler, George E. (Methodist) 3rd Arkansas Infantry (POW)
Curry, W. L. (Baptist) 50th Georgia Infantry
Doll, Penfield (Methodist) 18th Georgia Infantry
Dunlap, W. C. (Methodist) 8th Georgia Infantry
Frazier, Robert (Cumberland Presbyterian) 4th Alabama Infantry
Garrison, James A. (Unknown) 20th Georgia Infantry
Granbery, John C. (Methodist) 11th Virginia Infantry
Hudson, John (Methodist) 17th Georgia Infantry
McCarthy, F. M. (Baptist) 7th Virginia Infantry
McCauley, George (Unknown) 51st Georgia Infantry
McGruder, A. I. (Unknown) 2nd South Carolina Infantry
McRae, John H. D. (Methodist) 24th Georgia Infantry
Owen, William B. (Methodist) 17th Mississippi Infantry (POW)
Penick, William S. (Baptist) 53rd Virginia Infantry
Perry, William G. (Methodist) 44th Alabama Infantry (POW)
Porter, Rufus (Presbyterian) 2nd Georgia Infantry

Price, Blackford (Unknown) 48th Alabama Infantry
Roberson, William F. (Methodist) 15th Georgia Infantry
Simmons, W. A. (Methodist) 11th Georgia Infantry
Starr, William G. (Methodist) 47th Alabama Infantry
Tinsley, Peter (Episcopal) 28th Virginia Infantry (POW)
Treadwell, Henry B. (Baptist) 53rd Georgia Infantry

Second Corps (Lt. Gen. Richard Ewell)

Betts, Alexander D. (Methodist) 30th North Carolina Infantry
Brittain, J. M. (Baptist) 38th Georgia Infantry
Brooks, Henry E. (Baptist) 2nd North Carolina Battalion (POW)
Cameron, William E. (Presbyterian) 26th Alabama Infantry
Colton, James H. (Presbyterian) 53rd North Carolina Infantry (POW)
Denny, George H. (Presbyterian) 50th Virginia Infantry
Ellis, R. A. (Unknown) 13th Georgia Infantry
Gilmore, J. Harvey (Presbyterian) 21st Virginia Infantry (POW)
Grandin, Joshua M. (Methodist) 33rd Virginia Infantry
Gwaltney, William R. (Baptist) 1st North Carolina Infantry
Hall, Willis T. (Unknown) 26th Georgia Infantry
Hardie, Robert, Jr. (Methodist) 2nd Louisiana Infantry
Harding, Ephraim (Presbyterian) 45th North Carolina
Haslett, William (Unknown) 21st Georgia Infantry
Hopkins, Abner C. (Presbyterian) 2nd Virginia Infantry
Hubert, Darius (Roman Catholic) 1st Louisiana Infantry (WIA)
Lacy, B. Tucker (Presbyterian) Appointed chaplain-at-large to II Corps by Lt.
     Gen. T. J. "Stonewall" Jackson
Marshall, Asa M. (Baptist) 12th Georgia Infantry
McGill, John (Episcopalian) 52nd Virginia Infantry
Moore, Junius (Unknown) 21st North Carolina Infantry
Morton, Paul C. (Presbyterian) 23rd Virginia Infantry (POW)
Murphy, Joseph W. (Episcopal) 32nd North Carolina Infantry (POW)
Patterson, George (Episcopal) 3rd North Carolina Infantry
Pettigrew, J. L. (Baptist) 31st Georgia Infantry (POW)
Power, William C. (Methodist) 14th North Carolina Infantry
Sheeran, James (Roman Catholic) 14th Louisiana
Smith, Samuel H. (Methodist) 60th Georgia Infantry
Smulders, Egidius "Giles" (Roman Catholic) 8th Louisiana Infantry
Sparks, James O. A. (Methodist) 4th Georgia Infantry
Sprunt, James M. (Presbyterian) 20th North Carolina

Strickler, William M. (Unknown) 5th Louisiana Infantry
Thompson, Eugene W. (Methodist) 43rd North Carolina Infantry
Vass, Lachlan (Presbyterian) 27th Virginia Infantry
Walton, Edward P. (Baptist) 5th Virginia Infantry
Woodfin, Augustus B. (Baptist) 61st Georgia Infantry

Third Corps (Lt. Gen. Ambrose P. Hill)

Anderson, James Madison (Methodist) 40th Virginia Infantry
Anderson, John Monroe (Presbyterian) 12th South Carolina Infantry
Barrett, Edward B. (Baptist) 45th Georgia Infantry
Beauchelle, James N. (Unknown) 13th South Carolina Infantry (POW)
Bennick, Augustus R. (Methodist) 34th North Carolina Infantry
Carson, W. B. (Baptist) 14th South Carolina Infantry
Chambliss, J. A. (Baptist) Davis's Mississippi Brigade
Cline, James M. (Methodist) 52nd North Carolina Infantry
Cook, J. O. A. (Methodist) 2nd Georgia Battalion (POW)
Dobbs, Charles H. (Presbyterian) 12th Mississippi Infantry
Eatman, Thomas (Methodist) 33rd North Carolina Infantry
Frierson, Madison W. (Presbyterian) 2nd Mississippi Infantry
Houser, William, Sr. (Unknown) 48th Georgia Infantry
Hyman, John James (Baptist) 49th Georgia Infantry
Jones, William E. (Methodist) 22nd Georgia Infantry
Kennedy, Francis Milton (Methodist) 28th North Carolina Infantry
Meredith, J. Marshall (Episcopal) 47th Virginia Infantry
Moore, Alex W. (Methodist) 14th Georgia Infantry
Moore, Styring S. (Unknown) 26th North Carolina Infantry
Perkins, Edmund T. (Episcopal) 55th Virginia Infantry
Porter, Joseph D. (Presbyterian) 5th Alabama Battalion
Raines, A. G. (Baptist) 14th Alabama Infantry (POW)
Renfroe, John J. D. (Baptist) 10th Alabama Infantry
Smith, Aristides (Episcopal) 11th North Carolina Infantry
Stokes, James M. (Methodist) 3rd Georgia Infantry (POW)
Stough, Albert (Methodist) 37th North Carolina Infantry
Stroud, A. L. W. (Methodist) 13th Alabama Infantry
Tomkies, John H. (Baptist) 7th Tennessee Infantry
Watson, John Franklin (Presbyterian) 16th North Carolina Infantry
Whitten, Moses L. (Methodist) 9th Alabama Infantry (POW)
Williams, George T. (Episcopal) 1st South Carolina Infantry/13th North Caro-
    lina Infantry

Witherspoon, T. D. (Presbyterian) 42nd Mississippi Infantry (POW)
Wood, Franklin H. (Methodist) 22nd North Carolina Infantry

Cavalry Corps (Maj. Gen. J. E. B. Stuart)

Carson, Theodore M. (Episcopal) 7th Virginia Cavalry
Cooper, Robert E. (Presbyterian) Cobb's (Georgia) Legion
Davis, Richard T. (Episcopal) 6th Virginia Cavalry
Flinn, William (Presbyterian) Phillips (Georgia) Legion
Landstreet, John (Methodist) 1st Virginia Cavalry, aide-de-camp to Maj. Gen.
    J. E. B. Stuart
Meredith, William C. (Episcopal) 4th Virginia Cavalry
Pratt, H. B. (Presbyterian) Robertson's Brigade (4th and 5th North Carolina
    Cavalry)
Proctor, James A. (Methodist) 2nd North Carolina Cavalry
Sheppard, Samuel (Unknown) 17th Virginia Cavalry
Smith, Thompson L. (Episcopal) 14th Virginia Cavalry
Spiller, B. C. (Methodist) 13th Virginia Cavalry
Taylor, James B. (Baptist) 10th Virginia Cavalry
Wheelwright, William H. (Methodist) 9th Virginia Cavalry

Artillery (Brig. Gen. William Pendleton)

Chambliss, J. A. (Baptist) First Corps Artillery
Chapman, Marcus B. (Methodist) Washington Artillery (Louisiana), First
    Corps
Gilmer, Walker (Presbyterian) Col. William Nelson's Artillery, Second Corps
    Artillery Reserve
Nelson, James (Baptist) Second Corps Artillery
Oliver, Charles J. (Methodist) Troup Artillery (Georgia), First Corps
Wharey, James Morton (Presbyterian) Poague's Artillery Battalion, Third Corps

Missionary Chaplains:
Armstrong, George D. (Presbyterian) Missionary to Third Corps
Jones, J. William (Baptist) Missionary to Third Corps

Staff:
McKim, R. H. (Episcopal) staff of Brig. Gen. George Steuart, Third Corps;
    thereafter chaplain of the 2nd Virginia Cavalry.

Pendleton, William (Episcopal) Brigadier General, chief of artillery, conducted meetings of chaplains and provided Episcopal worship services. He was Robert E. Lee's pastor in Lexington, Virginia, after the war.

Detailed:
Gache, Louis-Hippolyte (Roman Catholic) 10th Louisiana Infantry, detailed to Lynchburg hospital after the Battle of Chancellorsville.

A total of 110 Confederate chaplains, two missionaries, and two chaplain staff officers served at Gettysburg; ninety regiments were without chaplains.

KIA: Killed in Action
WIA: Wounded in Action
POW: Prisoner of War

Appendix II

After the War: Biographical Notes on Selected Chaplains Who Served at Gettysburg

Lorenzo Barber (1821–1882) USA. Methodist minister, born in Windsor, Berkshire County, Massachusetts. Prior to the war, Barber was an insurance agent and Methodist Episcopal minister in Troy, New York, married to Marian A. (Williams) Barber. Chaplain Barber served first with the 3rd New York Artillery and then in the 2nd Regiment, United States Sharpshooters, beginning on December 31, 1862.

While transporting mail for his regiment, Chaplain Barber was captured by Confederate cavalry near Taneytown, Maryland, on or about July 1, 1863. Barber managed to escape, and though he lost the mailbags, he did return with two prisoners. Chaplain Barber was one of the best shots in his regiment. Using his own rifle and scope, he once hit a sheep grazing 400 yards away. On July 2, the 2nd US Sharpshooters fought at Bushman Farm, defending the high ground in front of Big Round Top. On July 3, they opposed Wilcox's Alabama Brigade in the center of the Union line. Wounded while fighting at Mine Run, Virginia, later in the war, Barber was appointed chief of sharpshooters for the Army of the Potomac and promoted to lieutenant colonel. He was honorably discharged near Petersburg in February 1865. Lorenzo Barber died in Troy, New York, in 1882 of a firearms accident while hunting.

Alexander D. Betts (1832–1919) CSA. Methodist minister, born in Cumberland County, North Carolina. Thrown while riding a steer at age 17, Betts could no longer work on a farm so he turned his energies toward an academic career. In 1855 he graduated from the University of North Carolina and entered the Methodist ministry the next year. On October 25, 1861, Betts accepted a commission as chaplain of the 30th North Carolina Infantry. He was with his regiment at Antietam, Gettysburg, and Winchester, Virginia. At Gettysburg he ministered to the wounded and buried the dead. During the second week in April 1865, while on leave in North Carolina, Betts received news that Lee had surrendered the Army of Northern Virginia. Betts first rode his mule to find Gen. Joseph E. Johnston's Army of Tennessee, but when Johnston surrendered soon thereafter, Betts went to Chapel Hill, where he was paroled by Federal officers. After the war Betts served as a pastor in Greenville, South Carolina. He died in 1919.

Louis Napoleon Boudrye (1833–1892) USA. Methodist Episcopal minister. Born in Franklin County, Vermont, of French-Canadian parents, Boudrye did not learn to read or write English until he was 17 years of age. He attended Newton Academy in Shoreham, New York, and taught school at Keeseville Academy in Keeseville, New York. Having experienced a conversion from his parents' Roman Catholic faith, he joined the Methodist Episcopal Conference in 1856. In 1860 he married Pearlie Schermerhorn, with whom he had seven children. On January 31, 1863, Boudrye joined the 5th New York Cavalry at Albany, New York. Six months later he was captured near Gettysburg and sent to Libby Prison in Richmond for three months. He returned to his regiment after his imprisonment ended and served with them until discharge on July 19, 1865. After the war Chaplain Boudrye wrote four books, including the *Historic Record of the 5th New York Cavalry*, published in 1868. Eventually he moved to Chicago, where he ran a French Mission. He died in Chicago in 1892.

James McDonald Campbell (1830–1864) CSA. Methodist minister, born in McMinn County, Tennessee. Campbell grew up on a farm in Alabama. Converted at age 15, he was admitted to the Alabama Conference on trial in 1853. In 1855 he was appointed as pastor to the Geneva Circuit in southeast Alabama under the supervision of his presiding elder (district superintendent), the Reverend Stephen F. Pilley. In 1861 Campbell enlisted in the 1st Georgia Infantry Regiment, training at Pensacola, Florida. In May 1861 he was elected chaplain and accompanied his regiment to Virginia. In April 1862 he resigned his position as chaplain to become captain of Company E, 47th Alabama Infantry Regiment. He was wounded at Cedar Mountain on August 8, 1862, but recovered and was present during the battles of Second Manassas, Fredericksburg, and Gettysburg. At Gettysburg he temporarily commanded the regiment during Lee's retreat into Virginia. Campbell was killed by a sharpshooter near Spotsylvania on May 15, 1864. Col. William C. Oates, later governor of Alabama, wrote that Major Campbell was "a good officer and a very gallant man. He did his whole duty manfully and well."[1]

William Corby (1833–1897) USA. Roman Catholic priest of the Congregation of the Holy Cross, born in Detroit, Michigan, to Daniel and Elizabeth Corby of Ireland and Canada, respectively. After working for four years in the real-estate business, William Corby went to the University of Notre Dame in South Bend, Indiana, to study for the priesthood. He took his final vows in 1860 after seven years of study. When the war began, Notre Dame sent seven priests to serve as chaplains to Union regiments, and Father Corby was one of

---

[1] John Wesley Brinsfield, Jr., *The Spirit Divided: Memoirs of Civil War Chaplains—The Confederacy* (Macon, GA: Mercer University Press, 2005) 24.

them. Corby joined the 88th New York Infantry in the "Irish Brigade" at their camp just outside Alexandria, Virginia. Father Corby served faithfully in that position for nearly three years, most notably at the battles of Antietam and Gettysburg, where he was the only chaplain for the brigade. After the war Father Corby was twice appointed president of the University of Notre Dame, where he remained until his election as provincial general of the Congregation of the Holy Cross in 1886. In 1893 his *Memoirs of Chaplain Life* was published by the Scholastic Press at Notre Dame, which led Corby to start a museum of artifacts from the Irish Brigade at the university. He did not live to complete that project, for he died on December 28, 1897, of pneumonia. On October 29, 1910, a bronze statue of Father Corby, sponsored by members of the Irish Brigade and the Catholic Alumni Sodality of Philadelphia, was dedicated on the battlefield at Gettysburg. A similar ceremony took place in May 1911 when a replica of the Gettysburg statue was unveiled in front of Corby Hall at Notre Dame, forever the home of "the fighting Irish."

William Reed Eastman (1835–1925) USA. Congregational minister, born in New York City. Eastman served at Gettysburg in the 72nd New York Infantry, III Corps, and his time of service was from January 1, 1863, to his discharge with his regiment on June 19, 1864. His wife was Laura Barnes Eastman (1846–1935). After the war Eastman was a member of the Military Order of the Loyal Legion of the United States and helped develop the State Library in Albany, New York. He died in Washington, DC, in 1925 at age 90 and was buried in Albany, New York.

John Cowper Granbery (1829–1907) CSA. Minister and bishop, Methodist Episcopal Church, South. Born December 5, 1829, in Norfolk, Virginia, Granbery graduated from Randolph-Macon College in 1848. He served as chaplain for the 11th Virginia Infantry Regiment and was wounded at Frazier's Farm in 1862, at which time he lost sight in one eye. Granbery returned to the Army of Northern Virginia as a missionary and surrendered in that capacity at Appomattox Court House on April 9, 1865. Appointed professor of Moral Philosophy and Practical Theology at Vanderbilt University in 1875, Granbery was elected a bishop of the Methodist Episcopal Church, South, in 1882. He died April 1, 1907, and was buried at Hollywood Cemetery, Richmond, Virginia.

John William Jones (1836–1909) CSA. J. William Jones was a Baptist minister, born in Louisa Court House, Virginia. He was educated at the University of Virginia and at the Southern Baptist Theological Seminary in Greenville, South Carolina. Ordained in 1860, Jones accepted a call to be the pastor of Little River Baptist Church in his home county east of Charlottesville. In May 1861 Jones enlisted as a private in the Confederate Army. A year later he was commissioned as the chaplain of the 13th Virginia Infantry Regiment. In 1863

Jones was appointed a missionary chaplain to Gen. A. P. Hill's Corps. In his ministry of three and a half years Jones baptized 520 soldiers and reportedly helped more than 2,000 soldiers make a personal confession of faith. After the war Jones became the Baptist chaplain at Washington College during the presidency of Robert E. Lee. Jones wrote a number of books, including *Christ in the Camp*, which documented the revivals that occurred in the Confederate armies during the war. Jones died in 1909, still a passionate witness to the presence of the Holy Spirit in the great revivals of his time.

Francis Milton Kennedy (1834–1880) CSA. Methodist minister, born in South Carolina, son of the Reverend and Mrs. William Kennedy of the South Carolina Conference. Educated in his father's parsonage, Kennedy was admitted to the South Carolina Conference when he was 20 years old. He served several pastorates in the northern part of the state. In 1862 he was a tract agent for the Confederate Army, distributing religious newspapers and tracts from Charlotte, North Carolina, to Richmond, Virginia. On January 3, 1863, Kennedy became the chaplain of the 28th North Carolina Infantry Regiment and reported for duty a week later. Chaplain Kennedy served at Gettysburg, where he thought Pickett's Charge was a mistake that could turn into a disaster. After the war he settled in Macon, Georgia, where he edited *The Southern Christian Advocate*. Kennedy died on February 5, 1880, and was buried in Macon.

Joseph B. O'Hagan, SJ (1826–1878) USA. Roman Catholic priest. Born in Ireland, Joseph O'Hagan's family emigrated to Nova Scotia when he was young. He joined the Jesuits in 1847 and studied in Europe, where he was ordained in 1861. Father O'Hagan served as the chaplain of the 73rd New York Volunteer Infantry in the Excelsior Brigade. He was a good friend of Joseph Twichell, chaplain of the 71st New York Volunteer Infantry in the same brigade and helped care for the wounded Maj. Gen. Daniel Sickles at Gettysburg. After the war, Father O'Hagan served many churches in Boston and in 1872 was appointed president of the College of the Holy Cross in Worchester, Massachusetts. At the end of his presidency, for reasons of health, he sailed on a ship bound for California. Stricken with apoplexy, he died on board the ship on December 15, 1878.

Charles James Oliver (1831–1911) CSA. Methodist minister, born in Warwick, England. Oliver emigrated with his parents to the United States at age 9. He grew up in Athens, near the University of Georgia, where he became fond of drama and the plays of William Shakespeare. Shortly before the war Oliver became a local Methodist preacher. On August 6, 1862, he enlisted as a private in the Troup Artillery, Cobb's Georgia Legion, and served as an artillery crew member in numerous battles including Antietam, Fredericksburg, Chancellorsville, and Gettysburg, where he was slightly wounded. Oliver functioned as the noncommissioned chaplain of the Troup Artillery, Cabell's Artillery Battalion, in Lt. Gen. Longstreet's Corps until Brig. Gen. William Pendleton, chief of the Artillery for the Army of Northern Virginia, sponsored his commission as chaplain for his unit. On September 12, 1864, Oliver received his commission from Richmond. In December 1864 he returned to Athens on furlough. Nothing further is known about his service during the war. In 1869 Oliver was appointed as pastor of the Methodist Church in Ringgold, Georgia, and then in 1873 retired to Athens, where his family had lived. He died in East Point, Georgia, in 1911 and was buried in Athens in a cemetery behind the University of Georgia.

James B. Sheeran (1819–1881) CSA. Roman Catholic priest of the Redemptorist Congregation, born in County Longford, Ireland, in 1819. At age 12 Sheeran emigrated to North America, first to Canada, then to New York, Pennsylvania, and finally to Monroe, Michigan, where he engaged in the tailoring business. While in Monroe he taught at a boys' school operated by the Redemptorist Fathers. About 1842 Sheeran married and had two children, a son and a daughter. Seven years later he became a widower and sent his daughter to board with the Sisters of the Immaculate Heart. In 1855 Sheeran joined the Redemptorist Congregation and was ordained to the priesthood in 1858. In 1859 he was stationed at the Redemptorist Church in New Orleans, and when his father Provincial asked for volunteers to act as chaplains for the Confederate Army, Father Sheeran volunteered. On September 2, 1861, he was assigned to the Army of Northern Virginia as chaplain of the 14th Louisiana Volunteer Infantry. After the Gettysburg Campaign, Father Sheeran accompanied his regiment to the Shenandoah Valley, where he was arrested on November 5, 1864, at Winchester, Virginia, by order of Maj. Gen. Philip Sheridan. Father Sheeran was confined to Fort McHenry, Maryland, until he convinced Gen. Sheridan to set him free. After the war Father Sheeran served as a pastor of the Catholic church in Morristown, New Jersey. He died in 1881 at the age of 62, leaving behind his handwritten *Journals* that described his experiences as a Confederate chaplain.

John H. W. Stuckenberg (1835–1903) USA. Lutheran pastor and professor, born in Bramasche, Germany. Emigrating with his family in 1839, Stuckenberg grew up in western Pennsylvania, southern Ohio, and southern Indiana. He entered Wittenburg College in 1852 and received his BA degree in 1857. He served a Lutheran church in Davenport, Iowa, for one year and then returned to Germany for two additional years of theological study at the University of Halle. Upon his return, Stuckenberg accepted a call to be the pastor for three churches in the Erie, Pennsylvania, area. Despising "the mean attempts"[2] of so many to avoid military service, Stuckenberg volunteered to serve as a chaplain in September 1862. From that time until his resignation in October 1863, Stuckenberg held the position of chaplain to the 145th Pennsylvania Infantry Regiment. He was at the battles of Fredericksburg, Chancellorsville, and Gettysburg, always up front or in hospitals with his men. When his brigade dwindled to the size of a regiment, with two other chaplains in place, Stuckenberg tendered his resignation to return to his pastoral charge in Erie. After the war Stuckenberg travelled to Germany on several occasions and returned to the United States to join the faculty at Wittenburg College. John Stuckenberg died suddenly on May 28, 1903, while on a trip to London. Both his remains and those of his wife, Mary, were eventually buried in the Gettysburg National Cemetery, the only Civil War chaplain still on the battlefield.

Peter Archer Tinsley (1833–1908) CSA. Episcopal priest, born in Powhatan County, Virginia, to John Brown Tinsley and Eliza Scott Trueheart. Peter Tinsley graduated from Hampden-Sydney College, Farmville, Virginia, in 1852. From 1859 to 1860 Tinsley was a student at the Virginia Theological Seminary, graduating with the Class of 1860. He was ordained a deacon by the Right Reverend William Meade, bishop of Virginia, on June 29, 1860, and appointed as rector of St. John's Church, Salem Parish, in Roanoke County. On May 13, 1861, Tinsley enlisted in the 28th Virginia Volunteer Infantry and was commissioned the same day to serve as their chaplain. On April 17, 1862, he traveled to Richmond, where he was ordained a priest by the Right Reverend John Johns at the Monumental Church. Tinsley returned and remained with his regiment throughout the war except for three months when he was detained as a prisoner. He was one of fifty Confederate chaplains who surrendered at Appomattox. After the war Tinsley served as chaplain of the University of Virginia for two years and then as rector of St. John's Church in Olney, Maryland, until 1869. From 1870 until 1901 he was the rector of the Church of the Advent in Cincinnati, Ohio. In 1885 he received an Honorary Doctor of Divinity degree from Kenyon College, Gambier, Ohio. From 1901 until 1908 he was rector emeritus, Church of the Advent, in Cincinnati. Tinsley died in Cincinnati on January 4, 1908, and was buried in Bedford County, Virginia.

Joseph Hopkins Twichell (1838–1918) USA. Congregational minister, born at Southington Corners, Connecticut. Twichell was the son of Edward Twichell, a tanner and a deacon in the local Congregational church. His mother

---

[2] David T. Hedrick and Gordon Barry Davis, Jr., eds., *I'm Surrounded by Methodists...Diary of John H. W. Stuckenberg, Chaplain of the 145th Pennsylvania Volunteer Infantry* (Gettysburg, PA: Thomas Publications, 1995) 1.

died when he was just 11 years of age, but he had eight siblings from his father's two marriages, so he was not alone in his young adult years. Twichell attended Yale College from 1855 to 1859, at which time he entered Union Theological Seminary in New York City to study for the ministry. When New York attorney Daniel Sickles raised a regiment, the 71st New York Infantry, to fight for the Union, Twichell's strong abolitionist sympathies led him to drop out of seminary to volunteer as Sickles's chaplain. Twichell was just 25 years of age and not yet ordained, a qualification he achieved in 1863 while on furlough. He remained with his regiment through all of the major battles in the Eastern theater, including the Battle of Gettysburg, where he ministered to Major General Sickles during the amputation of his leg. After the war Twichell returned to his studies, this time at Andover Theological Seminary in Massachusetts. With the help of Rev. Horace Bushnell of Hartford, Connecticut, Twichell became pastor of the Asylum Hill Congregational Church in that city. One of his parishioners was Samuel L. Clemens (aka Mark Twain), who became Twichell's friend and traveling companion. (Twichell's church was relatively affluent, which caused Twain to describe it as "The Church of the Holy Speculators.") Joseph Twichell retired from the ministry in 1912 at age 74. He died in Hartford on December 20, 1918, just after the end of World War I.

Thomas Dwight Witherspoon (1836–1898) CSA. Presbyterian minister. Born in Greensboro, Alabama, in 1836, Witherspoon spent eight years studying for the ministry, an unusual amount of time for most pastors of his generation. He was graduated from the University of Mississippi with a bachelor's degree in 1856 and a master's degree in 1859. He then enrolled at Columbia Theological Seminary in Columbia, South Carolina, graduating in 1859. Witherspoon served as pastor of the Presbyterian Church in Oxford, Mississippi, for one year before enlisting as a private in the 2nd Mississippi Infantry. Commissioned as a chaplain by President Jefferson Davis, upon petition of his friends, Witherspoon joined the 42nd Mississippi Infantry, with whom he served at Gettysburg. Remaining behind with the wounded of his regiment after the battle, Witherspoon was captured and imprisoned for three months. He rejoined his regiment and remained with the Army of Northern Virginia, surrendering with the 48th Mississippi Infantry at Appomattox. After the war Witherspoon served as pastor of the Second Presbyterian Church in Memphis, Tennessee, then as chaplain of the University of Virginia from 1871 to 1873. In 1882 Witherspoon accepted a call to the First Presbyterian Church of Louisville, Kentucky. He served also as moderator of the General Assembly of the Presbyterian Church, US, in 1884 and as professor of Homiletics and Pastoral Theology at the Louisville Presbyterian Theological Seminary from 1894 until his death on November 3, 1898.

Bibliography

Barrett, John G. *Yankee Rebel: The Civil War Journal of Edmund DeWitt Patterson.* Chapel Hill: University of North Carolina Press, 1966.

Bartlett, John. *Bartlett's Familiar Quotations.* New York: Permabooks, 1957.

Betts, Alexander Davis, DD. *Experience of a Confederate Chaplain 1861–1864.* Edited by W. A. Betts. Greenville, SC: privately printed, 1904.

Boritt, Gabor. *The Gettysburg Gospel.* New York: Simon and Schuster Paperbacks, 2006.

Boudrye, Louis Napoleon. "The Louis Napoleon Boudrye Papers," Wheaton (IL) College Archives and Special Collections, Series 1, Box 1, Item 10.

Bradford, Ned, ed. *Battles and Leaders of the Civil War.* New York: Appleton-Century-Crofts, 1956.

Bright, Robert. "Pickett's Charge at Gettysburg." *Confederate Veteran* 38/7 (July 1930).

Brinsfield, John Wesley. *The Spirit Divided: Memoirs of Civil War Chaplains—The Confederacy.* Macon, GA: Mercer University Press, 2005.

Brinsfield, John Wesley, William C. Davis, Benedict Maryniak, and James I. Robertson, Jr. *Faith in the Fight: Civil War Chaplains.* Mechanicsburg, PA: Stackpole Books, 2003.

Brock, R. A., ed. "Paroles of the Army of Northern Virginia." *Southern Historical Society Papers.* Vol. XV (1887).

Caba, G. Craig, ed. *Hospital Scenes after the Battle of Gettysburg.* Craig Caba: Gettysburg, PA, 1993.

Caskey, Thomas. *Caskey's Book: Lectures on Great Subjects.* Edited by G. G. Mullins. St. Louis, MO: John Burns Publishing Co., 1884.

Clay, James. "About the Death of General Garnett." *Confederate Veteran.* Vol. XXXIII (1905), as cited in Richard Rollins, ed., *Pickett's Charge: Eyewitness Accounts.* Torrance, CA: Rank and File Publications, 1994.

Clement, Maud Carter. *The History of Pittsylvania County, Virginia.* Baltimore, MD: Regional/Genealogical Publishing Company, 1937.

Coddington, Edwin B. *The Gettysburg Campaign: A Study in Command.* New York: Scribner's, 1968.

Corby, William. *Memoirs of Chaplain Life: Three Years with the Irish Brigade in the Army of the Potomac.* Edited by Lawrence F. Kohl. New York: Fordham University Press, 1992.

Coulter, E. Merton . *The Confederate States of America.* Baton Rouge, LA: LSU Press, 1950.

Curry, John P. *Volunteers' Camp and Field Book* (1862). Edited by William B. Sargeant and John W. Brinsfield. Macon, GA: Mercer University Press, 2009.

Dabney, Robert. *Life and Campaigns of Lt. General Thomas J. Jackson.* Harrisonburg, VA: Sprinkle Publications, 1983.

Davis, Jefferson. *The Rise and Fall of the Confederate Government.* Vol. II. New York: D. Appleton and Company, 1881.

Dobbs, Charles Holt. "Reminiscences of an Army Chaplain." *The Presbyterian Christian Observer.* Louisville, KY: Converse & Co., 1874.

Durkin, Joseph T., SJ, ed. *Confederate Chaplain: A War Journal of Rev. James B. Sheeran, c.ss.r. Fourteenth Louisiana, C.S.A.* Milwaukee, WI: The Bruce Publishing Co., 1960.

Ewell, Richard S. "The Gettysburg Campaign," US War Department, *The War of the Rebellion: Official Records of the Union and Confederate Armies.* Series I, Vol. XXVII, Part 2, Chapter 39.

Faust, Drew Gilpin. *This Republic of Suffering: Death and the American Civil War.* New York: Vintage Books, 2008.

Foote, Shelby. *The Civil War: A Narrative. Volume Two. Fredericksburg to Meridian.* New York: Random House, 1958.

Fry, B. D. "Pettigrew's Charge at Gettysburg." *Southern Historical Society Papers.* 7/2 (1879).

Gates, Henry Louis, Jr. "Did black men fight at Gettysburg?" *Nation* (July 1, 2013), as cited in http://www.theroot.com/articles/history/2013/07/did_black_men_fight_at_gettysbu rg.html.

Gourley, Bruce T. "Baptists and the American Civil War." *Baptist History and Heritage.* XLVII/2 (Summer 2013).

Hancock, Cornelia. *South after Gettysburg: Letters of Cornelia Hancock from the Army of the Potomac, 1863–1865.* University of Pennsylvania Press, original from the University of Michigan, digitized October 27, 2006.

Hedrick, David T. and Gordon Barry Davis, Jr., eds. *I'm Surrounded by Methodists...Diary of John H. W. Stuckenberg, Chaplain of the 145th Pennsylvania Volunteer Infantry.* Gettysburg, PA: Thomas Publications, 1995.

Hill, A. P. "Report of the Battle of Gettysburg." *Southern Historical Society Papers.* Vol. II. Edited by J. William Jones. Richmond, VA: George W. Gary, Printer, 1876.

Hird, Henry III, ed. *Gettysburg National Military Park Handbook.* St. Augustine, FL: Historic Print and Map Co., 2011.

"Historic Gettysburg—Adams County." *Gettysburg Civil War Field Hospital Tour.* Harrisburg, PA: The Hospital and Healthsystem Association of Pennsylvania, 2001.

Howard, Oliver O. "O. O. Howard Papers." Special Collections, Bowdoin (College) Library, Catalog Number M 91.8, Item 43, Number 19.

Jones, J. William. *Christ in the Camp or Religion in the Confederate Army.* Harrisonburg, VA: Sprinkle Publications, 1986.

Jones, J. William. *Personal Reminiscences, Anecdotes, and Letters of General Robert E. Lee.* New York: D. Appleton and Company, 1875.

Kennedy, Francis Milton. "Chaplain Francis Milton Kennedy's Diary, Confederate Diaries of the War." Morrow, GA: Georgia State Department of Archives and History, 1940.

Knauer, Kelly, ed. *Gettysburg: A Day-by-Day Account of the Greatest Battle of the Civil War.* New York: Time Books, 2013.

Lanning, Michael. *The Civil War 100.* Napierville, IL: Sourcebooks, Inc., 2007.

Lee, Fitzhugh. *General Lee.* Greenwich, CT: Fawcett Publications, 1964.

Lee, Robert E. "General Lee's Final and Full Report of the Pennsylvania Campaign and Battle of Gettysburg." Vol. II. Edited by J. William Jones. *Southern Historical Society Papers.* Richmond, VA: George W. Gary, Printer, 1876.

Loehr, Charles T. "The 'Old First' Virginia at Gettysburg." *Southern Historical Society Papers.* Vol. XXXII. Richmond, VA: George W. Gary, Printer, 1904.

Long, A. L. Colonel. *Memoirs of Robert E. Lee.* London: Sampson Low, Marston, Searle and Rivington, 1886.

Longstreet, James. *From Manassas to Appomattox: Memoirs of the Civil War in America.* Philadelphia: J. B. Lippencott, 1896.

Longstreet, James. "General James Longstreet's Account of the Campaign and Battle." *Southern Historical Society Papers.* Vol. V. Edited by J. William Jones. Richmond, VA: George W. Gary, Printer, 1878.

Luvass, Jay and Harold W. Nelson, eds. *Guide to the Battle of Gettysburg.* Lawrence: University Press of Kansas, 1994.

Martin, David G. *Gettysburg July 1.* Conshohocken, PA: Combined Publishing Co., 1996.

Maryniak, Benedict R. and John Wesley Brinsfield, Jr. *The Spirit Divided: Memoirs of Civil War Chaplains—The Union.* Macon, GA: Mercer University Press, 2007.

McLaws, Lafayette. "Gettysburg." *Southern Historical Society Papers* 7/2 (1879).

McNamara, Pat. "Father James Sheeran: Immigrant Priest and Confederate." *Patheos* (April 4, 2011) as cited in http://www.patheos.com/blogs/mcnamarasblog/2009/12/fr-joseph-b-o'hagan-s-j-1826-1878.html.

McNeil, Betty Ann, ed. *Dear Masters: Extracts from Accounts by Sister Nurses.* Emmitsburg, MD: Daughters of Charity of Saint Vincent de Paul, 2011.

Messent, Peter and Steve Courtney, eds. *The Civil War Letters of Joseph Hopkins Twichell.* Athens: University of Georgia Press, 2006.

Morley, Christopher, ed. *The Shorter Bartlett's Familiar Quotations.* New York: Permabooks, 1957.

Morse, Charles F. *Letters Written during the Civil War, 1861–1865.* Boston, 1898, as cited in http://www.masshist.org/collection-guides/view/fa0376.

Motts, Wayne E. *"Trust in God and Fear Nothing" Gen. Lewis A. Armistead, CSA.* Gettysburg, PA: Farnsworth House Military Impressions, 1994.

Pfanz, Harry W. *The Battle of Gettysburg.* Washington, PA: US National Park Service, 1994.

Rollins, Richard, ed. *Pickett's Charge: Eyewitness Accounts.* Torrance, CA: Rank and File Publications, 1994.

Sears, Stephen W. *Gettysburg.* Boston: Houghton Mifflin, 2003.

Shattuck, Gardiner H., Jr. *A Shield and a Hiding Place: The Religious Life of the Civil War Armies.* Macon, GA: Mercer University Press, 1988.

Simons, Ezra D. *A Regimental History: The One Hundred and Twenty-Fifth New York State Volunteers.* New York: Ezra D. Simons, 1888.

Smith, Edward Parmelee. *Incidents among Shots and Shell.* Memphis, TN: General Books, 2012.

Stockdale, Jim. *Thoughts of a Philosophical Fighter Pilot.* Stanford, CA: Hoover Institution Press, 1995.

Stuart, J. E. B. "General Stuart's Report of Operations." Edited by J. William Jones. *Southern Historical Society Papers.* Vol. II. Richmond, VA: George W. Gary, Printer, 1876.

Tagg, Larry. *The Generals of Gettysburg.* Campbell, CA: Savas Publishing Co., 1998.

Taylor, William B. to his mother, June 22, 1863. Gettysburg, PA: Gettysburg National Military Park Library, 1195 Baltimore Pike, Gettysburg, PA,17325.

Tinsley, Peter Archer. "Private Diary." John and Joyce Schmale Civil War Collection, Wheaton (IL) College Archives, Box 1, Folder 51.

Trimble, Isaac R. "Civil War Diary of I. R. Trimble," *Maryland Historical Magazine*. 7/1 (1922).

Trudeau, Noah. *Gettysburg: A Testing of Courage*. New York: Harper Collins, 2002.

"Union Officers in Richmond Prisons—A Complete Official List," *New York Daily Tribune*. XXIII/7,049 (Friday, November 6, 1863).

US War Department, *Revised United States Army Regulations of 1861*. Washington, DC: Government Printing Office, 1863.

US War Department, *The War of the Rebellion: Official Records of the Union and Confederate Armies*. Series I, Volume XXVII, Parts 1, 2, and 3. Washington, DC: Government Printing Office, 1880–1901.

Wagner, Margaret E., Gary W. Gallagher, and Paul Finkelman, eds. *The Library of Congress Civil War Desk Reference*. New York: Simon and Schuster, 2002.

Wiley, Bell I. *The Life of Johnny Reb and The Life of Billy Yank*. New York: Book-of-the-Month Club, 1994.

Wills, Gary. *Lincoln at Gettysburg: The Words That Remade America*. New York: Simon and Schuster, 1992.

Wisconsin Historical Society, Quiner Scrapbooks: Correspondence of the Wisconsin Volunteers, 1861–1865. v. 8, Seventh Infantry, CWQ UOO80264, Madison, Wisconsin.

Woodhead, Henry, ed. *Voices of the Civil War: Gettysburg*. Richmond, VA: Time-Life Books, 1995.

About the Author

Chaplain (Colonel-Retired) John Wesley Brinsfield is an adjunct faculty member at Wesley Theological Seminary in Washington, DC, and a retired minister of the United Methodist Church.

Dr. Brinsfield is a native of Atlanta and a graduate of Vanderbilt University. He has a Master of Divinity degree from Yale Divinity School, a PhD in Church History from Emory University, and a DMin in Ethics from Drew University. From 1972 to 1973 Dr. Brinsfield held a Woodrow Wilson Fellowship at Mansfield College, Oxford, and a Leopold Schepp Fellowship at Wesley House, Cambridge.

From 1969 to 2002, Dr. Brinsfield served as a chaplain in the Army, with teaching assignments at the US Army Aviation School, the Army Chaplain School, in the Department of History at the United States Military Academy at West Point, and at the US Army War College as director of Ethical Program Development and faculty instructor in World Religions. During Operation Desert Shield and Desert Storm, he served as a chaplain in the Army Personnel Command Headquarters in Riyadh, Saudi Arabia, in 1990 and 1991.

From 2002 to 2011 Dr. Brinsfield held the position of US Army Chaplain Corps Historian at Fort Jackson, South Carolina. After the attacks on the Pentagon and World Trade Center on 9/11, Chaplain Brinsfield interviewed more than sixty chaplains who assisted in the rescue/recovery operations. These interviews became the basis for two chapters in *Courageous in Spirit, Compassionate in Service: The Gunhus Years 1999–2003*, a tribute to the Army Chief of Chaplains, Maj. Gen. G. T. Gunhus, and the chaplains who served during that timeframe.

Dr. Brinsfield is the author or coauthor of nine books, including *Religion and Politics in Colonial South Carolina*; *Encouraging Faith, Supporting Soldiers: A History of the Army Chaplain Corps, 1975–1995*; *Courageous in Spirit, Compassionate in Service: The Gunhus Years 1999–2003*; *History of the Army Chaplaincy: The Hicks Years 2003–2007*; *Faith in the Fight: Civil War Chaplains*; *The Spirit Divided: Memoirs of Civil War Chaplains* (two volumes); *Volunteers' Camp and Field Book, 1862*, reprint; and *Spiritual Resilience for an Army at War: The US Army Chaplaincy, 2007–2011*, as well as numerous articles and editorials for the *Atlanta Journal-Constitution* and the *New York Times*.

John Brinsfield and his wife, Patricia, reside in Ringgold, Georgia. They have two daughters, Casey and Cindee, and one son, Ben.

Index

Adams, Charles Francis, Jr., 32
Adams, Hop, 109
African Americans, at Gettysburg, 104,
 109n46, 134
African Methodist Episcopal Church
 (Gettysburg), 134
aid stations, 136
Alexander, Edward Porter, 104, 106,
 107, 111, 113
Allen, E., 128
Allen, Henry, 76
Allen, R.C., 126
Ambrose, Stephen, 159
Anderson, George T., 79
Anderson, R.H., 14, 49, 88
Andersonville (GA), prison at, 145
Angle, The, 121, 162
Antietam, Battle of, 33, 75, 152
Archer, James, 49, 52, 54
Armistead, Lewis A., 113, 114, 119,
 122, 126, 150–51, 155, 162
Armstrong, Samuel C., 116–17, 150,
 158
Army of Northern Virginia. *See* Con-
 federate Army
Army of the Potomac. *See* Union Army
Artillerist's Manual, The, 97
Avery, Isaac, 91, 93

bands, 3, 93–94, 118, 123
Barber, Lorenzo (chaplain), 164, 181
Barber, Marian A. (Williams), 181
Barksdale, William, 86–87, 88, 114
Barlow, Francis C., 59, 63
Barlow's Knoll, 63
Barnes, James, 81, 87
Barnett, Thomas (chaplain), 56–58
Bartow, Francis, 4
Baxter, Henry, 60, 61, 66
Bennett, W.W. (chaplain), 166
Benning, Henry, 79
Berry, William W., 19

Betts, Alexander D. (chaplain), 30–31,
 119, 165, 181
Biddle, Chapman, 59–60
Biggs, Bail, 148
Big Round Top, 73, 80, 94, 181
Bingham, Henry, 150
Birney, David, 39
Blanton, Leigh, 163
Bouchelle, James N. (chaplain), 141
Boudrye, Louis Napoleon (chaplain),
 131–32, 182
Bradley, L.W., 127n11
Brinton, Jeremiah, 51
Brockenbrough, John, 61, 116
Brooke, John, 81, 82, 84
Brooks, Henry E. (chaplain), 30, 141,
 144
Brown, Hiram L., 84, 85
Brown, William Y. (chaplain), 7n19,
 128
Buchanan, James, 77
Buford, John, 34, 48, 49, 50–51
Bulkley, Charles H. A. (chaplain), 41
Burgwyn, Henry K., 62
Burlando, Francis, 137
Burnside carbines (.52-caliber), 50
Bushnell, Horace, 187
Butler, George E. (chaplain), 141
Butterfield, Daniel, 33, 106

Caldwell, John, 81
Calef, John, 50
Campbell, James McDonald, 182
Camp Letterman, 136, 139
Carleton, H.H., 125
Carroll, Samuel, 91
Carson, Lewis D., 144
Carter, Thomas H., 63
Caskey, Thomas W. (chaplain), 8, 168
Cemetery Hill, 70, 88, 90–91, 96, 98,
 116

98, 99; Excelsior Brigade, 39, 41,
77, 184; Farnsworth's Brigade, 131;
Gamble's Brigade, 49–50, 51; Gibbon's Division, 98, 106; Hall's Brigade, 121; Hancock's Divisions, 99;
Harrow's Brigade, 87, 121; Humphreys's Division, 79, 81; Iron Brigade, 52, 54, 55, 61; Irish Brigade
(88th New York Infantry Regiment), 32, 35, 81–82, 84, 93, 166,
183; Kilpatrick's Cavalry Division,
131; Meredith's Brigade, 61; New
York Brigade, 74; Paul's Brigade,
62, 65; Pennsylvania Brigade, 62;
Philadelphia Brigade, 121; Robinson's Division, 66, 98; Shaler's Brigade, 102; Stannard's Brigade, 121;
Third Division, 98; Union Division, 119; Vermont Brigade, 119,
123; Webb's Brigade, 98, 122;
Weed's Brigade, 80; ; Cavalry
Corps, 33, 34; First Corps, 32, 34,
42, 50, 60, 61, 62, 65, 67, 69, 72–
73, 98, 99, 102; Second Corps, 32,
35–37, 50, 60, 69, 72, 78, 81, 83,
84, 87, 91, 97–98, 115–16; Third
Corps, 32, 34, 39, 42–44, 49, 50,
72, 74, 77–78, 81, 82, 98, 99. 87;
Fifth Corps, 32, 70, 72, 74, 80, 81,
87, 99; Sixth Corps, 33, 72, 73, 99,
102; Eleventh Corps, 32, 34, 50,
59, 60, 61, 64–65, 72, 99, 102;
Twelfth Corps, 32, 34, 69, 70, 72,
74, 91, 99, 102; V Corps, 34; 1st
Maine Light Artillery, 115; 1st
Cavalry Division, 48; 1st Minnesota Infantry Regiment, 87, 88,
122n85, 163; 1st New York Independent Artillery Battery, 121; 1st
United States Artillery, 153; 2nd
Delaware Infantry, 84n39; 2nd
Maine Battery, 53; 2nd US Sharpshooters, 165, 181; 2nd Wisconsin
Infantry, 52; 4th United States Artillery, 98, 106, 121; 5th New York

Cavalry Regiment, 131, 182; 5th
US Artillery, 115; 6th Wisconsin,
59; 7th Michigan, 122n85; 7th
Wisconsin Infantry Regiment, 55,
56; 8th Connecticut Infantry,
165n39; 8th Illinois Cavalry, 49;
8th New York Cavalry Regiment,
51; 8th Ohio Infantry, 116, 117;
8th US Infantry Regiment, 74;
14th Brooklyn, 59; 15th Massachusetts, 122n85; 16th Maine Infantry,
65; 16th Michigan, 80; 19th Indiana Infantry, 55, 56–57, 61; 19th
Maine, 122n85; 19th Massachusetts Infantry, 121, 122n85; 20th
Maine Regiment, 80, 81, 153; 20th
Massachusetts Infantry, 121,
122n85; 20th Pennsylvania Emergency Militia Infantry, 46; 24th
Michigan Infantry, 55, 56, 62; 26th
Pennsylvania Emergency Militia
Infantry, 46; 27th Pennsylvania
Emergency Militia Infantry, 46,
47–48; 28th Pennsylvania Emer-
gency Militia Infantry, 46; 29th
Pennsylvania Emergency Militia
Infantry, 46; 30th Pennsylvania
Emergency Militia Infantry, 46;
31st Pennsylvania Emergency Mili-
tia Infantry, 46; 33rd Pennsylvania
Emergency Militia Infantry, 46;
42nd New York, 122n85; 44th
New York, 80; 52nd New York In-
fantry, 84n39; 54th New York
Volunteer Infantry, 63, 64; 56th
Pennsylvania, 53; 61st New York
Infantry, 84n39; 64th New York
Infantry, 84n39, 127; 69th Penn-
sylvania Regiment, 121; 70th New
York Infantry Regiment, 41; 71st
New York Infantry Regiment, 40,
41, 92, 129, 187; 71st Pennsylvania
Regiment, 121; 72nd New York
Infantry, 8, 41, 128, 183 ; 72nd
Pennsylvania Regiment, 121,